Designs of the Times

RotoVision

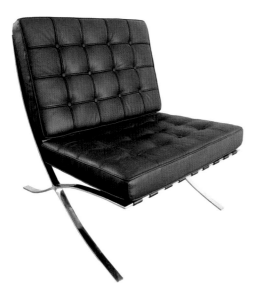
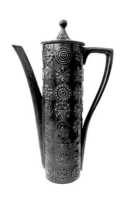
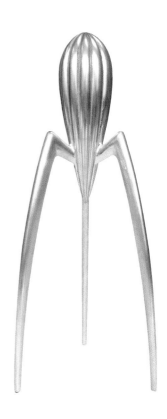

DESIGNS OF THE TIMES

Using Key Movements
and Styles For
Contemporary Design

Lakshmi Bhaskaran

A RotoVision Book

Published and distributed by
RotoVision SA
Route Suisse 9
CH-1295 Mies
Switzerland

RotoVision SA
Sales & Editorial Office
Sheridan House
114 Western Road
Hove BN3 1DD, UK

Tel: +44 (0)1273 72 72 68
Fax: +44 (0)1273 72 72 69
Email: sales@rotovision.com
Web: www.rotovision.com

10 9 8 7 6 5 4 3 2 1

ISBN: 2-88046-816-7

Art Director Luke Herriott
Book design by HDR Visual
Communication

Printed in Singapore by Star Standard
Industries (Pte) Ltd

Acknowledgments

I would like to thank all the designers and design companies who were so helpful in contributing images to this book. I'd also like to thank my editors, Kate Shanahan and Lindy Dunlop, and April Sankey and Luke Herriott at RotoVision.

Special thanks go to Josie Ballin and all at D&AD; Quentin Newark for all the help and advice; and to Jony for continuing to inspire me on a daily basis.

Bifur typeface:
A. M. Cassandre

ABCDEFGHIJKLMN OPQRSTUVWXYZ 1234567890 .,;:— '' ''' . ‹› ‹‹›› !?() Çç

1993

Illustration for the
Beautiful South's
album *0898*:
David Cutter

2003

Richard B. Fisher
Center for the
Performing Arts at
Bard College, New
York: Frank Gehry

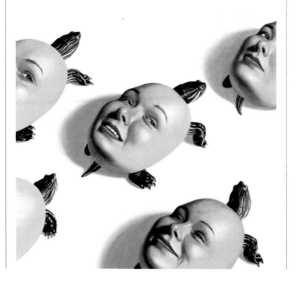

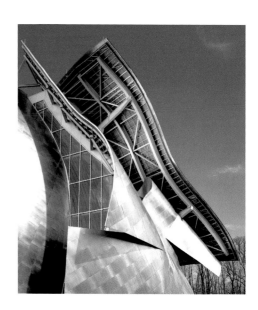

Contents

Introduction

From art to architecture and furniture to graphics, design in the twenty-first century has become a global phenomenon. Whether used as a means of communication or expression, to attract new audiences or inspire old, the language of design has become the soundtrack of choice in a world where too much is never enough. In short, design has become ubiquitous.

We now live in a society overwhelmed by choice, surrounded by products whose ability to transcend function has created a world dominated by esthetics and driven by consumerism. Mass production has been superceded by mass customization in a disposable age where goods are replaced rather than repaired. Design has infiltrated our everyday existence and become such an integral part of daily life that we expect no less. In fact we expect more and, as a result, demand more. Continually on the lookout for something different, for the next and best "big thing," we put pressure on the design industry and, more importantly, on designers to provide it.

In response to the ever-changing demands of the twenty-first century consumer, designers today increasingly find themselves looking to historicism for a helping hand. Applied to design, historicism is the practice of reusing earlier historical styles in art, design, and architecture. Yet, while borrowing from the past has long been recognized as an acceptable creative resource—look back to the Roman sculptors who borrowed from Greek tradition—this has not stopped a 150-year long debate over its legitimacy. While imitative historicism dominated much of nineteenth-century art and design, this approach was the very antithesis of everything modernism stood for in the twentieth-century. Determined to forge a new language of design, borrowing from the past was simply not an option in modernist circles—in fact, it was a

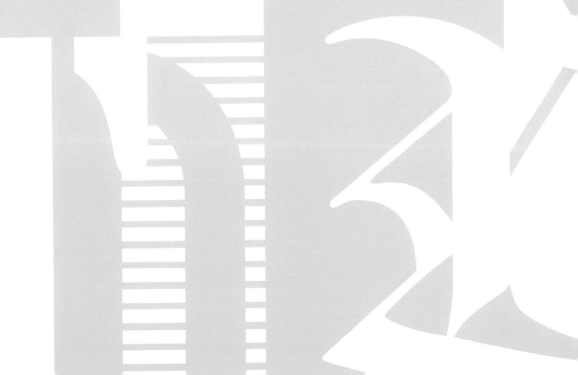

crime. It was not until the 1960s and the advent of postmodernism that this view was effectively challenged and designers began to freely explore the past once more.

Having come full circle, as we begin to find our feet in the twenty-first century, historicism is not only a legitimate area of creativity, it is an integral part of contemporary visual culture. We have moved beyond the time when a singular style was enough to capture the spirit of an age. Revolutionary advances in machinery and technology, once the primary motivators for designers and architects, no longer provide the stimulus they once did. Designers today find themselves immersed in choice, free to cherry pick from the plethora of stylistic attributes at their disposal, to mix and match past and present in search of the future.

Encapsulating the wide variety of styles that previously catered to distinct audiences, the sponge-like quality of

"twenty-first century modernism," and its ability to bypass the stylistic constraints that were once the very basis for identity, has led to a new body of expressions and global accents that have driven design to unprecedented levels of diversity. Former styles are continually revived, injected with a splash of contemporary kudos, and sent on their way with growing frequency and a level of transience more in line with the fashion industry than with other areas of design.

Using a combination of historical and contemporary examples spanning the fields of industrial design, furniture, graphics, art, and architecture, *Designs of the Times* is the ultimate source book for designers, students, and indeed anyone with an interest in design. Designed to inform and inspire in equal measure, the following pages will explore the key movements and styles that have come to define twentieth-century design. Each chapter illustrates

not only how a particular style has evolved over the years, but also how it can be applied to design today. In addition, each style's key figures and characteristics have been highlighted for quick reference, while a series of four timelines (classified by style, design, designer, and events) reveal the bigger picture.

Design is no longer simply a matter of form or function; it is a language and, like any language, must be fully understood before it can be used effectively. *Designs of the Times* provides the key to that understanding.

Key Movements and Styles

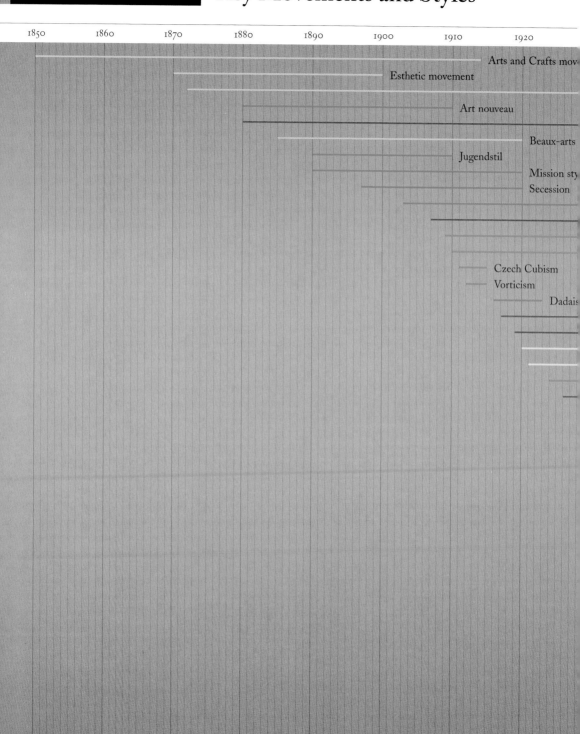

| 1850 | 1860 | 1870 | 1880 | 1890 | 1900 | 1910 | 1920 |

Arts and Crafts mov

Esthetic movement

Art nouveau

Beaux-arts

Jugendstil

Mission sty

Secession

Czech Cubism

Vorticism

Dadais

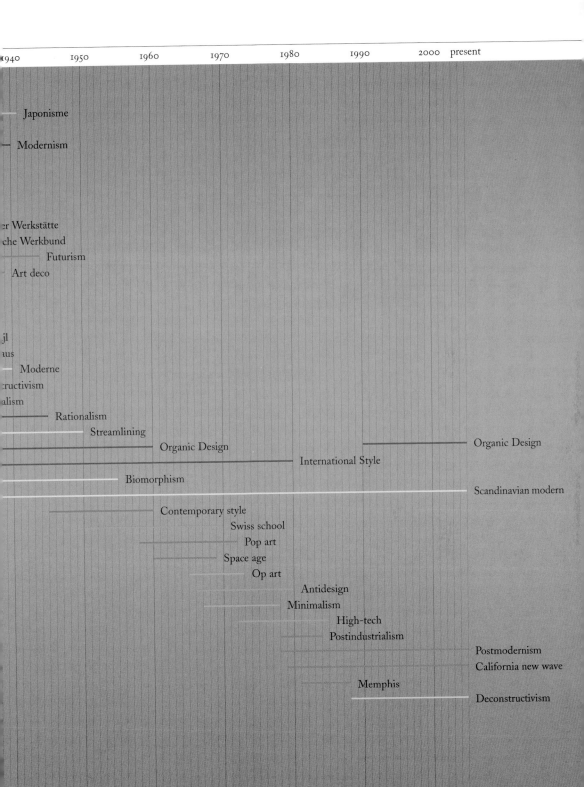

Japonisme

Modernism

er Werkstätte
che Werkbund
Futurism
Art deco

jl
aus
Moderne
structivism
alism
Rationalism
Streamlining
Organic Design   Organic Design
International Style
Biomorphism
Scandinavian modern
Contemporary style
Swiss school
Pop art
Space age
Op art
Antidesign
Minimalism
High-tech
Postindustrialism
Postmodernism
California new wave
Memphis
Deconstructivism

Designs

| 1900 | 1910 | 1920 | 1930 | 1940 | 1950 | 1 |

- Kodak Brownie camera *George Eastman*
- Hill House chair *Charles Rennie Mackintosh*
- Vienna stool *Otto Wagner*
- Sitzmaschine *Josef Hoffmann*
- Electric kettle *Peter Behrens*
- M1 typewriter *Camillo Olivetti*
- Czech Cubist chair *Vlastislav Hofman*
- Coca-Cola bottle *Alexander Samuelson*
- Red/Blue Chair *Gerrit Rietveld*
- Suprematist cross *Kasimir Malevich*
- Chaise longue *Le Corbusier, Jeanneret, and Perriand*
- Barcelona chair *Ludwig Mies van der Rohe*
- Moka Express coffeemaker *Alfonso Bialetti*
- Pencil Sharpener *Raymond Loewy*
- Savoy vase *Alvar Aalto*
- Ballpoint pen *Laszlo Biro*
- Lucky Strike packaging *Raymond L*
- Tupperware *Earl C. Tupper*
- Lounge Chair Wood (LCW)
- Ant chair *Arne Ja*
- Superleggera side
- Routemast
- Univers typ
- IBM lo
- Braun
- Helv

nheim Museum *Frank Gehry*

ng chair *Verner Panton*

Terminal, John F. Kennedy International Airport *Eero Saarinen*

ega TS502 radio *Richard Sapper and Marco Zanuso*

Stelton Cylinda Line *Arne Jacobsen*

Blow armchair *De Pas, D'Urbino, Lomazzi, and Scolari*

Furniture in Irregular Forms Side 2' *Shiro Kuramata*

Tizio table lamp *Richard Sapper*

Walkman TPS-L2 *Sony Design Team*

Carlton bookcase *Ettore Sottsass*

Macintosh I personal computer *Apple Computer*

Face 2 typeface *Neville Brody*

Alessi Bird Kettle *Michael Graves*

Nomos table *Foster and Partners*

Juicy Salif Lemon Squeezer *Philippe Starck*

Aeron office chair *Bill Stumpf and Don Chadwick*

Knotted chair *Marcel Wanders*

Jack Light *Tom Dixon*

iMac computer *Jonathan Ive and Apple Design Team*

Audi TT Coupe Quattro *Audi Design*

Apple iPod *Jonathan Ive and Apple Design Team*

Go chair *Ross Lovegrove*

Fresh Fat chairs *Tom Dixon*

Rolling Bridge *Thomas Heatherwick*

Kelvin 40 *Marc Newson*

iMac G5 *Jonathan Ive and Apple Design Team*

ay Eames

onti

as Scott

n Frutiger

Rand

osuper SK4 *Hans Gugelot and Dieter Rams*

ace *Max Miedinger*

Designers

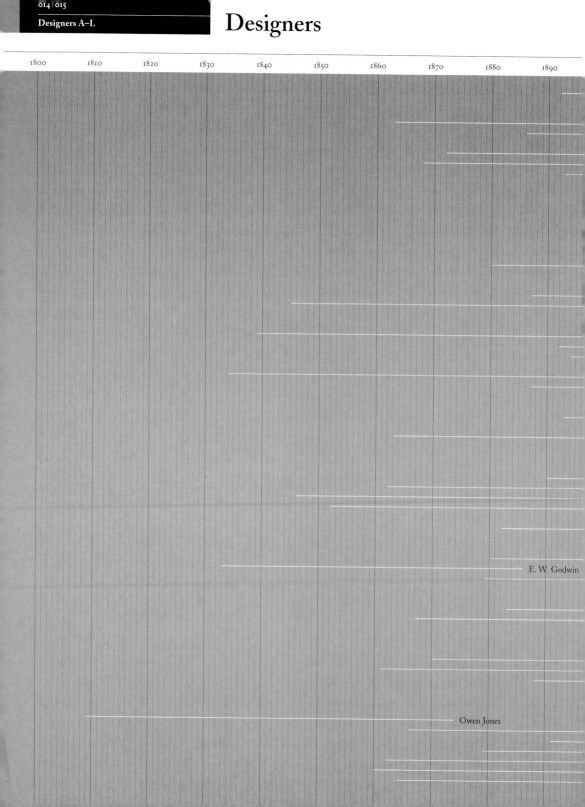

| 1800 | 1810 | 1820 | 1830 | 1840 | 1850 | 1860 | 1870 | 1880 | 1890 |

E. W. Godwin

Owen Jones

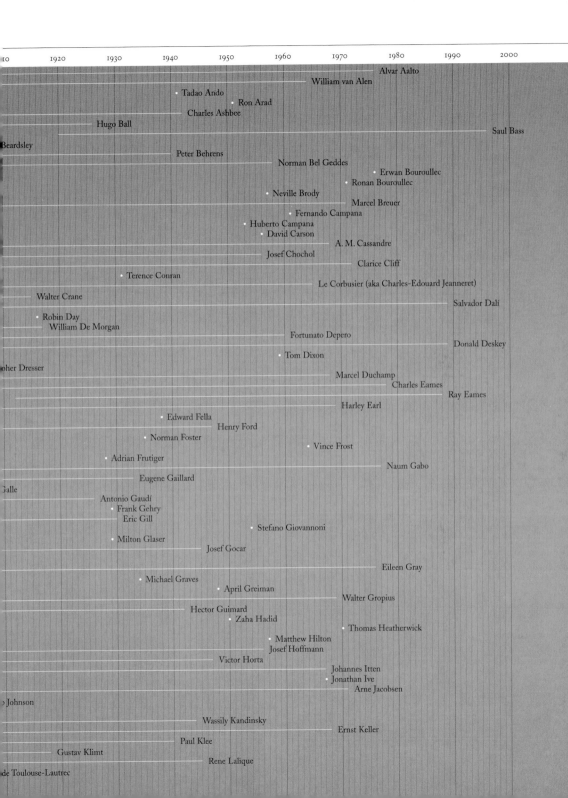

Alvar Aalto
William van Alen
Tadao Ando
Ron Arad
Charles Ashbee
Hugo Ball
Saul Bass
Beardsley
Peter Behrens
Norman Bel Geddes
Erwan Bouroullec
Ronan Bouroullec
Neville Brody
Marcel Breuer
Fernando Campana
Huberto Campana
David Carson
A. M. Cassandre
Josef Chochol
Clarice Cliff
Terence Conran
Le Corbusier (aka Charles-Edouard Jeanneret)
Walter Crane
Salvador Dalí
Robin Day
William De Morgan
Fortunato Depero
Donald Deskey
Tom Dixon
pher Dresser
Marcel Duchamp
Charles Eames
Ray Eames
Harley Earl
Edward Fella
Henry Ford
Norman Foster
Vince Frost
Adrian Frutiger
Naum Gabo
Eugene Gaillard
Galle
Antonio Gaudí
Frank Gehry
Eric Gill
Stefano Giovannoni
Milton Glaser
Josef Gocar
Eileen Gray
Michael Graves
April Greiman
Walter Gropius
Hector Guimard
Zaha Hadid
Thomas Heatherwick
Matthew Hilton
Josef Hoffmann
Victor Horta
Johannes Itten
Jonathan Ive
Arne Jacobsen
Johnson
Wassily Kandinsky
Ernst Keller
Paul Klee
Gustav Klimt
Rene Lalique
de Toulouse-Lautrec

1800	1810	1820	1830	1840	1850	1860	1870	1880	1890

A. W. N. Pugin

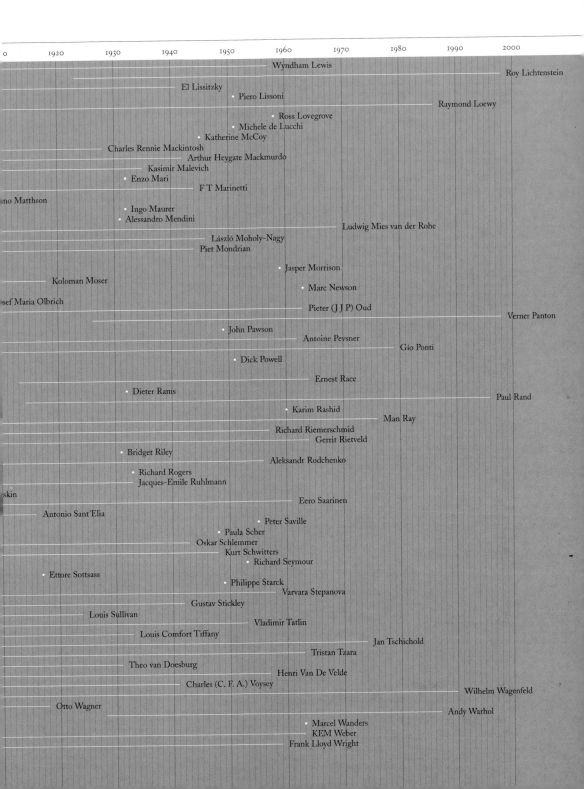

Wyndham Lewis

Roy Lichtenstein

El Lissitzky

Piero Lissoni

Ross Lovegrove

Raymond Loewy

Michele de Lucchi

Katherine McCoy

Charles Rennie Mackintosh

Arthur Heygate Mackmurdo

Kasimir Malevich

Enzo Mari

F T Marinetti

no Matthson

Ingo Maurer

Alessandro Mendini

Ludwig Mies van der Rohe

László Moholy-Nagy

Piet Mondrian

Jasper Morrison

Koloman Moser

Marc Newson

sef Maria Olbrich

Pieter (J J P) Oud

Verner Panton

John Pawson

Antoine Pevsner

Gío Ponti

Dick Powell

Ernest Race

Dieter Rams

Paul Rand

Karim Rashid

Man Ray

Richard Riemerschmid

Gerrit Rietveld

Bridget Riley

Aleksandr Rodchenko

Richard Rogers

Jacques-Emile Ruhlmann

skin

Eero Saarinen

Antonio Sant'Elia

Peter Saville

Paula Scher

Oskar Schlemmer

Kurt Schwitters

Richard Seymour

Ettore Sottsass

Philippe Starck

Varvara Stepanova

Gustav Stickley

Louis Sullivan

Vladimir Tatlin

Louis Comfort Tiffany

Jan Tschichold

Tristan Tzara

Theo van Doesburg

Henri Van De Velde

Charles (C. F. A.) Voysey

Wilhelm Wagenfeld

Otto Wagner

Andy Warhol

Marcel Wanders

KEM Weber

Frank Lloyd Wright

Events

| | 1800 | 1900 |

Movements and groups

- *1901* Societe des Artistes Decorateurs established, Fran[c]
- *1902* Cracow School initiated, Poland
- *1903* Wiener Werk[founded, Austria
- *1897* Vienna Secession founded, Austria

Companies and brands

- *1847* Siemens founded, Berlin
- *1883* AEG founded, Berlin
- *1892* General Electric founded, New York

Publications and exhibitions

- *1900* Exposition Universelle et Internationale, Paris
- *1904* Das En[
- *1895* Samuel Bing opens Art nouveau show[
- *1896* Die Jugend and Simplicissimus publishe[
- *1898* Heal's first furniture catalog publish[

World events

- *1900* Exposition Universelle et Internationale, Paris
- *1851* The Great Exhibition, London
- *1861* American Civil War begins
- *1876* Alexander Graham Bell designs first telephone

1911 Czech Cubism founded, Prague

1925 Bauhaus moves to Dessau, Germany

1914 AIGA founded, New York

1926 Rationalist movement founded by Gruppo 7, Italy

1915 Suprematism launched, Petrograd

Novecento movement founded, Italy

Design and Industries Association founded, London

Praesens group founded, Poland

1916 Dadaist movement founded, Zurich

1927 Cranbrook Academy of Art founded, Michigan, USA

Society of Arts and Crafts ustrial Design founded

1917 de Stijl founded, the Netherlands

Constructivism founded, Russia

1928 Bratislava School of Applied Art founded, Czechoslovakia

e Werkbund founded, Germany

1929 Union des Artistes Modernes (UAM) founded, Paris

09 Italian Futurist Manifesto published

1919 Bauhaus founded, Weimar, Germany

1911 IBM founded, New York

1921 Braun founded, Germany

Alessi founded, Italy

1923 Herman Miller furniture company founded, USA

1913 Citroën founded, Paris

1925 Chrysler Corporation founded, USA

Bang & Olufsen founded, Denmark

1927 Cassina founded, Italy

Olivetti founded, Italy

er founded, USA

1918 Matsushita founded, Japan

1909 Audi founded, Germany

1923 Bauhaus Exhibition, Weimar

1924 Manifeste du Surréalisme, France

1925 Exposition des Arts Décoratifs et Industriels, Paris

Hermann Muthesius

1914 Deutsche Werkbund-Ausstellung exhibiton, Cologne

BLAST launched

1928 *The New Typography*, Jan Tschichold, published

Domus magazine launched, Italy

1929 Museum of Modern Art (MoMA) founded, New York

1914 WWI begins

1925 Chromium made commercially available

1917 Russian Revolution

1918 WWI ends

1929 Wall Street Crash, New York

	1930	1940
Movements and groups	1930 Society of Industrial Artists, London	
	1932 Bauhuas moves to Berlin	1942 Utility Design Progr introduced, UK
	1933 Bauhaus closed	1943 Design Researc Unit established, UK
		1944 Counci Institute of I Design Cour
	1937 Exposition Internationale des Arts et Techniques dans la Vie Moderne, Paris	
Companies and brands	1930 Pininfarina design company founded, Italy	1943 IKEA founded,
	1934 Erco founded, Germany	1945 Bri
	Airstream founded, USA	
	1938 Tupperware founded, Massachusetts, USA	
	1938 Knoll International founded, New York	
Publications and exhibitions	1930 Stockholm Exhibition, Sweden	1940 Organic Design for the Home exh MoMA, New York
	1931 *An Essay on Typography*, Eric Gill, published	
	1932 The International Style exhibition, MoMA	
	1934 Machine Art exhibition, MoMA	
	1936 *Pioneers of the Modern Movement*, Nikolaus Pevsner, published	
	1937 Exposition Universelle, Paris	
	1939 New York World Fair, New York	
World events	1932 The atom is split for the first time	1940 Commercial television launched, U
	1933 New Deal, USA	1941 Japanese bomb Pearl Harbor
		1945 Firs on Hiros
	1936 First BBC television broadcasts, UK	WWII e
	1939 WWII begins	

1950   1960   1970

1952 Independent Group founded, London

1962 D&AD (British Design & Art Direction) founded, London

1953 Hochschule für Gestaltung, Ulm founded, Germany

1963 Archigram group founded, London

Icograda (International Council of Graphic Designers) founded, London

...al Design (COID) founded, UK

..., Chicago

..., London

1966 Archizoom Associati founded, Florence

Superstudio founded, Florence

1956 COID Design Centre opens, London

...ciety of Industrial Designers founded, USA

1968 Hochschule für Gestaltung, Ulm, Germany, closes

1950 Vitra founded, Basel, Switzerland

1960 Dieter Rams appointed Design Director at Braun

Bauhaus archive established, Darmstadt, Germany

1951 Tetra Pak created, Sweden

...d, Milan, Italy

1954 Pushpin Studios founded, New York

1963 Total Design founded, Amsterdam

...ce lighting founded, Italy

1964 First Habitat store opened by Terence Conran, London

...nics founded, Japan

1968 Coop Himmelb(l)au founded, Austria

...are founded, USA

1957 Casio founded, Japan

... Porsche founded, Germany

1958 First IKEA store opens, Sweden

1969 Frogdesign founded, Germany

1949 Kartell founded, Milan

1959 Artemide founded, Milan, Italy

IDEO founded, London

1951 Festival of Britain, London

1963 *Archigram* magazine launched, London

First Aspen International Design Conference, USA

1953 General Motors Motorama exhibition, New York

... Can Make It
...ion, London

1957 Council of Inustrial Design launches awards scheme, London

1966 *Complexity and Contradiction in Architecture*, Robert Venturi, published

... 'Low Cost Furniture'
...bition, MoMA, New York

1957 *Mythologies*, Roland Barthes, published

1949 'Design' magazine founded,
...Design Council, London

1958 *New Graphic Design* launched

1968 *2001: A Space Odyssey*, directed by Stanley Kubrick

1961 First manned spacecraft orbits earth

1961 Berlin Wall constructed

...s dropped
...Nagasaki

1955 First McDonald's restaurant opens, USA

1964 Tokyo Olympic Games

Disneyland opens, USA

1957 Launch of Sputnik satellite, USSR

1958 NASA founded, Washington DC

1969 Neil Armstrong becomes the first man to walk on the moon

	1970	1980

Movements and groups

- *1980* California New Wave founded, USA
- *1981* Japan Design Foundation fo
- Memphis Design Group founde
- *1982* Domus Academy founded, Milan
- *1975* Conseil Superier de la Creation Esthetique Industrielle founded, France
- *1976* Design for Need Conference, London
- *1977* Danish Design Council founded
- Design History Society founded, UK
- *1979* Ergonomi Design Gruppen founded, Sw

Companies and brands

- *1971* Nike founded, Portland, Oregon
- *1972* Pentagram founded, London
- *1983* Swatch founde
- *1976* Apple Computer founded, California
- Studio Alchimia founded, Italy
- *1979* Ergonomi Design Gruppen founded, Sto
- MetaDesign founded, Berlin

Publications and exhibitions

- *1971* *Design for the Real World*, Victor Papanek, published
- *1980* *The Face* magazine launched, Lond
- *1972* *Mythologies*, Roland Barthes, translated into English
- Italy: The New Domestic Landscape exhibition, MoMA, New York
- *1984* *Emigré* j
- *1977* Centre Georges Pompidou opened, France

World events

- *1980* Floppy disk introduced
- *1982* Falklands War
- *1974* Internet first developed, Vint Cerf, USA
- *1983* Compact disc la
- *1984* Apple M

gn mark implemented, Korea

- *1993* IKEA buys Habitat

- *1991* *Ray Gun*, designed by David Carson, published
- *Typography Now: The Next Wave*, Rick Poynor, published
- Benetton's *Colors* magazine launched, art directed by Tibor Kalman

shed

Journal of Design History launched, UK

nstructivist Architecture exhibition, 1A, New York

1989 Design Museum, London opens

Vitra Design Museum, Weil am Rhein, opens

- *2000* Tate Modern, London, opens
- *2001* Memphis Remembered exhibition, Design Museum, London
- Workshpheres exhibition, MoMA, New York
- *2004* History of Modern Design - In The Home exhibition, Design Museum, London

- *1990* Reunification of Germany
- *1991* Gulf War
- Civil War, Yugoslavia
- WorldWideWeb hypertext system used on the Internet for the first time

rketed
- Collapse of Communist regime, USSR
- *1993* Eurotunnel opens between England and France

1989 The Internet goes commercial

Berlin Wall demolished

- *2000* Wireless Application Protocol (WAP) mobile technology becomes widely available
- *2001* September 11 terrorist attacks, New York
- "War on Terrorism" begins with invasion of Afghanistan
- Apple introduces iTunes for the Macintosh
- *2003* US-led invasion of Iraq

Arts and Crafts movement

Origin

United Kingdom

Key characteristics

Simplicity of form

Plain, linear shapes

First phase: inspired by natural plant and animal forms

Second phase: more abstract, inspired by movement and mythical creatures

Key facts

Belief in the superiority of handcrafted objects over machine-made, machine production regarded as being degrading to both creator and consumer

Advocates of the Arts and Crafts ideal formed guilds and crafts societies, each with their own style, specialization, and leaders, to discuss and share ideas

Belief that good art and design could reform society and improve the quality of life of creator and consumer alike (important precursor to modernism)

See also

Modernism p 50

Mission style p 64

Established as a reaction to the effects of nineteenth-century industrialization, which its proponents felt had resulted in a degeneration of both the design and quality of goods, the Arts and Crafts movement advocated a simpler, more ethical approach to design and manufacture. The aim of the movement, which began in the UK, was to promote the ideals of traditional craft production and craftsmanship. It incorporated everyone from artists and architects to writers, designers, and craftsmen, united by their belief in the superiority of handcrafted over machine-made objects. The movement also regarded machine production as degrading to both creator and consumer. Typical Arts and Crafts designs were characterized by simplicity of form and the use of plain, linear shapes in a bid to embody the natural union between form, function, and decoration. In its purest form, decoration was derived from construction, as with the use of pegs and dowels as surface motifs in furniture design.

One of the first to make the connection between declining esthetic standards and the nation's moral standing was designer Augustus W. N. Pugin. Steadfast in the belief that it was possible to reform society through good design, Pugin chose the Gothic model—which in his view symbolized a truly Christian society—as his vehicle for change. Best known for his designs for the new Houses of Parliament (1835–1837), Pugin's artifacts and architecture provided an ongoing source of inspiration for many leading Arts and Crafts practitioners, including William Burgess, John Ruskin, and William Morris.

There were two phases of Arts and Crafts designers in the UK. Those in the first, led by Morris, took their inspiration from bird, plant, and animal forms, clearly visible in Morris' wallpaper designs of the time. Designers in the second phase, among them Arthur Mackmurdo of The Century Guild, took a more abstract approach. Some incorporated movement into their

designs, while others sought inspiration from exotic, mythical creatures. William de Morgan's ceramics, Walter Crane's pottery designs, and the colorful enameled metalware by architect and designer Charles Ashbee were all characteristic of this latter approach.

The crusade to put Pugin's theories into practice was led by Morris who, in 1861, established Morris, Marshall, Faulkner & Co. (renamed Morris & Co in 1874), to manufacture tapestries, furniture, and stained glass. Morris and his cohorts blamed industrialization and mechanization for many of the social problems in England at the time. As passionate socialists, they believed a return to traditional craftsmanship would help improve the lives of the poor in Victorian England and thus make the world a better place. It is somewhat ironic then that many of Morris & Co.'s handcrafted products were so costly to produce that they became affordable only to the wealthy industrialists that the Arts and Crafts movement so despised.

Inspired by the medieval crafts guilds, advocates of the Arts and Crafts ideal formed a series of guilds and crafts societies, each with their own style, specialization, and leaders, to discuss and share ideas. These included the Guild of St. George, The Century Guild, the Guild of Handicraft, the Cotswold School, and the Art Workers Guild, whose aim it was "to advance education in all the visual arts and crafts by means of lectures, meetings, demonstrations, discussions, and other methods; and to foster and maintain high standards of design and craftsmanship … in any way which may be beneficial to the community." The Art Workers Guild was formed by the amalgamation of two existing groups—a group of five young architects known as The St. George Society and The Fifteen, a group founded by writer and designer Lewis F. Day and designer/illustrator Walter Crane. Its impressive membership included the likes of Morris, Mackmurdo, Ashbee, and Charles Voysey.

While Morris & Co. existed under the formal structure of a company, and members of The Century Guild were united by their close working relationship, there was no such sense of unity for the Art Workers Guild, whose members continued to work from their own studios and workshops. It was this realization, as well as the need for a collective display and promotion of their work, that led to the concept of a public exhibition. Despite opposition, in 1888, the new group held its first exhibition at the New Gallery on London's Regent Street under the presidency of Walter Crane. Known as the Arts and Crafts Exhibition Society, it was from this exhibition that the Arts and Crafts movement took its name.

Although the Arts and Crafts movement began in the UK, a newfound appreciation of the decorative arts in the USA and across Europe soon developed. In Scandinavia and central Europe the movement fueled a resurgence in national styles, while the American attempt to import the Arts and Crafts ideal became known as the Craftsman movement, **mission style** or Golden Oak. In esthetic terms, the Arts and Crafts movement represented a key stylistic development in the decorative arts, but it was also steeped in the belief that good art and design could reform society and improve the quality of life of creator and consumer alike, hence it was an important precursor to **modernism**.

Writing desk:
Arthur H.
Mackmurdo

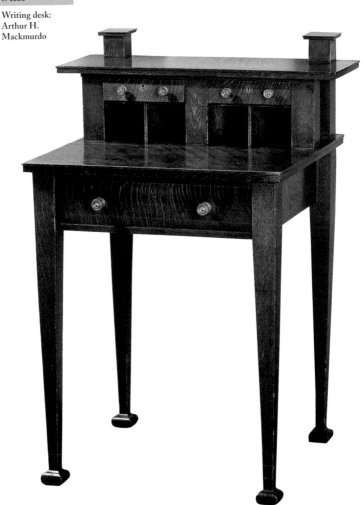

1895

Net Ceiling ceiling
paper: William
Morris

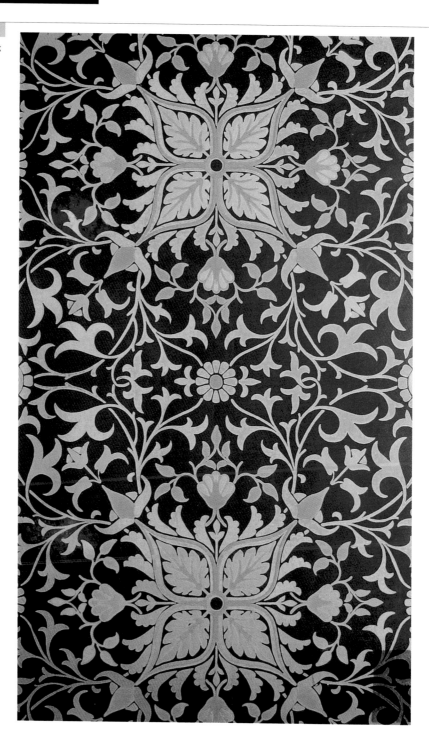

Enameled
silverwork: Charles
Robert Ashbee

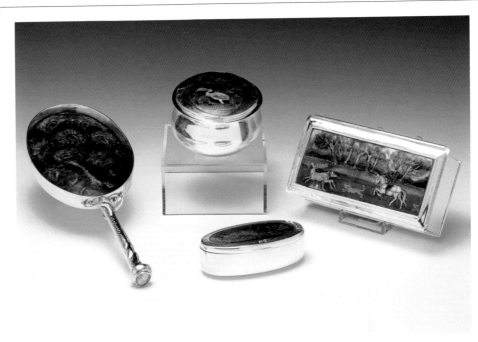

Decanter in green
glass with silver
mounts and
chrysophase set in
the finial: Charles
Robert Ashbee

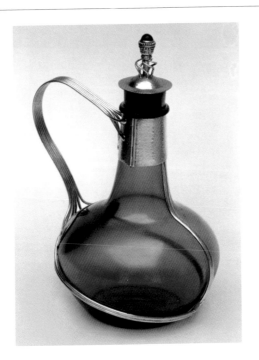

Regional variations	Country of origin	Key figures	Fields of work
Arts and Crafts movement	UK: 1st Phase	William Morris (1834–1896)	Socialist/Writer/Designer
		A. W. N. Pugin (1812–1852)	Architect/Designer/Theorist
		John Ruskin (1819–1900)	Philosopher/Artist/Art critic
	UK: 2nd Phase	William R. Lethaby (1857–1931)	Designer/Principal, Central School of Arts and Crafts, London (1896)
		Arthur H. Mackmurdo (1851–1942)	Architect/Designer
		Charles R. Ashbee (1863–1942)	Architect/Designer
		Charles F. A. Voysey (1857–1941)	Architect/Designer (furniture)/Principal Royal College of Art, London (1897–189…
		William De Morgan (1839–1917)	Designer (ceramics)
		Walter Crane (1845–1915)	Designer/Illustrator
		Gustav Stickley (1857–1942)	Designer (furniture)/Craftsman
Craftsman/Golden Oak/mission style	USA	Charles P. Limbert (1854–1923)	Designer (furniture and lighting)
		Elbert G. Hubbard (1856–1915)	Former soap salesman

English Guilds and Crafts Societies	Location	Founder/Leader
Guild of St. George (1872)	London, UK	John Ruskin (1819–1900)
The Century Guild (1882–1888)	London, UK	Arthur Mackmurdo (1851–1942)
		Selwyn Image (1849–1930)
St. George's Art Society (1883)	London, UK	Gerald Horsley (1862–1917)
		William R. Lethaby (1857–1931)
		Mervyn Macartney (1853–1932)
		Ernest Newton (1856–1922)
		E. S. Prior (1852–1932)
Art Workers Guild (1884)	London, UK	Founders of the St. George's Art Society together with members Oak/mission style of The Fifteen, including Walter Crane (1845–1915) and Lewis Foreman Day (1845–1910)
Guild of Handicraft (1888)	London, UK	Charles R. Ashbee (1863–1942)
Arts and Crafts Exhibition Society (1888)	London, UK	Walter Crane (1845–1915)
Glasgow School (1890s)	Glasgow, UK	Charles Rennie Mackintosh (1868–1928)

International Guilds and Crafts Societies	Location	Founder/Leader
Guild of St. George (1872)	East Aurora, nr Buffalo, NY, USA	Elbert Hubbard
The United Crafts (1898–1915)	Syracuse, NY, USA	Gustav Stickley
Darmstadt Artists Colony (1899)	Grand Duke Ernst Ludwig of Hesse	Darmstadt, Germany

Later Applications

Sponge Vase:
Moooi and
Droog Design
A joint project,
Marcel Wanders'

Sponge Vase is made
from a real sea
sponge, dipped in
liquid porcelain and
dried out. The sponge

is then burned away
in a ceramic oven,
leaving only the
creature's fragile
shape, set rigid.

Guest services
directory at the
Hotel Pattee, Perry,
Iowa, USA: Sayles
Graphic Design
The directory is
reminiscent of the
hotel's 1913 origins

and link to the
railroad industry.
The book is made
of brown leather
accented with colors
found in the hotel's
interior: red, green,
and dark yellow.

The cover is high-
lighted with an
embossed copperplate
affixed to the center,
and the binder is
lined with the actual
wallpaper used in the
main lobby.

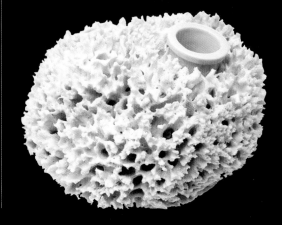

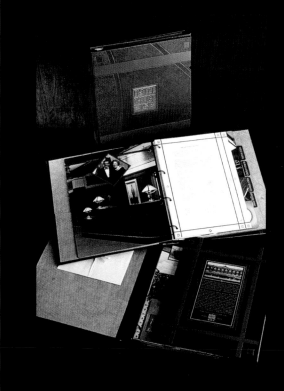

Exhibition catalog:
Area Designed to
accompany Jill
Ritblat's exhibition
One Woman's
Wardrobe at the

Victoria and Albert
Museum in London,
Area's exhibition
catalog heralded a
return to craft-based
values in the late

nineties. The catalog
folds out from a
handbag to reveal a
wealth of beautiful
imagery and
typographic forms.

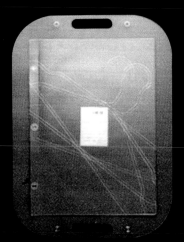

Later Applications

Logo for Arts and Crafts conference held at Hotel Pattee, Perry, Iowa, USA: Sayles Graphic Design

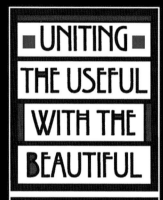

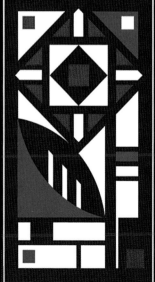

Crocheted lampshade: Electricwig Cotton was used to crochet the lampshade which was then stiffened with a mix of sugar and water.

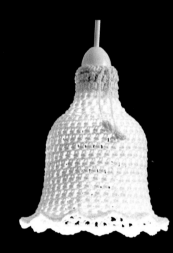

Style Riot: Grayson Perry Perry was awarded the 2003 Turner Prize for his classically shaped ceramic vases decorated with figures, objects, and text.

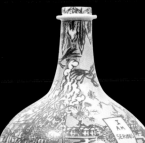

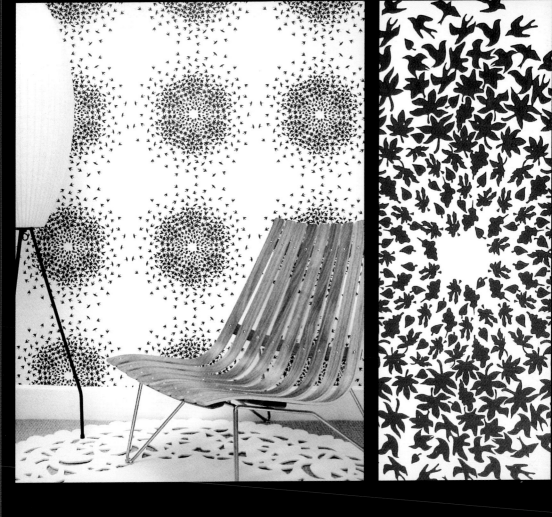

Esthetic movement

During the second half of the nineteenth century, developments in British art, architecture, and design led to the creation of the Esthetic movement, a modern style of Victorian design that ran largely in parallel to the **Arts and Crafts movement** and sought to elevate the status of all objects to works of art. Driven by slogans such as "art for art's sake," the Esthetic movement, like the Arts and Crafts movement, was a reaction to the excesses of the Gothic revival. However, in contrast with the Arts and Crafts movement, estheticism rejected the idea that art should have any social or moral purpose. In architecture it was characterized by plain materials, and in the decorative arts by the arts and craftsmanship of Japan and China.

The Esthetic movement initially offered a contrast to the opulence of the classical styles, having simplicity, honesty, and plainness as its primary objectives. However, decorative interpretation, combined with Japanese and other ethnic influences, eventually led to the corruption of these original ideals. The movement was initiated by Christopher Dresser and Owen Jones, both of whom believed good design

should be both appropriate to function and fit for purpose. Having only recently opened up to the West, the high-quality craftsmanship and use of abstract and geometric forms that characterized Japanese design also had a profound influence on the style. While Godwin westernized Japanese and Chinese forms to create his Anglo-Japanese furniture, western forms were orientalized; ceramics adopted oriental shapes and forms and Tiffany & Co., in New York, produced silver pieces with Japanese motifs. The Japanese influence could also be seen in Europe, especially France where **Japonisme** flourished in ceramics, metalware, and glass.

The Esthetic movement had many supporters, all united by the desire to move away from the rigidity of early Victorianism toward a freer view of art and design. The movement succeeded in capturing the imagination of the masses through a series of international exhibitions—held between 1871 and 1878 in London, Vienna, Philadelphia, and Paris—and workshops held by the likes of Morris & Co., London, and Cottier & Co., New York. Home decorating manuals, such as *Hints on Household Taste*

1878

Toast rack:
Christopher Dresser
(Historical reproduction by Alessi, 1991.)

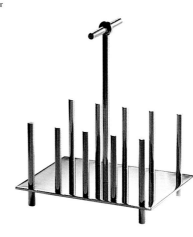

and *The House Beautiful* provided an additional vehicle through which to spread the word. The latter, by Clarence Cook, reiterated the importance of selecting from different eras and harmoniously combining disparate elements to create a coherent, beautiful whole. The movement also incorporated the architectural style of E. W. Goodwin, with its extensive use of red brick with decorative motifs, overly tall chimneys and stepped gables, Pre-Raphaelite painters such as Edward Burne-Jones, and the writings of Oscar Wilde. London's Liberty store became *the* place to source the latest works by the movement's leading practitioners. The Esthetic movement was influential over art and design in Europe, eventually leading to **art nouveau** and **secessionism**.

House and Studio for F. Miles Esq., Chelsea: E. W. Godwin

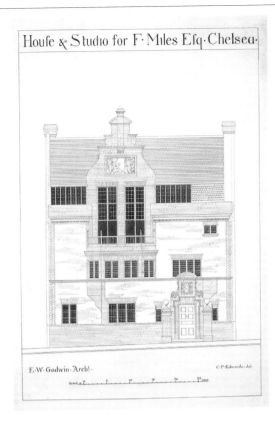

Esthetic interior, English School, showing works by William Morris and William de Morgan.

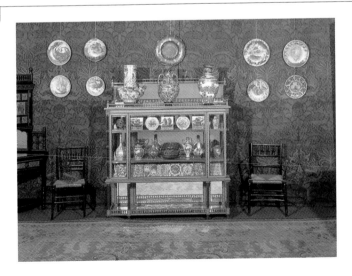

1881

My Lady's
Chamber,
frontispiece to *The
House Beautiful*:
Clarence Cook

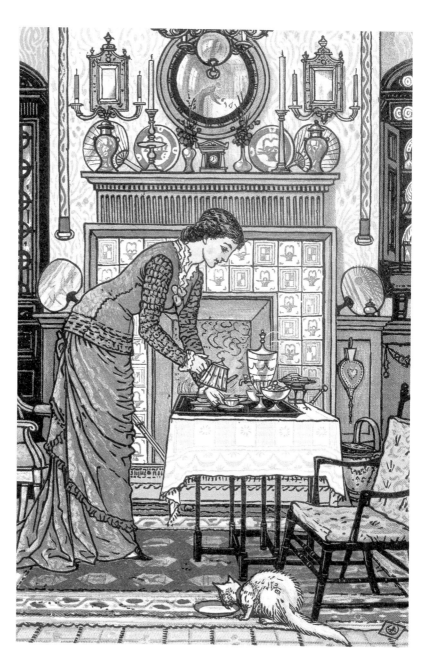

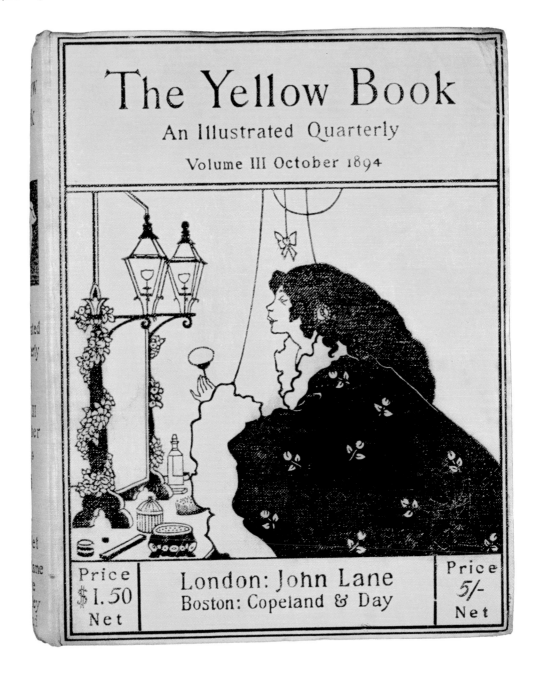

The Yellow Book

An Illustrated Quarterly

Volume III October 1894

Price
$1.50
Net

London: John Lane
Boston: Copeland & Day

Price
5/-
Net

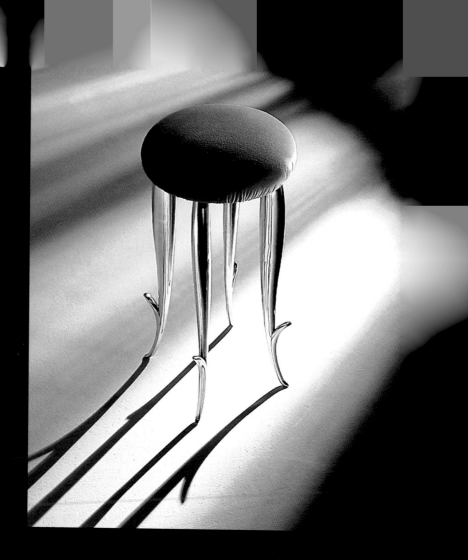

Royalton bar stool:
Philippe Starck
for XO

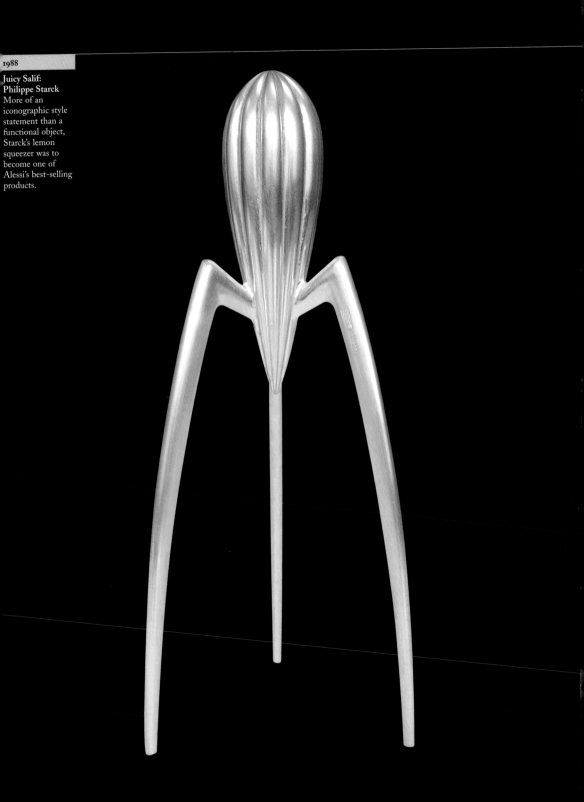

Juicy Salif:
Philippe Starck
More of an
iconographic style
statement than a
functional object,
Starck's lemon
squeezer was to
become one of
Alessi's best-selling
products.

Japonisme

By the late nineteenth century, many **art nouveau** designers found themselves looking to the East, and especially to Japan, for inspiration. As Japan finally opened up to the West, following some 200 years in isolation, the sudden influx of traditional Japanese crafts—from ceramics and metalwork to architecture, printmaking, and painting—had a profound effect on designers and collectors alike. The Paris *Exposition Universelle* of 1867 introduced Japanese craft and culture to the West and brought many Japanese visitors to the city. In 1872, the French art critic Philippe Burty described this newfound Japanese-influenced style as Japonisme.

Western enthusiasm for Japanese decorative and graphic art was fed by its exposure through art dealers, import shops, museum exhibitions, world fairs, and, of course, word of mouth. One of the most important

figures in the history of Japonisme was the Parisian dealer Samuel Bing who, in 1888, founded the journal *Le Japon Artistique* as a means of raising the profile of "crafts" in Europe. This was achieved, in part, by highlighting work from Japan where there was no distinction between fine and applied art. Bing dealt in woodcuts, ceramics, lacquers, and sword guards, and held several special exhibitions in his galleries.

A number of natural themes, including animals, insects, and plants, emerged as a common motif, fueled by a growing appreciation of early woodblock prints, pottery, and other fine arts from Japan. The 2-D, richly patterned surfaces of Japanese woodblock prints, by artists such as Hiroshige, influenced a number of Western designers at this time. This influence can be seen in the flowing, organic themes of art nouveau.

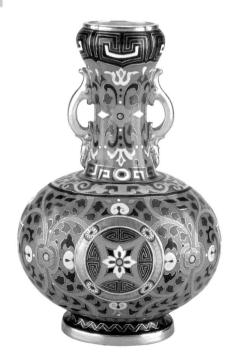

c. 1870

Dummy vase: Christopher Dresser
This vase is decorated in imitation of cloisonné enamelware.

Henri de Toulouse-Lautrec's brilliant assimilation of woodblock prints led him to forge a poster style free of Western perspective and modeling.

In France during the 1870s, Japonisme flourished in ceramics, metalware, and glass. In Paris, exhibitions of Ukiyo-e art were held to great acclaim as the popularity of Japanese style spread through the fine and decorative arts, and the rest of the design world. In eighteenth- and nineteenth-century Japan, the Ukiyo-e Floating World school of printmaking included artists such as Hiroshige, whose nonheroic, everyday subject matter was mass-produced as woodcuts, cheap enough for the average Japanese person to afford. Although not considered fine art in Japan, they had a huge impact on the decorative arts in continental Europe. Graphic designers including Toulouse-Lautrec were especially influenced by

Ukiyo-e, as was designer and writer Christopher Dresser, who traveled to Japan to find goods to import for sale by Liberty of London. The store opened in 1875 selling ornaments, fabrics, and objets d'art imported from Japan and the East. It also commissioned local designers to create homewares in the Japanese style. Dresser's deep interest in Japanese art, which began in the early 1860s, influenced his entire esthetic, and he was instrumental in making Japanese art and design better known both in the UK and in the US. Western appreciation for Japanese graphic art and objects quickly intensified as Japanese-influenced style entered the lexicon of Western artistic expression. Around the same time, exposure to the West increasingly influenced Japanese artists and audiences.

Japonisme also provided some of the central concepts of twentieth-century **modernism**. The grid structures

characteristic of many Japanese interiors were echoed in a sideboard by Charles Rennie Mackintosh. Their simple palettes and asymmetric lines, detailed craftwork and elegant accessories, such as fans and kimonos, were all eagerly soaked up by designers in the West. The greatest impact of the Far East, however, was the move toward decoration as a valid means of artistic expression.

1860–1895

Teapot: Honoike of Yokohama

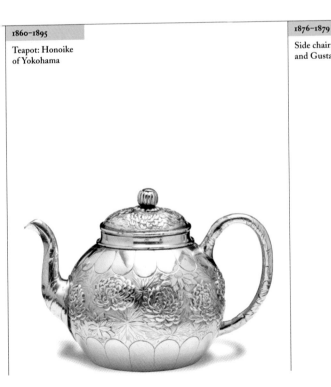

1876–1879

Side chair: Christian and Gustave Herter

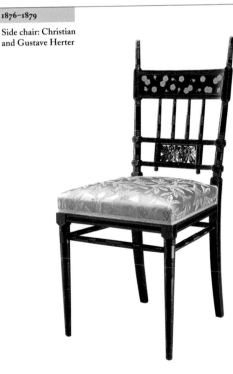

Compagnie
Francaise des
Chocolats et des
Thès poster:
Theophile
Alexandre Steinlen

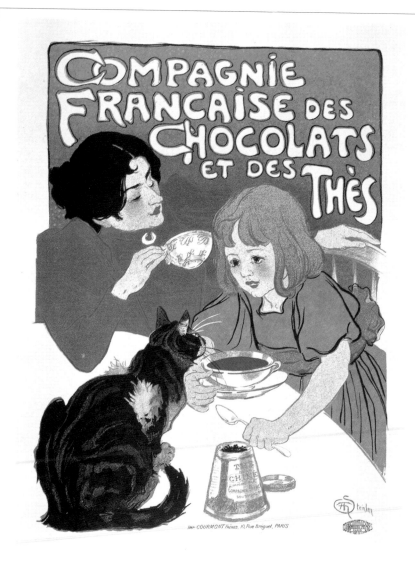

Key figures	Fields of work
Henri de Toulouse-Lautrec (1864–1901)	Artist
Christopher Dresser (1834–1904)	Designer (metalwork, ceramics, glassware, industrial design)
Samuel Bing (1838–1905)	Art dealer/Promoter
Félix Braquemond (1883–1914)	Artist

Later Applications

Shu Uemura joined forces with Japanese artist Ai Yamaguchi, whose work combines Edo esthetics with a contemporary pop-art edge, to create the artwork for this limited-edition set of cleansing oils.

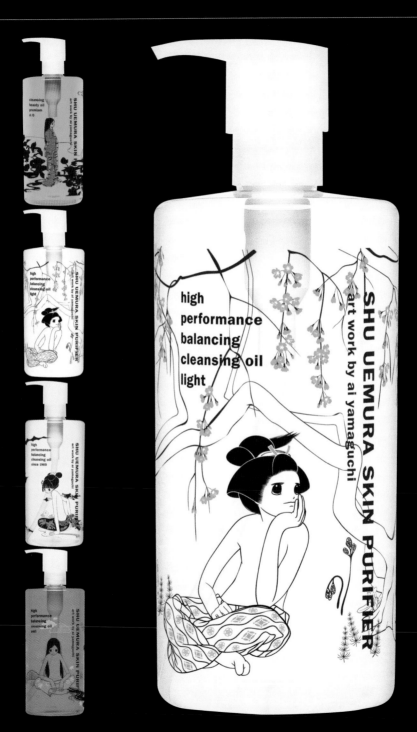

Art nouveau

Art nouveau is the name attributed to a universal design style that emerged in Europe in the late 1880s, a time when designers and architects were looking to forge a future based on the new. Inspired by the British **Arts and Crafts movement**, art nouveau rejected historicism and, for this reason, is often described as the first truly modern, international style. Its characteristic organic foliate forms, sinuous lines, and curvilinear whiplash motifs inspired some of the most fundamental forms of this unique style.

Despite its many regional variations, not to mention the outstanding talents of its individual designers, the art-nouveau (new art) styles had a number of shared goals. The introduction of new forms, embrace of mass production, and focus on the natural as a source of inspiration were common to all. **Japonisme**, with its use of white space and simplicity of form, also played a crucial role in the evolution of art nouveau. This was particularly evident in graphic design and can clearly be seen in the work of poster artists such as Henri de Toulouse-Lautrec, Alphonse Mucha, and Aubrey Beardsley.

In Spain, France, England, and the USA, art-nouveau designs were dominated by curvilinear whiplash motifs, while in Scotland and Germany, they were predominantly identified as rectilinear. Charles Rennie Mackintosh' architecture, interiors, and furniture designs for the Glasgow School of Art remain some of the best examples of rectilinear art nouveau. As with any design style, there were exceptions to th rule, with some designers opting to combine curvilinear and rectilinear lines within their work.

A key exponent of art nouveau in the UK was Liberty, while in France the style was clearly divided into two group the Nancy School, founded by Emile Gallé in 1901; and the Paris School, which developed as a result of Hector Guimard's work with Victor Horta. Gallé's botanical knowledge and interest in the natural world was manifested in his decorative use of exotic plant forms and insects, including his marquetry designs for furniture. His curvilinear surface patterns of intertwining leaves are classic examples of Nancy designs of the time.

1882

Details of the
Sagrada Familia,
Barcelona, Spain:
Antoni Gaudí

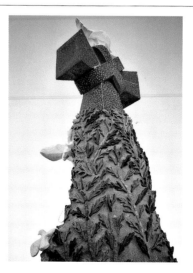
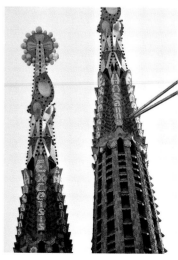

Staircase of the
Horta House,
Brussels, Belgium:
Victor Horta

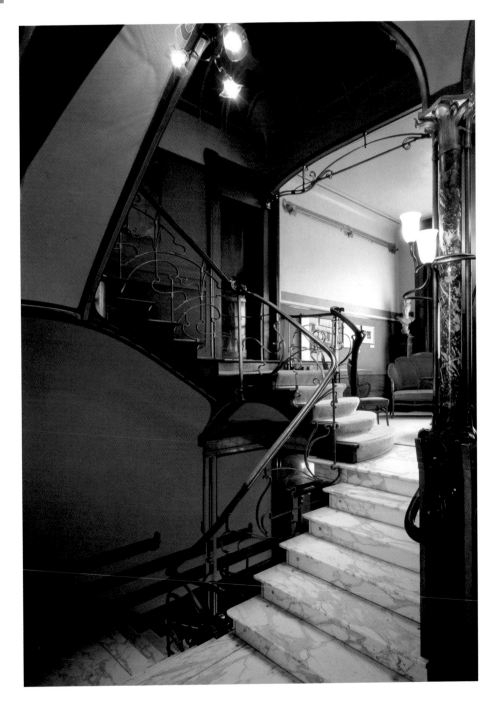

1900

Abbesses metro
station, Paris:
Hector Guimard

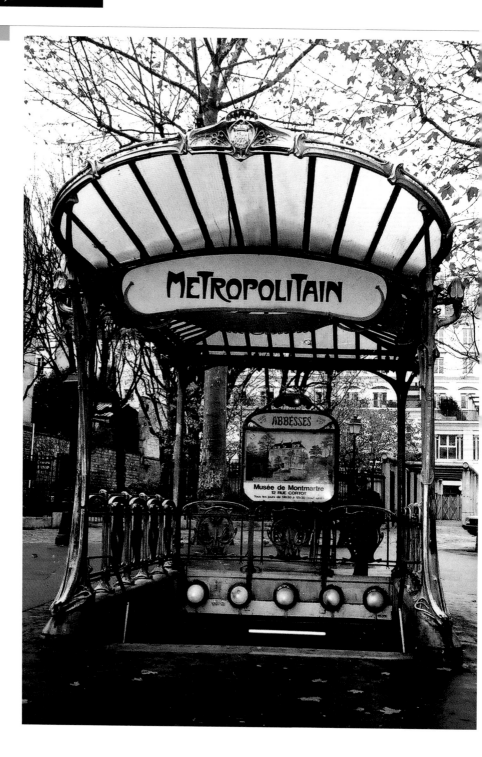

Art nouveau remained predominantly architectural in Belgium, where Horta's Hotel Tassel became one of the first architectural responses to the style. The Belgian architect's ironwork and use of stemlike columns became known as the Horta Line. Guimard's influence, seen to best effect on his entrances for the Paris Mètro, became definitive of the Style Guimard in France. In Paris, the scene centered on a group of artists brought together by Samuel Bing, who exhibited their work in his gallery, L'Art Nouveau. In Spain, Modernismo began to take hold thanks to the work of Antoni Gaudí, while the Germans opted for the name **jugendstil** to describe their interpretation of the style.

Parc Guell,
Barcelona, Spain:
Antoni Gaudí

Plate 54: Alphonse Mucha Design for an art-nouveau alphabet published by Librarie Centrale des Beaux Arts.

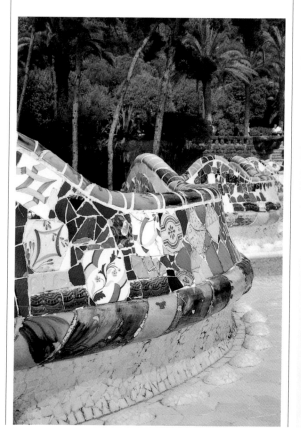

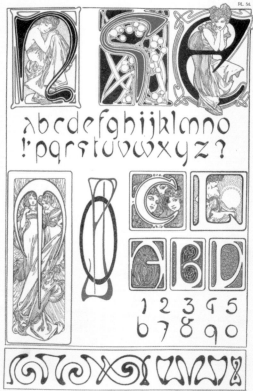

1902

**Electric fan:
H. Frost & Co** The curvilinear, sinuous lines are characteristic of art nouveau.

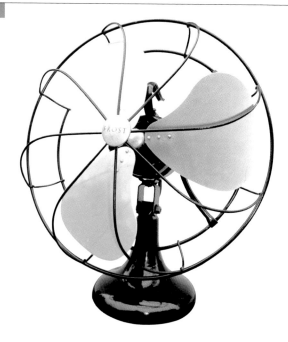

1904

Fragranced lip balms: Perfumería Gal Still sold today in the original art-nouveau packaging.

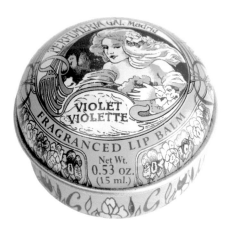

1905–1907

Facade of the Casa Batllo, Barcelona, Spain: Antoni Gaudí The design of this building was inspired by colors and shapes found in marine life.

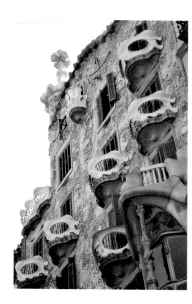

Interior of Casa
Mila ("La Pedrera"),
Barcelona, Spain:
Antoni Gaudí

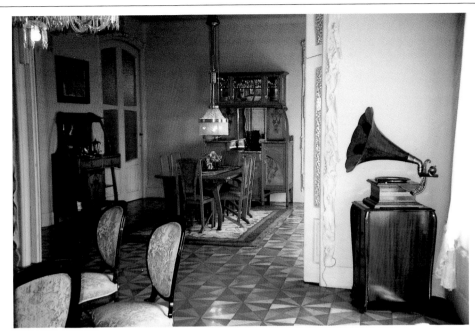

The decorative
elements of this
pewter teapot were
influenced by
natural plant forms.

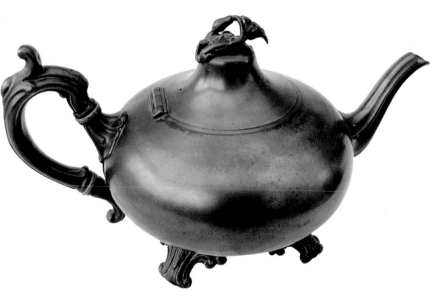

Later Applications

Art-nouveau
border designs.

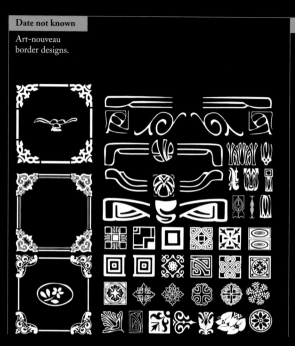

Art nouveau–style
typefaces:
Gismonda: Sam
Wang; Harquil:
Lisa Wade; Isadora:
Sam Wang; Paris
Metro: David
Rakowski;
Rudelsberg: David
Rakowski; Sarah
Caps: Sam Wang

Gismonda

Harquil

ISADORA

PARIS METRO

Rudelsberg

SARAH CAPS

Regional variations	Country of origin	Key figures	Fields of work
Art nouveau (also known as le style moderne in France)	UK France Belgium USA	Charles Rennie Mackintosh (1868–1928)	Architect/Designer
		Hector Guimard (1867–1942)	Architect/Furniture designer
		Émile Gallé (1846–1904)	Designer/Glassmaker
		Henri de Toulouse-Lautrec (1864–1901)	Artist
		Victor Horta (1861–1947)	Architect/Designer
		Henri van de Velde (1863–1957)	Architect/Industrial designer/Painter/Art critic
		Louis Comfort Tiffany (1848–1933)	Glassmaker/Jeweler/Painter/Designer/Interior decorator
Jugendstil	Germany/Scandinavia	Peter Behrens (1868–1940)	Graphic artist/Architect/Designer
		Richard Riemerschmid (1868–1957)	Architect/Designer
Secession/Sezession/Vienna secession	Austria	Josef Franz Maria Hoffmann (1870–1956)	Architect/Designer
		Otto Wagner (1841–1918)	Architect/Designer
		Josef Maria Olbrich (1867–1908)	Artist/Architect/Designer
		Koloman Moser (1868–1918)	Painter/Designer/Metalworker/Graphic
Modernismo/modernista	Spain	Antoni Gaudí (1852–1926)	Architect/Designer

**The Light Bar:
Philippe Starck**
Starck's acclaimed
design for The
Light Bar at the
St. Martin's Lane
Hotel, London,
hints at the
rectilinear style of
art nouveau
popularized by
Charles Rennie
Mackintosh in the
late 1890s.

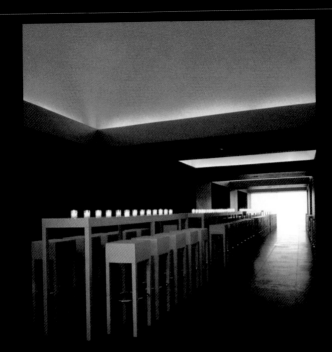

**Glasgow 1999
typeface:
MetaDesign**
Commissioned by
Glasgow and
designed by
MetaDesign,
Glasgow 1999
gives the heritage
of Charles Rennie
Mackintosh a
contemporary twist.

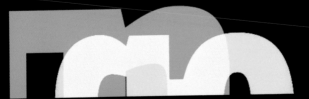

Glasgow is Scottish in its stone, Eur

but we've tried to give the typeface *Glasgow 1999* some special features.

Modernism

The leading design movement of the twentieth century, modernism emerged as a result of the growth in industrialization that occurred from the nineteenth to the twentieth century. Following the war, as the movement began to gain momentum, modernist theories and principles became increasingly influential in the planning and rebuilding of many European cities. A number of moral debates paved the way for the development of modernism, including that put forward in Nikolaus Pevsner's seminal book, *Pioneer's of the Modern Movement* (1936). The underlying principles of modernism are best represented in the work of Le Corbusier; other notable early modernists include Adolf Loos, Peter Behrens, Walter Gropius, and Mies van der Rohe.

The development of modernism is ofte explained architecturally, a point symptomatic of architecture's dominand over craft and design at the time. Havin come to the realization that the High Victorian style they were witnessing wa the result of corruption and greed, early pioneers of modernism—William Morr and A. W. N. Pugin—took it upon themselves to reform society by way of a new approach to design: developing well-designed and executed products fo everyday use. Although both advocated craftsmanship over industrial productio they also encouraged the need for and importance of functionality, simplicity, and appropriateness in design. Moreove they stressed that it was the moral responsibility of designers and manu-facturers alike to produce such goods.

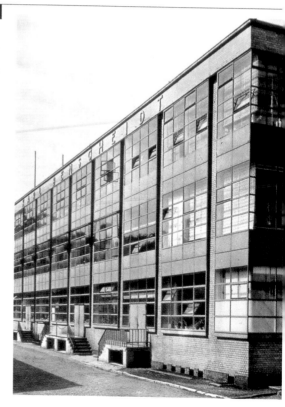

1910–1911

Fagus Shoe Factory: Walter Gropius and Adolf Meyer Gropius and Meyer's factory remains a seminal structure in the history of modern architecture.

**Table lamp:
Wilhelm
Wagenfeld**
This famous nickel,
silver, and glass
design was created
for the Bauhaus
workshops in
Weimar, Germany,
and is often
referred to simply
as "the Bauhaus
lamp." As
Wagenfeld
commented years
later, the Bauhaus
designs were
intended to be
industrial products,
and indeed looked
like them, but in
fact they were
handcrafted.

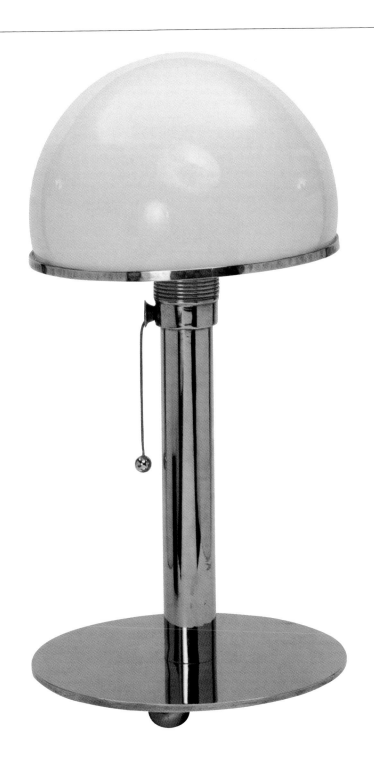

It was this idea that design could be used as a democratic tool for social change that was to have a fundamental impact on the development of modernism. In Adolf Loos' *Ornament und Vebrechen* (Ornament and Crime), he linked excessive decoration with the debasement of society, while *Form ohne Ornament* (Form without Ornament) highlighted the virtues of plain, rationally based designs. This emphasis on the purging of ornament was a concept promoted by the **de Stijl** movement, while **constructivism** and **futurism** celebrated the machine, and **Bauhaus**, under the directorship of Walter Gropius, was established to bring unity to the arts and put the reforming ideals of modernism into practice. Through its promotion of functionalism, and its use of state-of-the-art materials and industrial methods, Bauhaus had an enormous impact on modernism, creating a new language of design, that infiltrated everything from interiors and furniture to metalware, ceramics, graphics, and architecture.

By 1927, an **International Style** of modernism had emerged. Championed by Le Corbusier, **minimalism** and Industrial Style were just two modernist subdivisions characteristic of this new reductivist machine esthetic. 1930s fashion was also influenced by the International Style, taking geometric abstraction to extremes, as well as using industrial materials and severity of form purely for stylistic purposes. As a result, modernism soon lost its original moral bearings, but all was not lost, as the modernist baton was passed to Scandinavian designers such as Alvar Aalto, whose pioneering work humanized form through **organic design**, and inspired a whole new generation of modernist designers.

Exemplified by the International Style that dominated US architecture in the 1920s and 1930s, modernism has since evolved into various regional trends, from Brutalism to Rectilinearism. Unlike the majority of design styles, modernism had no single manifesto or "members". Rather, it encompassed a variety of different people united by a shared esthetic and set of common value

Modernism's concept of modernity and desire to exploit the latest materials and technology was expressed with simple forms, smooth finishes, minimal surface modeling, no applied or integral decoration, and the use of white space.

1925

Laccio tables:
Marcel Breuer

MR Side Chair: Ludwig Mies van der Rohe This classic design by the master of modernism has spawned a multitude of imitations across the globe.

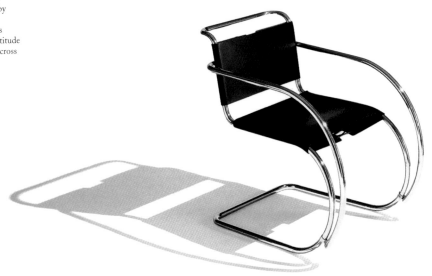

Futura typeface: Paul Renner The prototype for this family of geometric sans-serif typefaces.

abcdefghijklmnopqrstuv
wxyz fiflß&
ABCDEFGHIJKLMNOPQR
STUVWXYZ
1234567890
.,:;-—__'' """.‹›«»*%‰
!?¡¿()[]/†‡§$£¢ƒ

German Pavilion,
International
Exposition,
Barcelona: Ludwig
Mies van der Rohe
While constructed as
a temporary building,
van der Rohe's design
used permanent
materials—steel,
glass, marble, and
travertine. The
design of the single-
story building was
asymmetric and
fluid, ensuring
a continuous
flow of space.

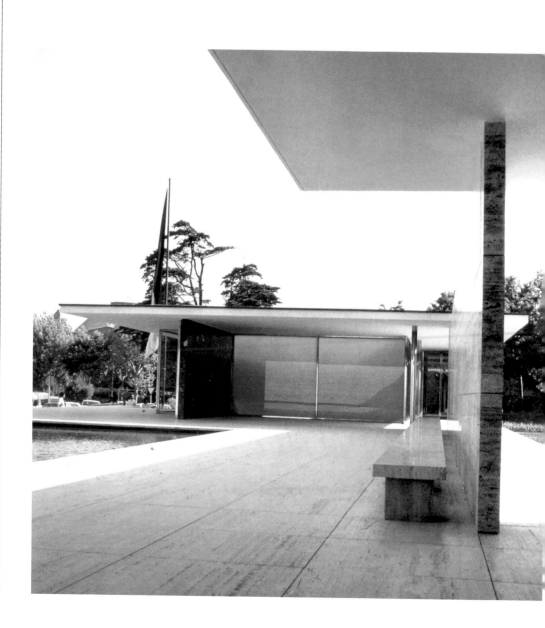

Pontresina Engadin poster: Herbert Matter
Matter completely understood modernism's new approach to visual communication. Here he uses montage and extreme scale change—from the large head to the small skier—to integrate image and text with startling effect.

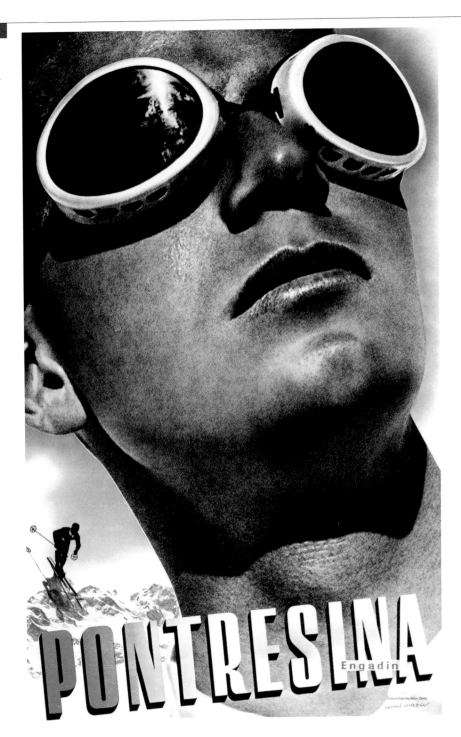

Later Applications

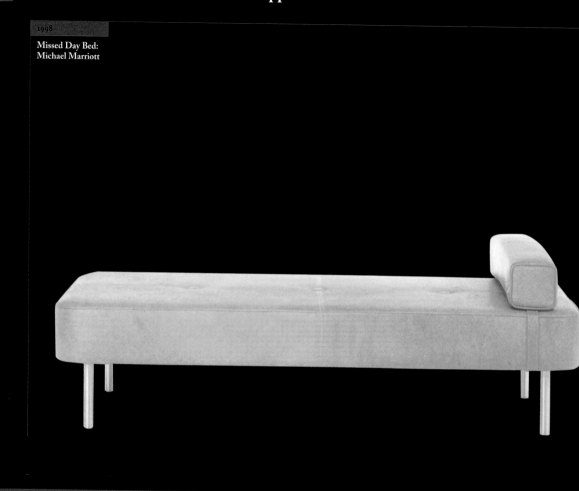

1998

**Missed Day Bed:
Michael Marriott**

Key figures	Fields of work
Charles-Edouard Jeannerer-Gris Le Corbusier (1887–1965)	Architect
Adolf Loos (1870–1933)	Architect/Designer
Peter Behrens (1868–1940)	Graphic artist/Architect/Designer
Walter Adolph Gropius (1883–1969)	Architect
Ludwig Mies van der Rohe (1886–1969)	Architect/Designer

Strands of modernism	Country of origin
de Stijl	Denmark
Constructivism	Russia
Futurism	Italy
Bauhaus	Germany

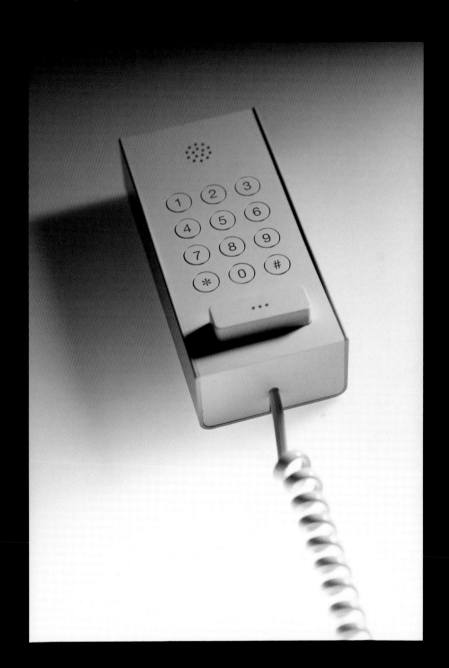

**Second phone:
Sam Hecht for
Muji**

Beaux-arts

Origin

France

Key characteristics

Grandiose buildings with stone finish

Monumental classical ornamentation (balustrades, balconies, columns, cornices, and pilasters)

Grand stairways

Large arches

Symmetrical facades

Key facts

The beaux-arts style combined classical Greek and Roman architecture with Renaissance ideas

The Ecole des Beaux-Arts academie established itself as the only school teaching this architecture

Advocates of the movement felt that beauty could be an effective device for social control

Famous beaux-arts buildings

Boston Public Library (1887–1895), Charles Follen McKim (1847–1909) of McKim, Mead, and White

Grand Central Terminal, New York (1907–1913), Reed and Stern with Warren and Wetmore

New York Public Library (1897–1911), Carrere and Hastings

Palace of Fine Arts, San Francisco (1913–1915), Bernard R. Maybeck

See also

Postmodernism p 216

Also known as beaux-arts classicism, academic classicism, and classical revival. The beaux-arts (fine art) style originated from the Ecole des Beaux-Arts in Paris during the second half of the nineteenth century, and was incorporated into architecture and interior design, as well as objects such as furniture and textiles. Beaux-arts was characterized by order, symmetry, formal design, grandiosity, and elaborate ornamentation. The beaux-arts style combined classical Greek and Roman architecture with Renaissance ideas, resulting in an eclectic neoclassical style noted for its paired columns, patterns within patterns, high parapets, domes, projecting facades, balustrades, pilasters, and pavilions. Due to the size and grandiosity of the buildings, the beaux-arts style was predominantly used for public buildings such as museums, railway stations, libraries, and banks, although during the Gilded Age (the era in American history from the end of the Civil War to the turn of the century), the style was adopted by some wealthy industrialists for their own private homes. As a result, in the USA the style led to planned neighborhoods with large, showy houses, wide boulevards, and vast parks, courthouses, and government buildings.

The Ecole des Beaux-Arts itself was an officially sponsored school of art and design, established in 1819 as the sole successor to a number of royal arts academies that had previously existed in France. Before long, it had established itself as the *only* school of architecture, with students traveling from around the world to attend. Many American architects, including Raymond Hood,

Charles Follen McKim, Louis Sullivan, and John Russell Pope studied at this legendary school, where they were taught about the esthetic principles of classical design. Students at the school worked in ateliers, under the guidance of an established architect. Famous teachers included Charles Garnier, the architect responsible for the Paris Opera House, Henri Labrouste, whose early use of iron and glass can be seen in his Paris libraries, and Victor Laloux. The students' work was then judged in a competition by a panel of professionals. Like the **Bauhaus**, the Ecole des Beaux-Arts was an important model, not just for what was designed, but as a way *to* design.

The beaux-arts movement was also concerned with formal design and city planning, and in the late nineteenth century inspired the so-called City Beautiful movement, which sought to improve the urban environment through beautification in architecture and landscaping in the hope that "… American cities would be brought to cultural parity with their European competitors through the use of the European beaux-arts style; and create a more inviting city center in which to work and spend money." (*The City Beautiful: The 1901 Plan for Washington DC.*). Influenced by the beaux-arts architecture of Europe and working on the premise that beauty could be an effective device for social control, American city-shapers designed civic centers, grand boulevards, and parks in a quest for urban beauty. The first expression of this was The White City, created for the World's Columbian Exposition of 1893. Said to epitomize city

Key students of the Ecole des Beaux-Arts, Paris	Fields of work
Raymond Hood (1881–1934)	Architect
Charles Follen McKim (1847–1909) of McKim, Mead, and White	Architect
John Russell Pope (1874–1937)	Architect

planning and architectural cohesion, this grand example of beaux-arts planning saw individual buildings—all of uniform cornice height, with the same decoration, and painted bright white—formed into a carefully grouped ensemble. The style's popularity waned in the 1920s, and the buildings were soon considered ostentatious. It wasn't until later in the twentieth century that **postmodernists** rediscovered an appreciation of beaux-arts ideals.

1897–1911

Detail of the facade of the New York Public Library: John Carrere and Thomas Hastings

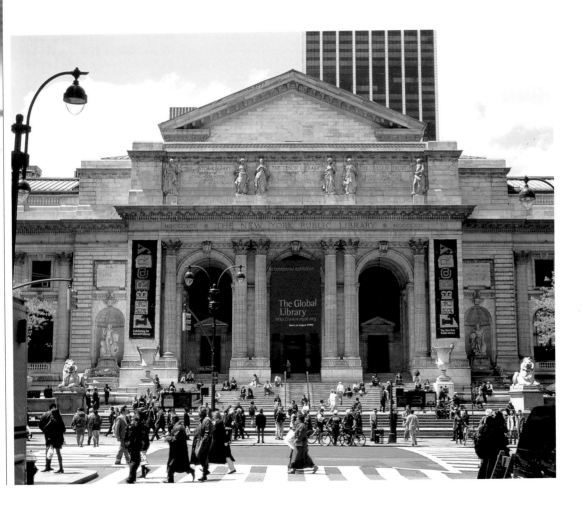

Jugendstil

Key characteristics

Geometric and naturalistic forms

Undecorated surfaces

Energetic, organic designs inspired by advances in science and technology

Key facts

The German and Scandinavian interpretation of art nouveau was inspired by the vernacular and had a simplicity of form and a startling modernity

Advocated the use of natural forms as a means of reforming design, and in turn society

Workshops devoted to the applied arts were set up with the aim of producing honest domestic wares through ethical manufacturing practices

Jugendstil (youth style) refers to the German and Scandinavian interpretation of **art nouveau** that became prevalent during the 1890s. Closely associated with the Vienna Secession and **Wiener Werkstätte**, the style takes its name from the decorative arts journal *Jugend*, founded in Munich in 1896, which described itself as a "Periodical for Art and Life."

Jugendstil designers advocated the use of natural forms as a means of reforming design, and in turn society. Their work ranged from simple household articles to large wall mosaics, jewelry, glass design, and architecture. Interiors and architecture inspired by the vernacular, simplicity of form, and a startling modernity characterized many designs. Jugendstil developed later than art nouveau in the rest of continental Europe as many German designers were still committed to the revivalist trends that had characterized design through the second half of the nineteenth century. However, by the 1890s, designers were ready for a new, fresh alternative to historicism. Advances in science and technology provided a new, deeper understanding of nature that inspired jugendstil designers to inject a newfound energy into their work. In the same vein as the **Arts and Crafts movement**, several workshops devoted to the applied arts were set up across Germany with the aim of producing honest domestic wares through ethical manufacturing practices. These included the cooperative set up in Darmstadt, and supported by the Grand Duke Ernst Ludwig of Hesse, the Dresdener Werkstätten für Handwerkskunst (Dresden Workshops for Artist Craftsmanship), and the work

1897

Lady's bureau:
Henri van
de Velde

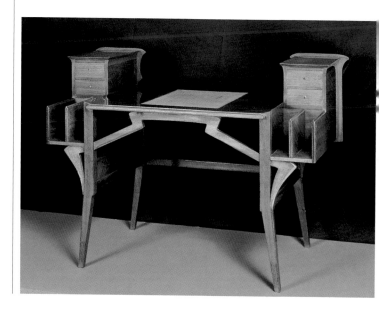

hops established in Munich in 1897 by
Bruno Paul, Vereinigte Werkstätten für
Kunst im Handwerk (United Workshops
for Artist Craftsmanship). The majority
of important jugendstil designers,
including Eckmann, Obrist, and Endell,
continued to work out of Munich.

Jugendstil can be divided into two
distinct phases: pre-1900 and post-1900.
Pre-1900, the designs being produced
were similar to those of the British Arts
and Crafts movement, with the emphasis
on "floral" art—naturalistic and
representative forms—as seen in the
graphic and applied arts of the time.
Folk themes were also commonplace.
Post-1900, however, designs took on
a more abstract, dynamic form, inspired
by the philosophies of Belgian architect
Henri van de Velde. Van de Velde
believed firmly in the importance of art

**Tropon lithograph:
Henry van de
Velde** It has been
suggested that
the swirling
configuration in
this poster for
Tropon food
concentrate was
inspired by the
separation of
egg yolks from
egg whites.

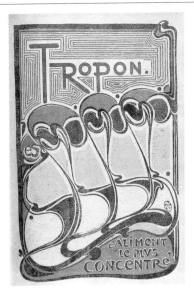

**Behrens typeface:
Peter Behrens**

abcdefghijklmnopqrst
uvwxyz ß&
ABCDEFGHIJKLMNOP
QRSTUVWXYZ
1234567890
.,:;-–—'' "".‹›«»*%
!?¡¿()[]/†‡$£¢€

education for improving quality of life, including the local economy, and it was this thinking that led to his being commissioned to design the Weimar Kunstgewerbeschule (School of Applied Arts) in 1904, of which he became director until 1914.

In addition to *Jugend*, the publication of other art journals, such as *Pan* (Berlin, 1895) and *Simplicissimus* popularized the jugendstil esthetic. In Austria, the end of jugendstil came in the lead up to WWI, when a group of designers and architects set up the **Deutsche Werkbund**.

Date not known

Facade of Jugendstil residence, Riga, Latvia.

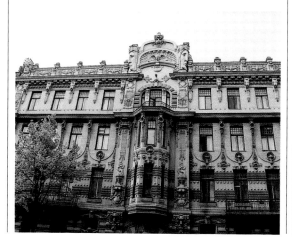

1903

25–29 Jauniela Street, Riga, Latvia: Wilhelm Bokslaff

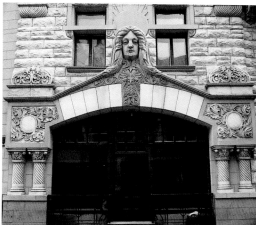

Key figures	Fields of work
August Endell (1871–1925)	Architect/Sculptor/Designer
Herman Obrist (1862–1927)	Sculptor/Designer
Bernhard Pankok (1872–1943)	Designer/Graphic artist
Richard Riemerschmid (1868–1957)	Architect/Designer
Bruno Paul (1874–1968)	Architect/Cabinetmaker/Designer/Teacher
Henri van de Velde (1863–1957)	Architect/Industrial designer/Painter/Art critic

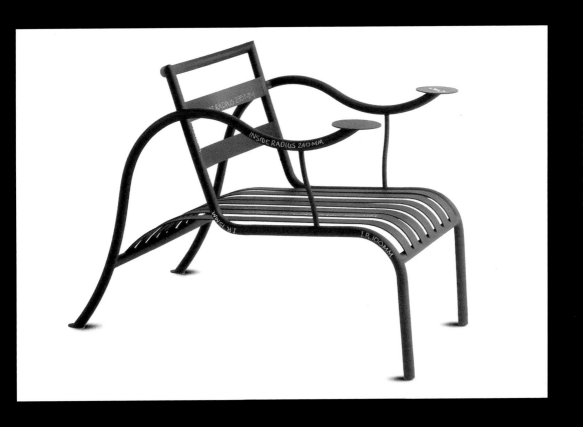

Mission style

Key characteristics

Bold rectilinear designs

Exposed joinery

Simple forms

Key facts

Inspired by the British Arts and Crafts movement

A strong emphasis on craftsmanship

The Roycroft workshops handicraft community had more than 500 workers at its peak, in 1910

See also

Arts and Crafts movement p 24

Also known as the craftsman movement and Golden Oak. Inspired by the British **Arts and Crafts** movement, a number of American designers, including Gustav Stickley, began to take a serious interest in the writings of John Ruskin and William Morris. Following a trip to Europe in 1898, during which he met the likes of Charles Voysey and Charles R. Ashbee, Stickley returned to the USA to set up his own workshop to design and build furniture in this radical new style. With a strong emphasis on craftsmanship, the bold, rectilinear lines and exposed joinery of Stickley's designs were seen to resemble the furniture of the California missions, hence the term mission style. Stickley also published his own magazine, *The Craftsman* (1901–1916), as a vehicle for his ideas, designs and products. Early issues also incorporated the work and ideas of both

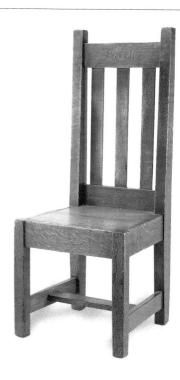

c. 1905–1912

Desk chair:
Roycroft Shop

Key figures	Fields of work
Gustav Stickley (1858–1942)	Craftsman/Furniture designer/Manufacturer/Entrepreneur
Charles P. Limbert (1854–1923)	Furniture designer/Maker
Elbert Green Hubbard (1856–1915)	Furniture designer
Greene & Greene: Charles Sumner (1868–1957) and Henry Mather (1870–1954)	Architects/Designers

Ruskin and Voysey, and played a key role in introducing British **Arts and Crafts** to a new American audience.

Also inspired by the ideas of Morris was Elbert G. Hubbard, a former soap salesman who, in 1893, after visiting Morris' workshops and press in England, decided to set up his own handicraft community in East Aurora, New York. Established along the same lines as the Guild & School of Handicrafts, the Roycroft workshops produced "Mission" furniture, leather and metalwork, while the Roycroft Press published the community's magazine *The Philistine*. In 1903, the Roycroft Inn was built to house the community's ever-increasing number of visitors, and furnished with simple, linear furniture designed by the Roycrofters, as the workers were known. The community flourished, employing more than 500 workers at its peak in 1910.

The Roycroft Shops operated until 1938 by which time, his business over extended and designs costly to manufacture, changing public tastes and the sobriety induced by WWI led to Stickley's bankruptcy and a decline in the popularity of the mission style.

Later Applications

2000

Trico Café furniture: Michael Marriott Solid wood table and chairs designed around a plank of wood of standard proportions.

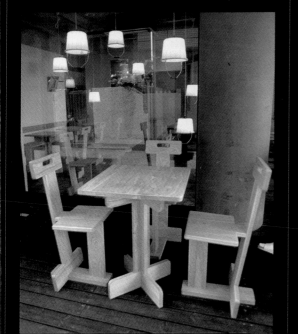

2001

Double-decker table: Marcel Wander for Moooi The simple structure and bold, rectilinear lines give the piece a solid functional appearance reminiscent of the mission style.

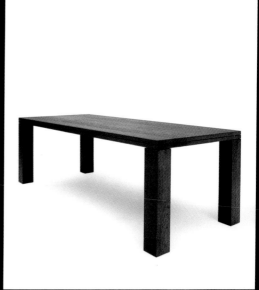

Secession

Also known as secessionism and Wiener sezession. Secession was the name given to groups of artists in Germany and Austria that seceded from the official arts academies in pursuit of their own artistic direction. These included the Munich secession (1892) and the Berlin secession (1899). The most influential, however, was the Gesellschaft bildender Künstler Österrichs (Association of Austrian Artists) or Vienna secession.

Established in 1897 by a group of artists and architects disaffiliated from Vienna's Künstlerhaus, members of the Vienna secession refused to accept the conservative standards propagated by the Academy, opting instead to pursue their own creative vision as an independent association. Although the group consisted of artists and architects, a number of its members—Hoffmann, Moser, and Olbrich included—also designed ceramics, furniture, and metalware.

Created with the aim of bringing architecture and the decorative arts closer together, the group went on to produce posters, prints, drawings, glass, ceramics, metalwork, and textiles, as well as promoting its ideas through its own magazine, *Ver Sacrum* (Sacred Spring). The organization was based at the Secession Building in Vienna, designed by Josef Olbrich in 1898. The Secession Building eventually became the group's

1899–1901

The Stadtbahn, the Vienna underground railway: Otto Wagner

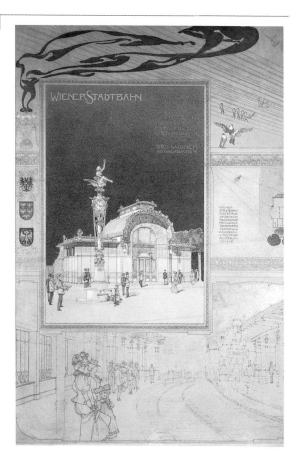

ermanent exhibition space, although : was not completed in time for the first ecession exhibition, which was held at he Horticultural Hall in Vienna.

In addition to the Secession Building itself, notable architectural vorks of Vienna secessionism include Dtto Wagner's design of the Vienna tadtbahn transit line (1899–1901) and he Purkersdorf Sanatorium by Josef Hoffman (1904–1906).

In 1900 the group held the landmark VIII Wiener Sezession exhibition, entirely devoted to the decorative arts, with installations by Charles Rennie Mackintosh, Charles Ashbee, and Henry an de Velde. Although the secession's

early work was created within the art-nouveau style, following this exhibition the group's designers opted for an increasingly rectilinear esthetic—as seen in the geometric form of the Purkersdorf Sanatorium and its furniture, by Koloman Moser. In 1903 Hoffman and Moser founded the **Wiener Werkstätte** as a means to produce and sell works by members of the Vienna secession.

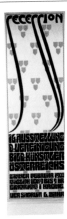

1903

Poster for the 14th Vienna Secession exhibition: Alfred Roller

1900

A Josef Maria Olbrich interior as shown in *Deutsche Kunst und Dekoration.*

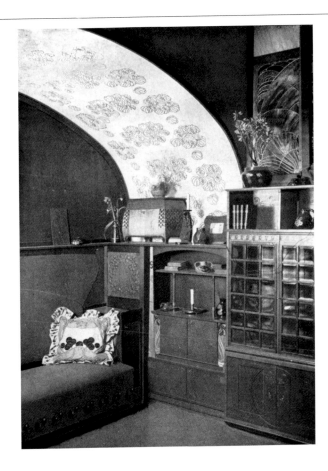

Later Applications

Decades OS typeface: Corey Holms The typography of the Vienna Secession was the influence for this typeface, designed for a vintage couture boutique in Los Angeles.

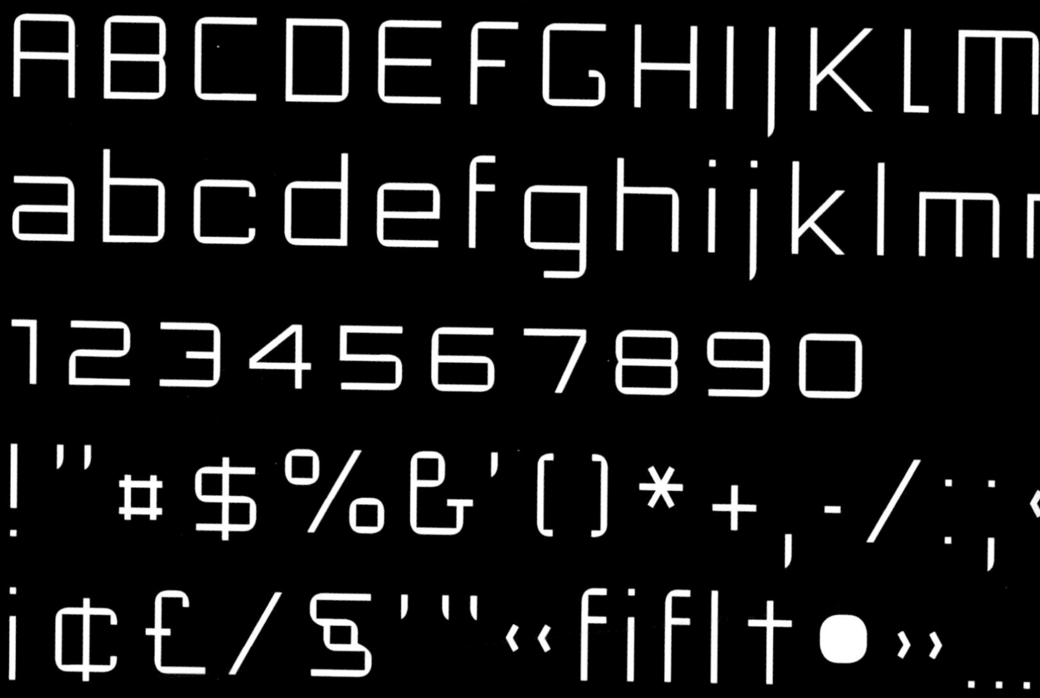

ABCDEFGHIJKLM

abcdefghijklm

1234567890

!"#$%&'()*+,-/:;

¡¢£/§'"‹‹fiflt•›...

Founding members	Fields of work
Gustav Klimt (1862–1918)	Artist
Carl Moll (1861–1945)	Artist
Josef Engelhart (1864–1941)	Artist
Josef Maria Olbrich (1867–1908)	Artist/Architect/Designer
Koloman Moser (1868–1918)	Painter/Designer/Metalworker/Graphic artist
Josef Franz Maria Hoffmann (1870–1956)	Architect/Designer

OPQRSTUVWXYZ

opqrstuvwxyz

' ? ° - x

. ¿ Ɔ Ø Œ æ ı ø œ ß ™

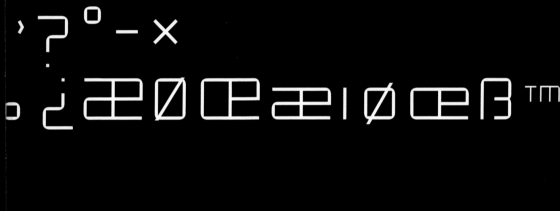

decadesinc

decadesinc vintage couture and accou trements **cameronsilver** 8214-1/2 melr ose avenue los angeles california 90046 usa tel 323-655-0223 fax 323-655-0172 w ww.decadesinc.com

Wiener Werkstätte

Origin

Vienna

Key characteristics

Pre-WWI : Abstract patterns, geometric motifs—chequerboards, squares, grids

Post-WWI: More ornamental, seventeeth-century Baroque influences, sense of opulence

Key facts

Promoting equality between designer and craftsman was central; all designs produced by the workshops bore the monograms of both

Overtook the secession as the leading progressive Viennese arts and crafts organization, employing more than 100 workers

A refusal to compromise on quality in return for affordability limited the potential mass appeal of the Werkstätte's designs

See also

Arts and Crafts movement p 24

Secession p 66

Art deco p 86

Established in Vienna in 1903 with the aim of sustaining high-quality craft manufacture, the Wiener Werkstätte, Produktiv-Gemeinschaft von Kunsthandwerkern in Wien (Vienna Workshops, Production Cooperative of Artist Craftsmen in Vienna) was a development of the Vienna **secession**.

The cooperative was founded by two of the secession's leading members, Josef Hoffmann and Koloman Moser, along with wealthy banker Fritz Wärndorfer. The Wiener Werkstätte took its lead from British **Arts and Crafts** initiatives, especially Charles Ashbee's Guild of Handicraft to which it had a similar

1905–1911

Palais Stoclet, Brussels: Josef Hoffmann

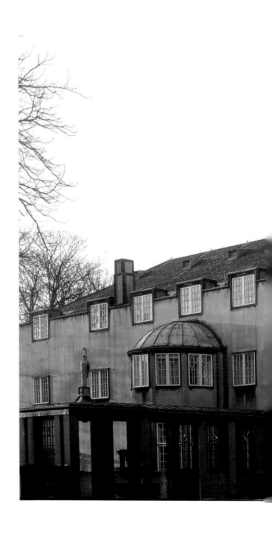

mission, described by Hoffmann as the need to develop "an intimate relationship between the public, the designer, and the craftsman, and to create good, simple things for the home."

Promoting equality between designer and craftsman was central to the Werkstätte's philosophy and as a result, all designs produced by the workshops bore the monograms of both. By 1905, the distinctly modern style of the Wiener Werkstätte had overtaken the secession as the leading progressive Viennese arts and crafts organization, employing more than 100 workers. Housed in a series of small studios, each devoted to a different craft from cabinetmaking to bookbinding—there was also a design studio and an architectural practice. During its reign the Werkstätte produced furniture, graphics, metalware, textiles, jewelry, clothing, glassware, wallpaper, and ceramics by more than 200 designers,

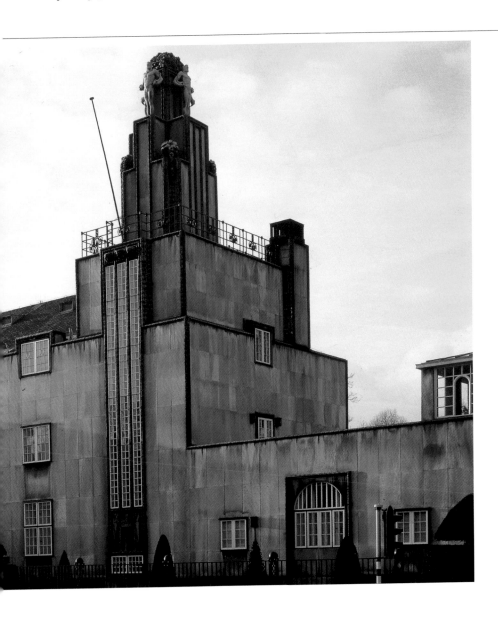

1912

Printed silks:
Edward Wimmer
(top); Lotte
Froemmel (bottom)

Wimmer and
Froemmel designed
these silks for the
Wiener Werkstätte.

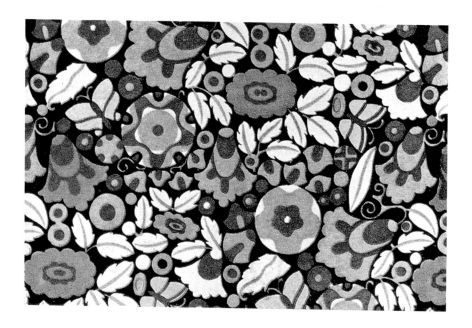

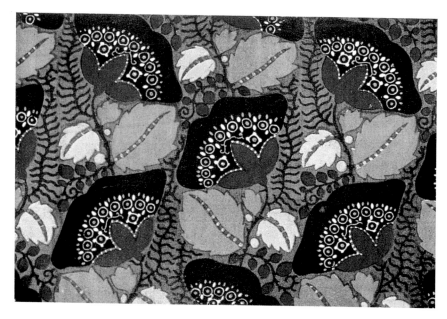

as well as three notable Gesamtunstwerk (complete artwork) projects: Hoffmann's Purkersdorf Sanatorium (1904–1906), the Cabaret Fledermaus theater (1907), and the Palais Stoclet (1905–1911).

The Werkstätte's early secessionist style was epitomized in the rectilinear form and elaborate construction of the Palais Stoclet in Brussels. However, from about 1915, consumer demand dictated a more opulent style and Werkstätte designs began to take on a more ornamental quality, as seen in the richness of Dagobert Peche's interior and furniture designs. By the 1920s, women were becoming involved with the workshops. Several were trained by Moser at the Vienna School of Applied Arts, among them Therese Trethan (painted furniture) and Jutta Sika (ceramics and glass). Through the use of bold, dramatic forms, contrasting black- and-white color schemes, and geometric refinement, Hoffmann and Moser's Werkstätte designs provided a much needed antidote to the ornament and exuberance of continental **art nouveau**.

The Werkstätte was initially established as a means of producing simple, quality products for the home. However, Hoffman's refusal to compromise on quality in return for affordability, while ensuring excellence, limited the potential mass appeal of the Werkstätte's designs. As a result, the workshops found themselves producing nothing more than fashionable decorative arts for the wealthy. The style was not confined to Austria; in 1919 the opening of a sales headquarters on New York's Fifth Avenue opened up a whole new market in the USA as examples of the new Viennese style began to crop up across the city. Unfortunately, its increasingly opulent style eventually became indistinguishable from the stylistic attributes of **art deco**, which had already had its day.

The Werkstätte held exhibitions in Berlin (1904) and Hagen (1906) in Germany, and in Vienna and Brünn (1905) in Austria, as well as participating in international exhibitions including the Cologne Werkbund-Ausstellung (1914) and the Paris Exposition Internationale des Arts Décoratifs (1925).

Date not known

Glass vase: Josef Hoffmann

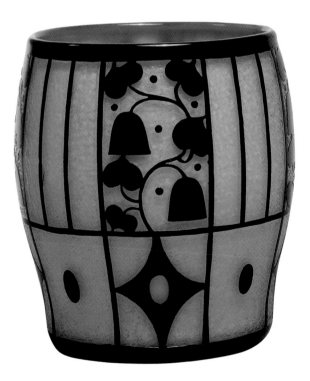

The decoration in this theater, as shown in its poster for Cabaret Fledermaus, was a Gesamtunstwerk (complete artwork) project, and exemplifies the Wiener Werkstätte movement.

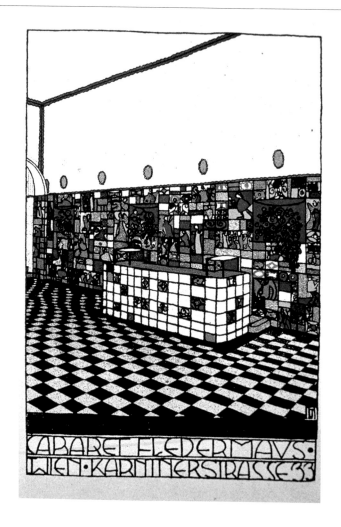

Key figures	Fields of work
Josef Franz Maria Hoffmann (1870–1956)	Architect/Designer
Koloman Moser (1868–1918)	Painter/Designer/Metalworker/Graphic artist
Otto Prütscher (1880–1949)	Architect/Furniture Designer/Jeweler/Designer
Michael Powolny (1871–1954)	Sculptor/Ceramicist/Teacher
Carl Czeschka (1878–1960)	Architect/Painter/Graphic designer (jewelry, stained glass, embroidery)
Jutta Sika (1877–1964)	Ceramicist/Glassware designer

1991

**Folding bookcase:
Jan Konings and
Jurgen Bey for
Droog Design**

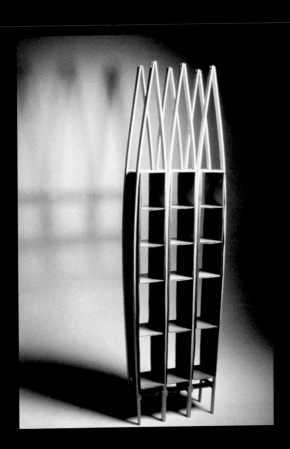

1983

**Tea and coffee
Piazza service:
Paolo Portoghesi
for Alessi**
The set echoes
the decorative style
of the early
twentieth-century
Wiener Werkstätte.

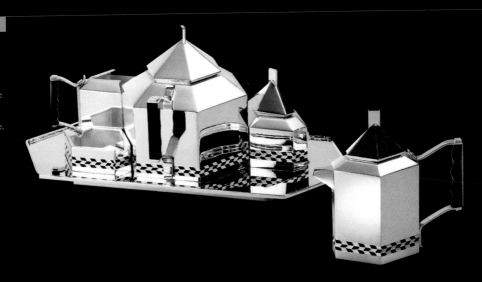

Deutsche Werkbund

Founded in 1907, with the aim of bridging the gap between industry and design, the Deutsche Werkbund sought to replace the naturalistic forms of **jugendstil** with a more formal, functional, and utilitarian language of design. The group did not, however, advocate a return to the craft and craftsmanship of the **Arts and Crafts movement**. Rather, it argued for the moral and esthetic importance of design in response to the belief that the industrialization of Germany was a threat to its national culture.

The group's founder members consisted of 12 designers—including Richard Riemerschmid, Bruno Paul, Josef Maria Olbrich, and Peter Behrens—12 manufacturers, and workshops such as the **Wiener Werkstätte** and the Vereinigte Werkstätten für Kunst im Handwerk (United Workshops for Artist Craftsmanship). Within its first year, membership of the Deutsche Werkbund had reached more than 500, and at its peak the group had more than 3,000 members.

The Deutsche Werkbund also held a number of exhibitions to promote its ideas. In 1914 they arranged a major exhibition in Cologne. This featured, most notably, Walter Gropius' steel-and-glass model factory, Henry van de Velde's Werkbund Theatre, and Bruno Taut's glass-brick pavilion.

In 1927, the Werkbund held a much-publicized exhibition of housing, entitled Die Wohnung (The Dwelling), in Stuttgart. It incorporated an entire housing estate, Weissenhof Siedlung, the houses of which were furnished with tubular steel furniture designed by the exhibition's architectural director Ludwig Mies van der Rohe, along with Marcel Breuer and Le Corbusier. Other participants in the project included Peter Behrens, Walter Gropius, and Adolf Loos.

c. 1910

Window display of Tropon goods, image from *Deutsche Werkbund Jahrbuch.*

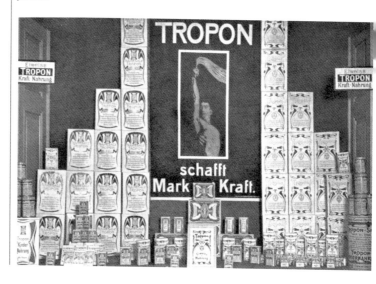

From 1912–1920 the Werkbund published its own yearbook, featuring articles and illustrations of its member's designs, along with the contact details and skills of all its members in a bid to promote collaboration. The group also published its own magazine, *Die Form* (1925–1934).

However, despite its best efforts to reconcile craft and industry, the internal conflict within the group—between Henry van de Velde and Hermann Muthesius—almost led to its demise. Muthesius' opposition to the use of ornament as a means of artistic validity, and belief in

practicality as the basis for expressing contemporary cultural values, did not sit well with van de Velde, who favored greater artistic freedom. The debate between the two began with Muthesius' 10-point program, which concentrated on the need to refine typical objects, but

Deutsche
Werkbund
Ausstellung poster:
Peter Behrens

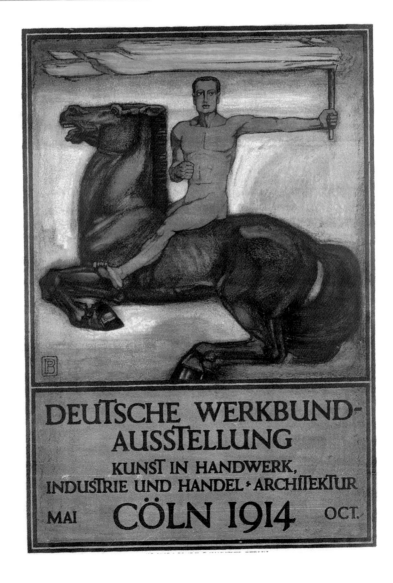

was immediately challenged by van de Velde's protest about the importance of individual artistic inspiration. This standardization versus individualism debate, which became known as the Werkbundstreit, continued, although it soon became apparent that industrial production and standardization was the only answer if the country was to make any sort of progress following the devastation of WWI.

In 1934 the Werkbund was dissolved due to increasing pressure against **modernism** from the Nazi regime.

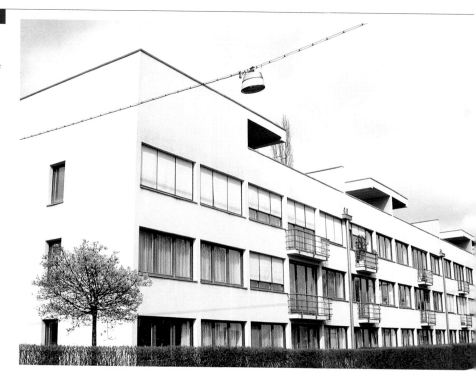

1926–1932

Apartment block Weissenhof, Stuttgart: Ludwig Mies van der Rohe Built for the Werkbund's Vice President.

Key figures	Fields of work
Richard Riemerschmid (1868–1957)	Architect/Designer
Bruno Paul (1874–1968)	Architect/Cabinetmaker/Designer/Teacher
Peter Behrens (1868–1940)	Graphic artist/Architect/Designer
Josef Maria Olbrich (1867–1908)	Artist/Architect/Designer
Hermann Muthesius (1861–1927)	Architect/Designer/Theorist
Henri van de Velde (1863–1957)	Architect/Industrial designer/Painter/Art critic
Walter Adolph Gropius (1883–1969)	Architect

MR Side Chair: Ludwig Mies van der Rohe, from design by Mart Stam In 1927 the Werkbund held the influential exhibition Die Wohnung (The Dwelling), which included the Weissenhof Housing Estate, an experimental group of model apartment buildings built in a suburb of Stuttgart. Under the direction of Mies van der Rohe, a number of important architects, including Mart Stam and Marcel Breuer, collaborated on the project, designing furniture for the apartments. The MR chair, developed from Mart Stam's 1924 design for a cantilevered chair, was introduced by van der Rohe at the Stuttgart exhibition and has remained in production ever since.

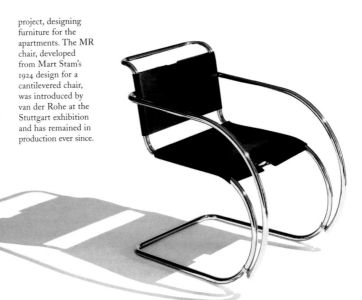

Kabel typeface: Rudolf Koch

abcdefghijklmnopqrstuv
wxyz fiflß&
ABCDEFGHIJKLMNO
PQRSTUVWXYZ
1234567890
.,:;-——''""·‹›«» *%‰
!?¡¿()[]/†‡§$£¢ƒ

Futurism

Italian futurism was perhaps the first movement in the history of art to be engineered and managed like a business. Founded in 1909 by the Italian writer and poet Filippo Tommaso Marinetti, initially as a literary movement, futurism introduced the use of the manifesto as a public means to advertise its artistic philosophy, and also as a polemic weapon against the academic and conservative world. Marinetti, along with his supporters, penned numerous manifestos, not only on literature, but also on music, dance, performance, painting, and architecture. Marinetti's first futurist manifesto, written in French and published in Parisian newspaper *Le Figaro* before any of the new futurist art existed, typified his understanding of the power of the media to work for him and to propagate his ideas.

The impact of radically new forms of technology had a profound effect on Western culture at this time; they were at the core of the futurist enterprise. The futurists loved speed, noise, machines, and cities. They embraced technological progress and celebrated the potential and dynamism of the modern age. Giacomo Balla was the first designer to experiment with the practical application of futurist theory in the decorative arts, closely followed by the designer and artist Fortunato Depero. Depero even went so far as to set up a craft workshop for futurist art in Rovereto that operated throughout the 1920s.

In art, paintings were characterized by dynamic and abstract geometric forms, while in book design the futurists rejected traditional typographical forms and page designs in favor of expressive typography and structure. Like the futurist painters, Marinetti used his poetry and book work to express modern life. He abandoned traditional grammar, punctuation, and format to create vivid, pictorial typographic pages. Marinetti's theories were widely influential and resulted in the production of hundreds of futurist books. Virtually anonymous covers disguised the explosive pages

within as traditional typefaces were eschewed in favor of newly designed typefaces that leaked across the pages without any respect for the so-called "rules of layout."

Futurists viewed the design and production of a book as symbolic of the machine age. Modern materials and methods were employed, as seen in Fortunato Depero's famous 1927 *Depero Futurista* (also known as *The Nailed Book*). This was held together by two aluminum bolts—a true manifesto of the machine age. Depero's innovation was no means confined to the cover. Inside a wealth of typographic innovations jumped from the pages; different typefaces, text formed into various shapes, different papers and colors were all used. The book had neither up nor down, right nor left, so that in order to read the text, it had to be turned round and round again.

In architecture, the futurist esthetic was largely promoted through the architectural proposals of Sant'Elia. It was characterized by raw, unfinished surfaces, violent coloring, and sweeping dynamic forms. Sant'Elia died in 1916, but his *Manifesto of Futurist Architecture* exerted a strong influence on the members of **de Stijl,** who received it the following year.

Zang Tumb Tumb:
F. T. Marinetti
The cover for this
book, written and
designed by
Marinetti,
exemplifies the
futurist esthetic.

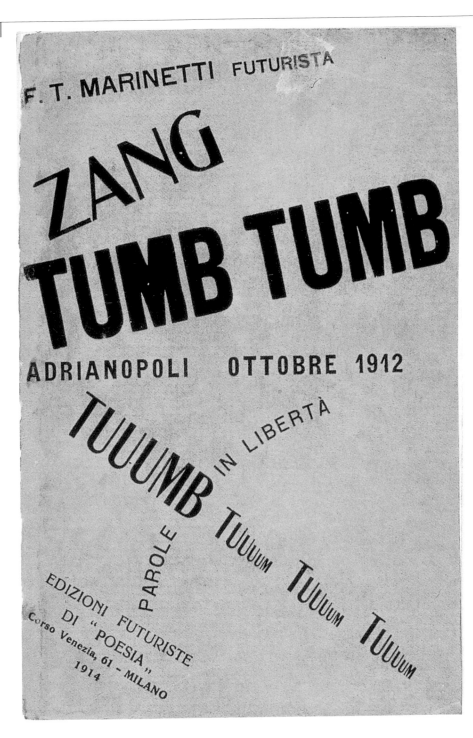

1914

Electric Power
Plant: Antonio
Sant'Elia

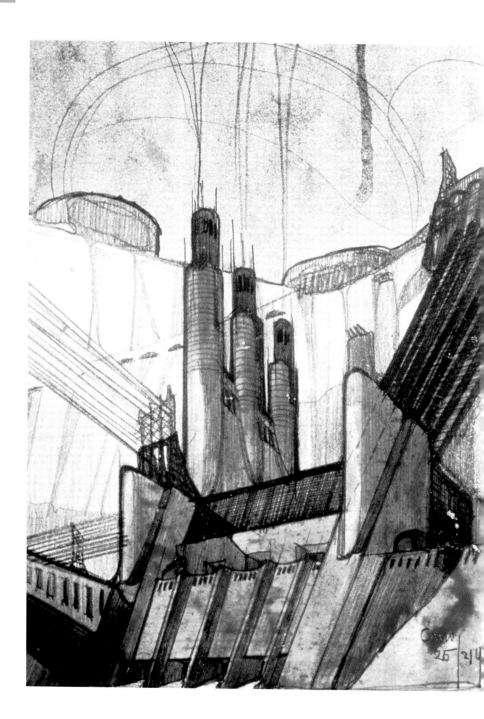

War Party tapestry:
Fortunato Depero

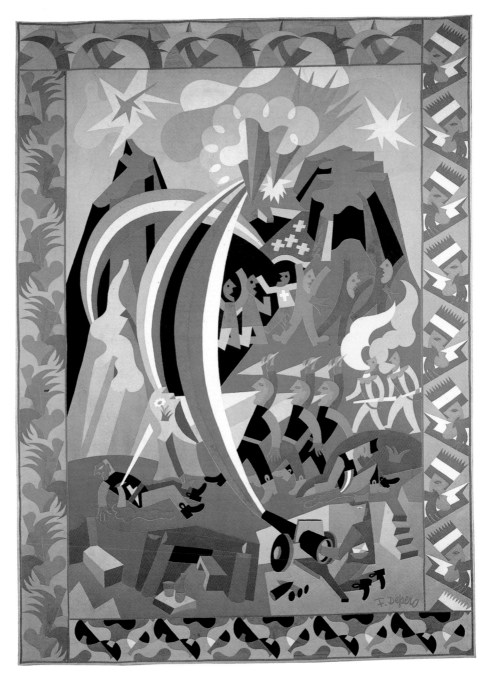

1996

Il Futurismo typeface: Alan Kegler Inspired by the handdrawn lettering and graphic design of the Italian futurists. The letterforms are meant to be slightly irregular to give a feel for the original handdrawn characters.

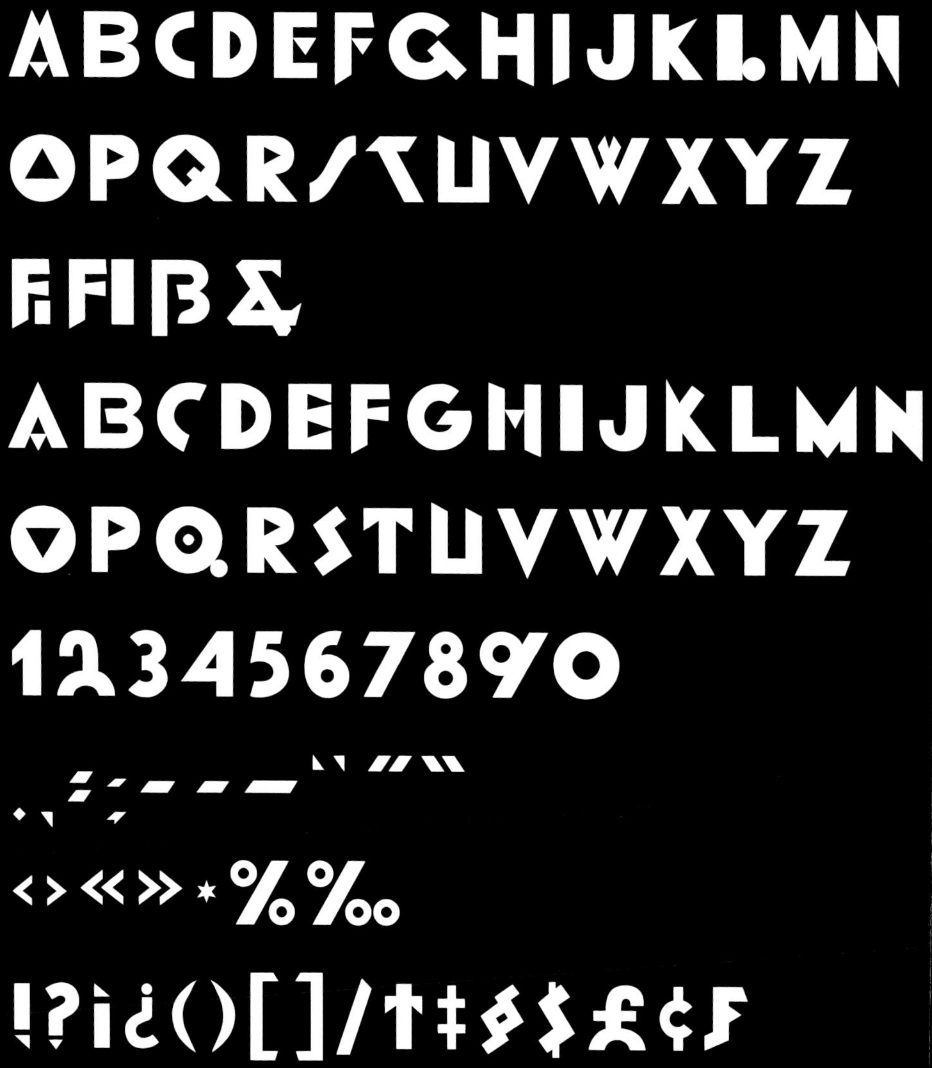

ABCDEFGHIJKLMN
OPQRSTUVWXYZ
FFIB&

ABCDEFGHIJKLMN
OPQRSTUVWXYZ
1234567890

< > << >> * % ‰

¡?¿()[]/†‡§£¢F

Key figures	Fields of work
Filippo Tommaso Marinetti (1876–1944)	Writer
Giacomo Balla (1871–1958)	Artist/Designer
Antonio Sant'Elia (1888–1916)	Architect
Fortunato Depero (1892–1960)	Artist/Furniture designer

MAXXI: National Center of Contemporary Arts, Rome, Italy: Zaha Hadid

Hadid is renowned for the futuristic architectural paintings and drawings she creates during the production phase of her work. The concept for this project is based on the idea of "irrigating" the large urban field with linear display surfaces, weaving a dense texture of interior and exterior spaces.

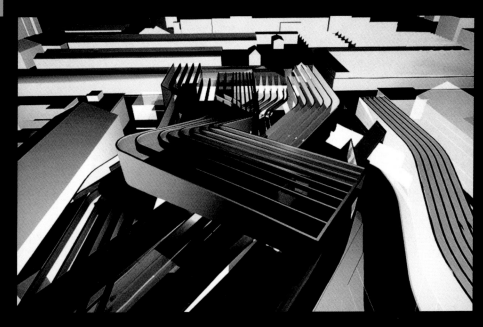

Book-End: Sara de Bondt for Shift

Reminiscent of the infamous mechanical binding that characterized Fortunato Depero's 1927 *The Nailed Book*, here stacks of back issues of *Shift* publications are drilled through and held together with industrial screws to create bookends.

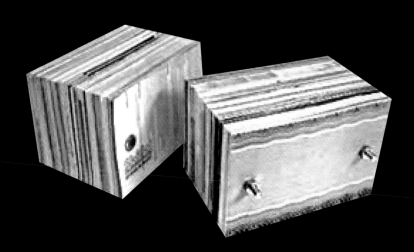

Art deco

Origin

France

United States

Key characteristics

Geometric, stepped forms

Bright colors

Sharp edges, rounded corners

Expensive materials: enamel, ivory, bronze, and polished stone

Mass-production materials: chrome, colored glass, Bakelite

Key facts

Influenced by costume design and fashion

Celebrated travel, speed, and luxury with vivid colors and flat, angular shapes

Geometric styling and Eygptian and Aztec influences

See also

Futurism p 80

Czech Cubism p 96

Constructivism p 126

Also known as modernistic and style moderne, prior to 1925. Art deco is an international decorative style that emerged in France during the 1920s. Initially inspired by the brilliant colors and costume designs of Diaghilev's Ballet Russes and the fashions of Paul Poiret, the art-deco style was also influenced by the abstract, simplified shapes exemplified in the avant-garde paintings of the **constructivists**, cubists, fauvists, and **futurists**. The discovery of Tutankhamun's tomb by Howard Carter in 1922 inspired the Egyptian styling that became an inherent part of the art-deco style. The esthetic transformed the skylines of cities from New York to Shanghai, and influenced the design of everything, from fashion to furniture, Hollywood films to luxury liners.

The style was named after the 1925 Paris Exposition des Arts Décoratifs et Industriels Modernes, an international showcase for the best in contemporary design. At this event, the USA was notable only for its absence. It has been said that America was not represented because at that time it had no art deco to contribute, but if this *was* the case, it didn't remain that way for long thank to two outstanding pieces of art-deco architecture—the Chrysler Building and the Empire State Building, both of which rose to dominate the New York skyline in 1930.

In France, the highly elaborate art-deco style was aimed primarily at the luxury market. It permeated virtually every design discipline, from paintings by Polish-born artist Tamara de

Date not known

Silver money box with typical simplified shape.

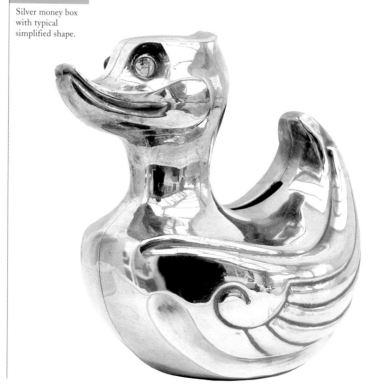

Lempicka (1898–1980), to graphics and stage designs by Robert Delaunay (1885–1941) and Sonia Delaunay (1885–1980), and glasswares by René Lalique. Advertising posters adopted simplified forms and bold silhouettes, such as those created by Cassandre for the ocean liner Normandie (1935). Celebrating their newfound fascination for travel, speed, and luxury, art-deco graphic artists used vivid colors and flat, angular shapes to convey their admiration.

Interiors and furnishings saw the development of two distinct styles, each with its own set of esthetic values: the Boudoir style of the 1920s, which used luxury materials to create the exotic, oriental style of Jacques-Émile Ruhlmann's furniture designs; and the sleek, modernist approach reflected in the works of Le Corbusier and his associates. By the 1920s, American designers also sought inspiration from machine and industrial forms, adopting repeated and overlapping geometric patterns, colorful rectilinear images, chevrons and lightning bolts (symbolizing electricity), and the ubiquitous zigzag designs. As a result, the style progressed from its highly decorative beginnings in the 1920s to the elegant functionalism of the 1930s.

Hollywood Style

In the USA, art deco was characterized by glamor, fantasy, and escapism. Inspired by Hollywood film sets and fashions, Hollywood Style could be seen everywhere from the extravagant productions on Broadway to interiors and skyscraper architecture. Eygptian and Aztec influences and geometric styling dominated American architecture and the decorative arts during the early 1930s. Classic examples of art-deco architecture include the Chrysler Building, the Empire State Building, and the Rockefeller Center in New York City. In the UK, Hollywood Style was reflected in the lavish, dramatic interiors of the numerous Odeon Cinemas in and around London, including the Leicester Square Odeon with its leopard-skin upholstery and gold-rippled walls.

Date not known

Art deco–style wooden clock.

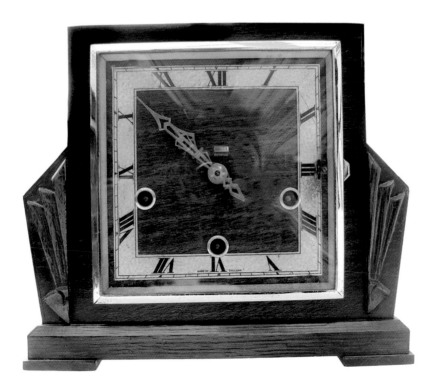

1927

Worth evening
dress, fashion plate
from Gazette du
Bon Ton, 1925:
Georges Barbier

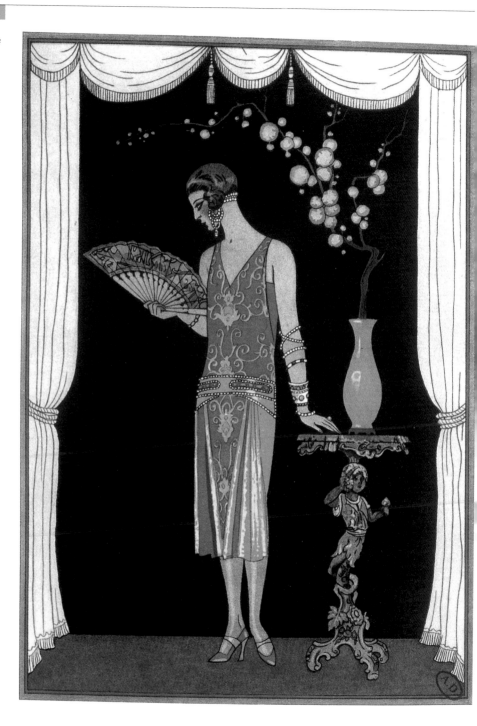

**The Chrysler
Building,
New York:
William van Alen**

**Bifur typeface:
A. M. Cassandre**
Designed by poster
artist A. M.

Cassandre, Bifur is
remarkable for its
visually exciting
two-tone deco look

and dramatic
simplification of
letterforms.

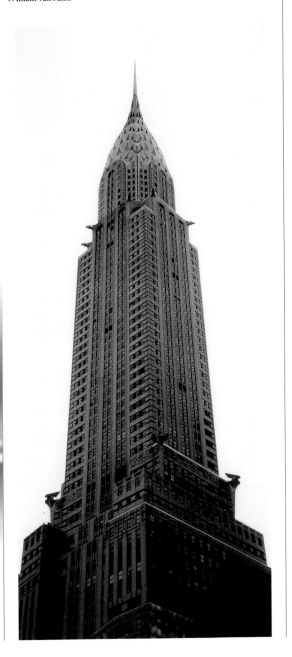

ABC
DEF
GHIJ
KLM
NOP
QRS
TUV
WX
YZ

1935

Interior of the De
La Warr Pavilion,
Bexhill, UK: Eric
Mendelsohn and
Serge Chermayeff

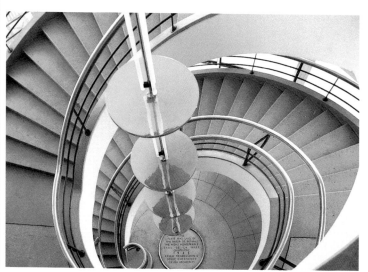
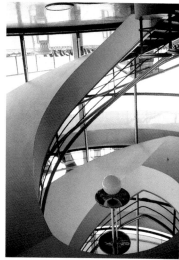

c. 1935

Peach-glass table:
James Clark Ltd.
of London

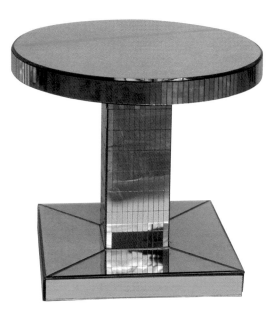

RCA Victor
Special portable
phonograph:
John Vassos

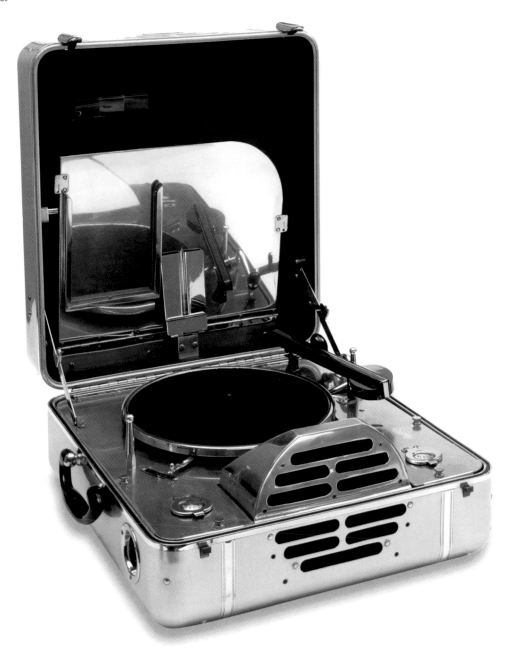

1936–1937

Marine Court:
K. Dalgleish,
R. K. Pullen
It is thought that
Marine Court, in

Hastings, UK,
was modeled on the
prestigious Queen
Mary liner.

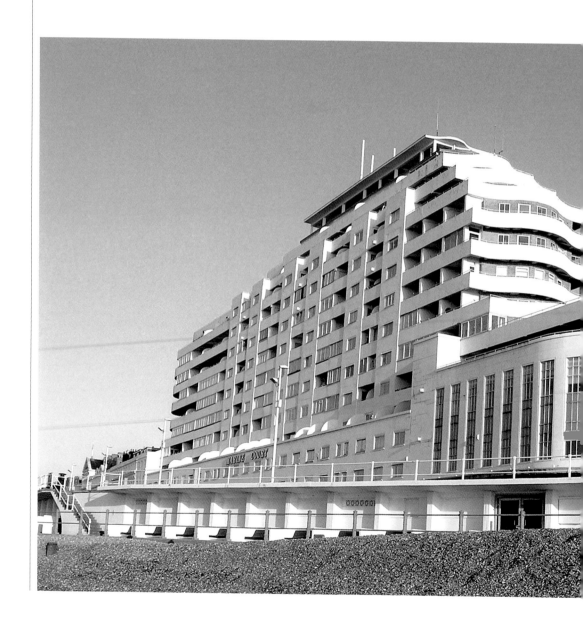

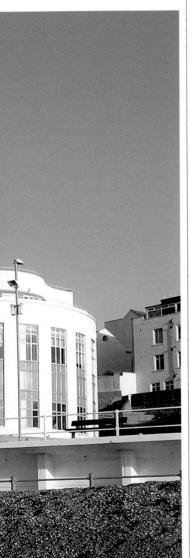

Star Cinema,
Leeds. In the UK,
Hollywood Style
was reflected in
numerous cinemas
dotted in and
around London
and other cities.

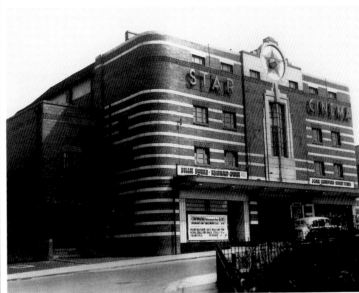

Later Applications

1969

**Biba logo: John
McConnell**
This early logotype
has a distinctly art-
deco feel.

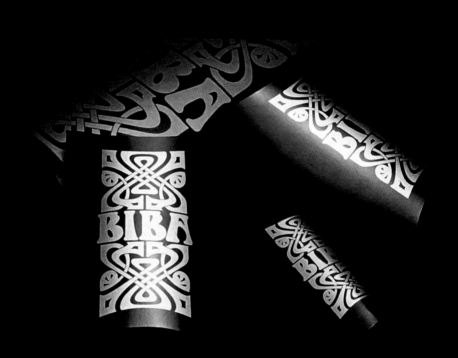

Regional variations	Key figures	Fields of work
Art deco (Paris, France)	Jacques-Emile Ruhlmann (1879–1933)	Designer/Decorator
	René-Jules Lalique (1860–1945)	Designer (glassware, jewelry, furniture)/Painter/Sculptor
	A. M. Cassandre (1901–1968)	Graphic designer
Moderne (New York, USA)	Donald Deskey (1894–1989)	Industrial/Furniture/Interior designer

**Crystal Palace
Ball chandelier:
Tom Dixon for
Swarovski**
Dixon's chandelier
captures the glamor
of the art-deco era.

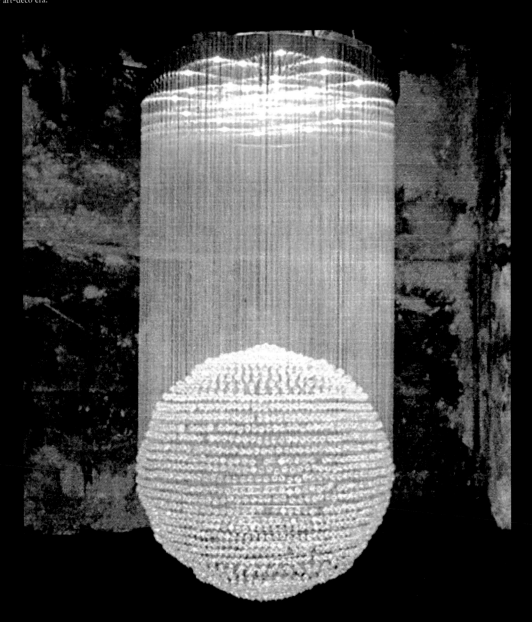

Czech Cubism

Origin

Prague

Key characteristics

Prism-like and crystalline motifs applied to architecture, furniture, ceramics, and jewelry

Angled, zigzag planes

Key facts

A short-lived, but highly original and influential movement

Believed in breaking up the vertical and horizontal surfaces of conventional design

Incorporated angled and zigzag planes into the design of everyday objects

See also

The influence of **art nouveau** on **modernism** was particularly obvious in Prague where a group of architects and designers, inspired by a combination of **secession** objects and Cubist sculptures and paintings, formed an important, albeit short-lived movement that became known as Czech Cubism. Sharp points, slicing planes, and crystalline shapes were the trademarks of this unique, avant-garde group. Centered around the Skupina Vytvarych Umelcu (Group of Creative Artists), established in Prague in 1911, it created original and dramatic early Modernist ceramic, glass, and furniture designs. The Skupina maintained close links with Parisian Cubism, organizing the Third Group Exhibition, which brought works by Pablo Picasso, André Derain, and Georges Braque to Prague. The group also founded its own magazine *Umeleck Mesicnik* (Artistic Monthly).

Four young, multitalented designers trained in the ateliers of leading rationalist architects Otto Wagner and Jan Kotera, were behind the bulk of Prague's Czech Cubist legacy. Both acquainted with and inspired by the Cubism of Picasso and Braque, and desperate to find a new style they could call their own, Pavel Janák, Josef Gocar, Josef Chochol, and Vlastislav Hofman adapted painters' cubist principles, and

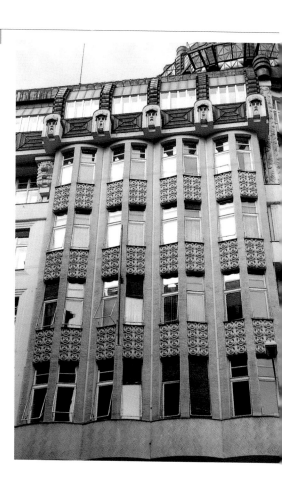

Date not known

Cubist building, Prague, Czech Republic.

tretched them not only to another imension, but also to everyday life. Opposed to the seccession and **Arts and Crafts** ideas that had been introduced to Czech design by their tutors, Wagner nd Kotera, the Czech Cubists believed hat an object's true internal energy ould only be released by breaking up he vertical and horizontal surfaces that estrain and repress it in conventional esign. By incorporating angled and igzag planes into the design of everyday bjects, they succeeded in transforming hem into dynamic works of art. Czech Cubists regarded the crystal as the ideal atural form, while the pyramid was seen s the pinnacle of architectural design. Luckily for them, Bohemia's culturally dventurous elite was open to these adical ideas and happily financed the ubist transformation of everything from ups and saucers, to desks and chairs, illas, and office buildings.

The group also rejected the ationalism that existed in architectural ractice and the use of applied lecoration in architecture, opting instead o apply Pyramidal Cubism to building acades with decorative applications of lanted facets, folds, and fractures. This pproach to architectural design was xemplified in Josef Chochol's Hodek partments in Prague.

In 1912, Gocar and Janák set up Prazske Umemecke Dilny (Prague Artistic Workshops). Based on the working practice of the **Wiener Werkstätte**, they adopted traditional methods and materials to create architectural, sculptural furniture, while their inexpensive glazed ceramics and glass, produced by the Artel Cooperative in Prague, ensured that, in part at least, they were able to fulfil their commitment to integrate Cubist principles into everyday life.

The Studio Corner ceramic dish: Pablo Picasso

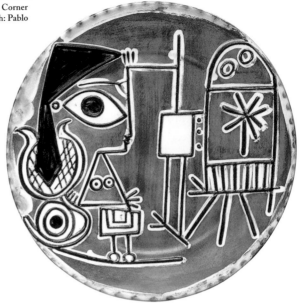

Ceramic collection: Clarice Cliff
Selection of Cubist ceramics including a conical bowl with a geometrical design (front right) by Clarice Cliff.

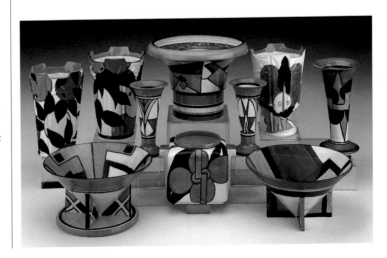

Later Applications

1942

America's Answer! Production poster: Jean Carlu
Translating Cubist influence into symbolic architectonic imagery, Carlu's seamless integration of the visual and verbal to create an intense symbol saw the designer receive an award from the New York Art Directors Club for this poster, of which more than 100,000 were distributed throughout the USA.

1989

Pyramide du Louvre: I. M. Pei

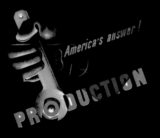

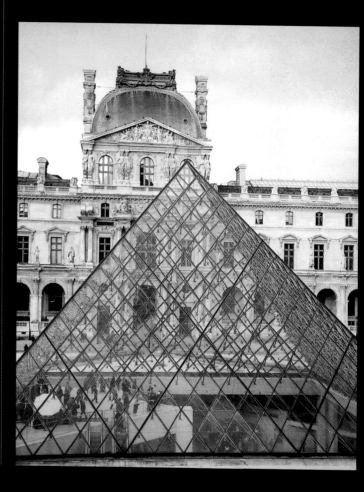

Key figures	Fields of work
Josef Chochol (1888–1978)	Architect/Furniture designer/Theorist
Josef Gocar (1880–1945)	Architect
Pavel Janák (1882–1956)	Architect/Designer/Teacher
Vlastislav Hofman (1884–1964)	Architect/Designer/Painter

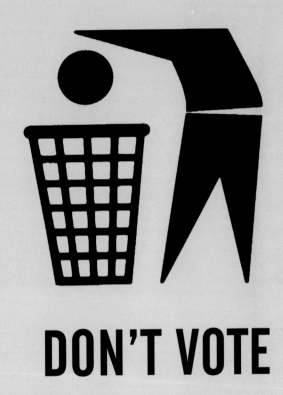

DON'T VOTE

Vorticism

Considered to be the only British avant-garde movement to make an original contribution to European **modernism**, vorticism may not have lasted long, but its typographical adventurousness was cited as one of the major forerunners of the revolution in graphic design in the 1920s and 1930s. Closely related to both **futurism** and **Cubism**, the movement was named by Ezra Pound in 1913, although artist Wyndham Lewis had been painting in the style for at least a year prior to this and is often regarded as the movement's founder and central figure. The vorticist movement represented a sustained act of aggression against the moribund and moderate Victorianism that Lewis and Pound regarded as stifling the artistic energies of the new generation in England.

The vorticists produced two issues of their own journal *BLAST*, edited by Lewis, in which the two vorticist Manifestos were published, in 1914 and 1915. The large-format magazine, with its radical typography and design, also incorporated works by Pound and T. S. Eliot, as well as by the vorticists themselves. *BLAST* made an important contribution to twentieth-century typography and remains a leading example of modernist expression.

Although the vorticist style had its roots in Cubism, it was the **futurist** idea of dynamic art capturing the modernity of the era that most inspired the movement. Despite this, the vorticists were harshly critical of the futurist's naive enthusiasm for modernity, preferring instead to create their own style of geometric abstraction to celebrate the new consciousness of humanity in a mechanized urban environment.

The mechanism of war was the primary focus for both futurists and vorticists and, as a result, provided great inspiration for both. However, while the futurists glorified war, the vorticists held a cautious respect for it; they appreciated the power of the machine, but also recognized its potential danger to society. This combined fear and respect for roboticism was expressed through their art, in particular through Jacob Epstein's famous sculpture The Rock Drill, the most celebrated of all the vorticist works.

The group held just one exhibition, at the Doré Gallery in London, in 1915—before vorticism was disrupted and finally extinguished by WWI—in which several of the group served as combatants and war artists.

The Wrestlers tray:
Henri Gaudier-
Brzeska for Omega
Workshops

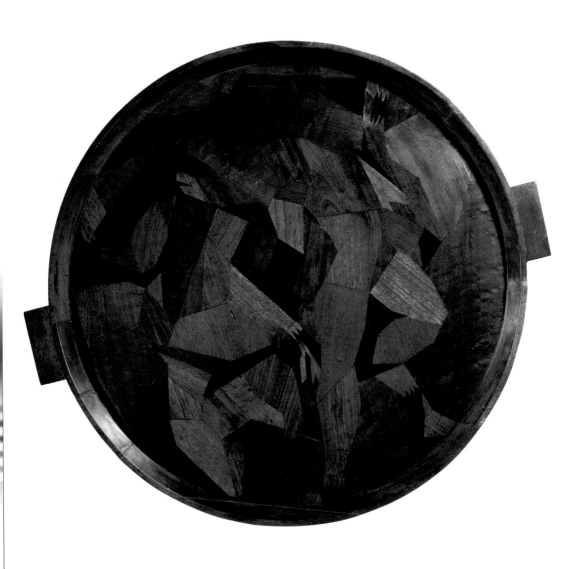

1915

Cover for *BLAST* magazine: Wyndam Lewis
This second and final issue of the magazine featured the second manifesto of the Vorticist movement.

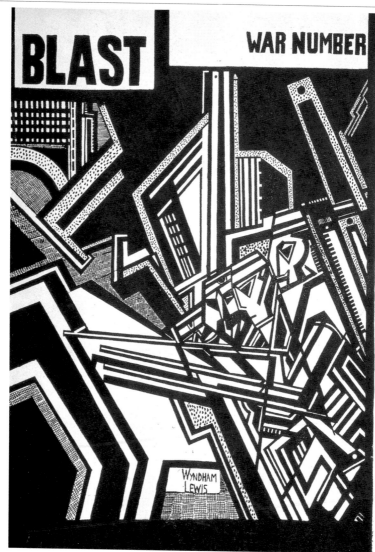

Key figures	Fields of work
Wyndham Lewis (1882–1957)	Artist/Writer
Ezra Pound (1885–1972)	Poet
Jacob Epstein (1880–1959)	Sculptor
Henri Gaudier-Brzeska (1891–1915)	Sculptor

Vorticist
composition:
Edward Alexander
Wadsworth

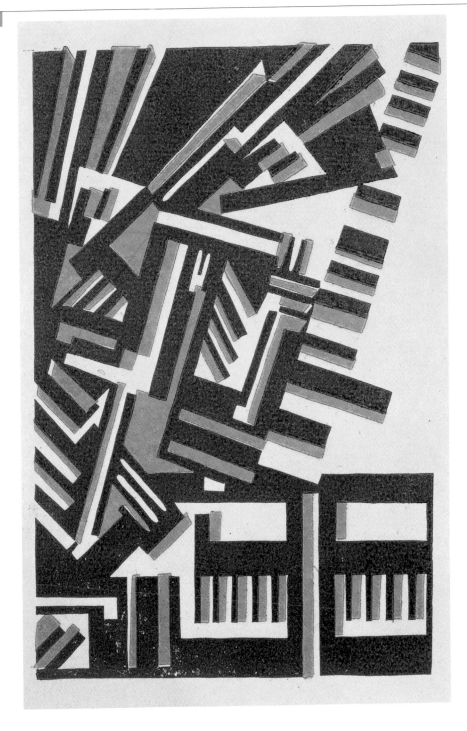

Dadaism

Key characteristics

No formal characteristics

Close relationship between word and image

Multiple type forms and line dimensions

Bold use of type: capital-lower case, condensed,
light-semibold type

Use of photomontage

Key facts

Focus on new materials, new ideas, and
new people

Main influence was on graphic design and in
particular typography

No formal characteristics

There is much controversy as to who founded the dada movement, not to mention when and where! Most believe it began in Zurich during WWI and then spread to New York, Paris, and Germany. Dada began as a literary movement, but soon grew to include poetry, performance art, collage, and photomontage. The spirit of dada was all about living in the moment and for the moment. Moreover, it was all about the newest materials, new ideas, and new people. The key characteristic of dadaism was the very fact that it had no formal characteristics, unlike the majority of other art styles and movements. Its only program was to have no program, and this is what gave the movement its explosive power to unfold freely in any direction, liberated from social or esthetic constraints. The fact that dada occurred in neutral Switzerland amidst the chaos of WWI is also of great significance: this was one of the few countries in which an amalgam of totally different characters could come together to form such a revolutionary movement. The fusion of personalities and ideas that occurred fueled the tensions and incompatibilities of character, origin, and attitude for which dada was renowned.

Founded by the poet and skeptic Hugo Ball at the beginning of 1916, dada's beginnings have been traced to the Cabaret Voltaire. In the first dada publication Ball wrote "The present booklet is published by us with the support of our friends in France, Italy, and Russia. It is intended to present to the Public the activities and interests of

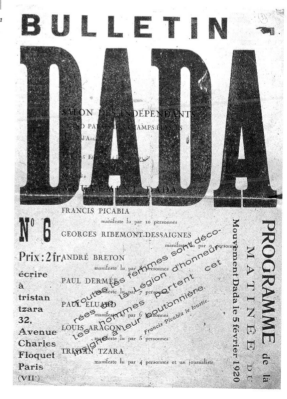

1920

Front cover, *Bulletin Dada* No. 6: Marcel Duchamp

Collage M2 439:
Kurt Schwitters

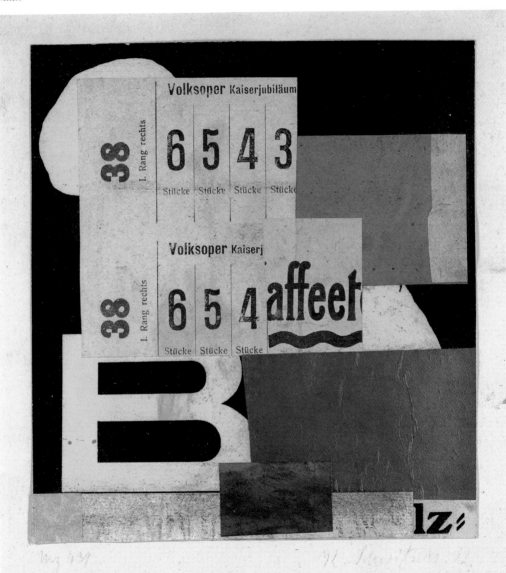

the Cabaret Voltaire, which has as its sole purpose to draw attention, cross the barriers of war and nationalism, to the few independent spirits who live for other ideals. The next objective of the artists who are assembled here is the publication of a revue internationale. La revue paraîtra à Zurich et portera le nom 'dada.' Dada dada dada." (Zurich, 15 May 1916). Another key figure was poet and essayist Tristan Tzara, who was responsible for many of the first dada texts, including *La Premiére Aventure Cèleste de Monsieur Antipyrine* (*The First Heavenly Adventure of Mr. Antipyrine*) 1916, *Vingt-cinq poémes* (*Twenty-Five Poems*) 1918, and *Sept Manifestes Dada* (*Seven Dada Manifestos*) 1924.

In design terms, dada did not really infiltrate the worlds of industrial design or architecture, but it did have a significant impact on graphic design, in particular typography. This period also saw the introduction of Photomontage as a new art form by the Berlin Dada group. Many of the earliest dada montages were used as covers and illustrations for magazines and manifestos of the movement. The dada influence on typography broke with most printing traditions and was distinguished by the close relationship between word and image, and the use of multiple type forms and line dimensions. Traditional horizontal and vertical dimensions were reinterpreted to create new layouts that incorporated lines, surfaces, and often, techniques that bore no visible relevance to the rest of the work, such as engravings. Syntactic elements like capital-lower case, condensed, light-semibold, etc., were used extensively. The legibility of texts may have suffered, but the content was emphasized.

While the original dada movement lasted only until 1923, the movement never really came to an end. In 1980, it saw a new and powerful revival when all the dada manifestos, which had previously been so difficult to find, were released by German publishers, reprinted true to the originals. A music group named itself after the Cabaret Voltaire and in 1982, the first dadaist conference since 1945 took place, in Germany.

In the last 20 years, formal and contextua dadaist influences have been used as important style elements in typography and graphic design. The work of two of the most influential graphic designers in the USA—David Carson and Edward Fella—was influenced by dadaism. In the UK, the punk movement exhibited dadaist tendencies in the mid-1970s, as seen in the graphics of Jamie Reid. In Germany, Thomas Nagel and Alex Branczyk brought dadaist freedom to th design of techno music and the digital world. The rebellious and inquiring principles of dada place it not just as an influential movement of the early twentieth century but also as a model for the present and the future.

Regional variations	Key figures	Fields of work
Zurich dada 1915–1920	Hugo Ball (1886–1927)	Author
	Tristan Tzara (1896–1963)	Poet/Essayist
	Marcel Janco (1895–1984)	Artist
New York dada 1915–1920	Marcel Duchamp (1887–1968)	Artist/Poet
Berlin dada 1918–1923	Johannes Baader (1875–1955)	Artist
	Raoul Hausmann (1886–1971)	Artist
	Richard Huelsenbeck (1892–1974)	Writer/Artist
Hannover dada 1919–1921	Kurt Schwitters (1887–1948)	Artist/Graphic designer/Typographer/Set designer/Poet
Cologne dada 1920–1922	Max Ernst (1891–1976)	Painter/Poet
	Johannes Baargeld (1892–1927)	Artist
	Hans Arp (1887–1966)	Sculptor/Painter/Poet
	Alfred Grunwald (1884–1951)	Author/Libbretist/Lyricist
Paris dada 1919–1922	Jacques Vaché (1896–1918)	Soldier

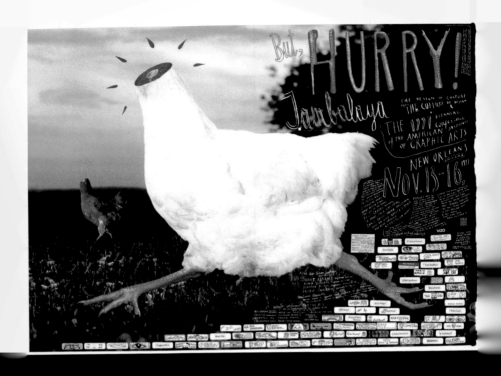

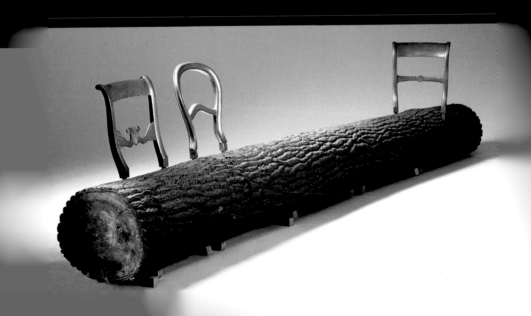

de Stijl

Also known as neoplasticism and elementarism. De Stijl (the Style) is the name attributed to the small group of architects, designers, artists, thinkers, and poets founded in the Netherlands in 1917 around the art journal of the same name. Led by the painter and architect Theo van Doesburg, the group, which included the likes of Piet Mondrian, Jacobus Johannes Pieter Oud, and Gerrit Thomas Rietveld, advocated a purification of art and design, eliminating natural forms and subject matter in favor of geometric abstraction, and the use of primary and noncolors (i.e. black and white). These aims were set out in the group's first manifesto, published in 1918. In addition to promoting its own work and ideas, the de Stijl journal also featured the work of the Russian **constructivists**, Italian **futurists**, and the **dadaists**. Neo-plasticism (new plastic art) was the term adopted by Mondrian to describe the qualities that de Stijl artists endeavored to achieve in their work; the creation of a universal esthetic language in favor of a simple, logical style that emphasized construction and function, and that would be appropriate for every aspect of modern life.

Responding to the chaos brought about by WWI, the de Stijl movement came at a time when order was valued above all else in the Netherlands. The multidisciplinary nature of the group's membership was integral to its success, enabling it to produce everything from graphics and paintings to interiors, textiles, and architecture, all united by a common visual language. The movement's work is instantly recognizable through its use of straight, horizontal and vertical lines, and block colors. Its philosophy, which had its roots in functionalism, was epitomized in the paintings of Piet Mondrian and the designs of Gerrit Thomas Rietveld. As the artist most closely associated with de Stijl, Mondrian's abstract paintings concentrated on the harmonious composition of line, mass, and color; the relationship between positive and negative elements in an arrangement of nonobjective forms and lines. Rietveld translated these principles into three dimensions with pieces such as his Red/Blue chair. Structure, emphasizing the intersection of planes through the use of contrasting colors and exaggerated junction points, was also integral to Rietveld's work. It is the Schroeder House, however, complete with furniture and decoration all designed by Rietveld, that stands as the most complete realization of the de Stijl esthetic.

The de Stijl journal was published until Theo van Doesburg's death in 1931, after which the movement gradually dissolved. De Stijl achieved international acclaim by the end of the 1920s. The dematerialist approach evident in its buildings, interiors, and furniture made a fundamental contribution to **modernism**.

Composition IX,
opus 18: Theo van
Doesburg

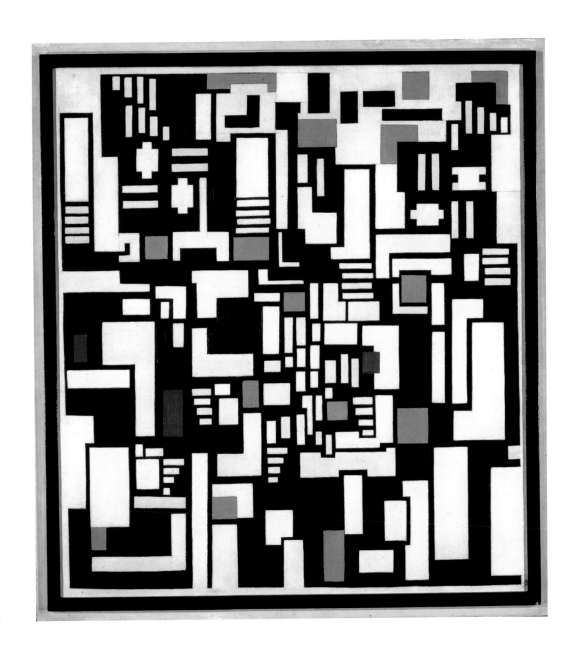

1917

De Styl poster:
Theo van
Doesburg and
Vilmos Huszar

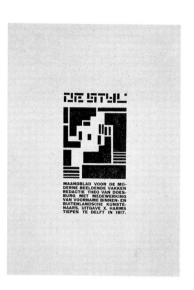

1918

Red/Blue chair,
early edition:
Gerrit Thomas
Rietveld

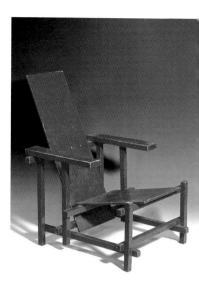

1923-1924

Schroeder House:
Gerrit Thomas
Rietveld

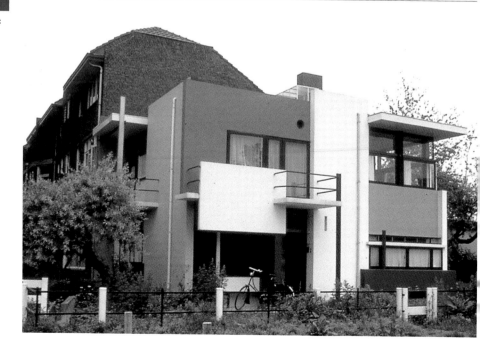

Composition in
Red and Blue:
Piet Mondrian

Later Applications

1995

**De Stijl typeface:
Theo van Doesburg,
Richard Kegler,
Michael Want**
The typeface features
three rigid, balanced,
and angular fonts,
and a set of
geometric extras.

ABCDEFGHIJ

fifLß&

ABCDEFGHIJ

1234567890

.. .. - - — '' ""'' ‹ ›‹

' , ' ,

!?¡¿()[]/††§

MNOPQRSTUVWXYZ

MNOPQRSTUVWXYZ

% ‰

f

Later Applications

The White Stripes *De Stijl* **album: concept by The White Stripes** The album features designs, sculptures, and sketches by Paul Overty, Gerrit Thomas Rietveld, Theo van Doesburg, Vilmos Huszar, and Georges Vantongerioo. In addition to naming their second album after the Dutch design movement, the band also dedicated it to Rietveld. All of The White Stripes' albums to date have featured the limited red-white-black color scheme associated with de Stijl.

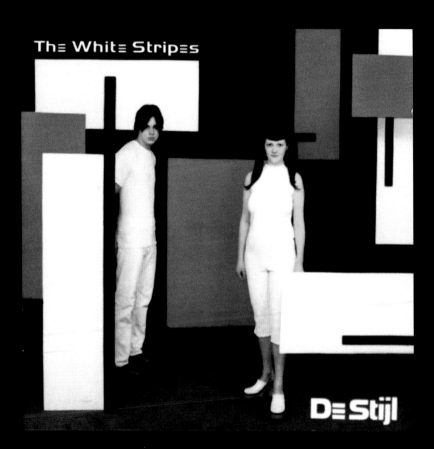

Key figures	Fields of work
Theo van Doesburg (1883–1931)	Architect/Painter/Stained-glass artist/Theorist
Piet Mondrian (1872–1944)	Artist
Jacob Johannes Pieter Oud (1890–1963)	Architect/Town planner/Designer
Gerrit Thomas Rietveld (1888–1964)	Architect/Furnituremaker/Designer

Pastoe installation
for Nu. 90 Jaar
Pastoe (Now. 90
Years Pastoe):
Experimental Jetset
for the Centraal
Museum, Utrecht

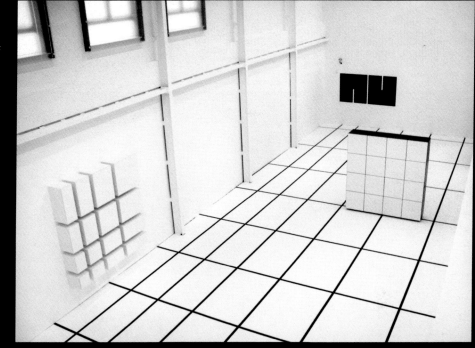

2003

L Bed: For Use,
for Interlübke

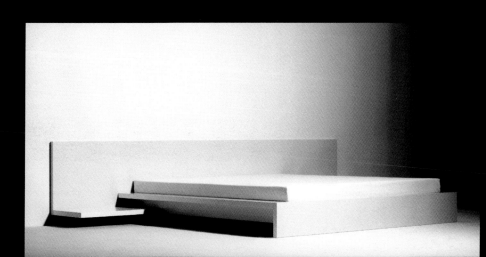

Bauhaus

The style most associated with **modernism**, the Bauhaus style of design takes its name from the German design school, Staatliches Bauhaus, Weimar. Referred to simply as Bauhaus, it was founded in 1919, in Weimer, Germany by the architect Walter Gropius. Gropius firmly believed in the idea of the Gesamtkunstwerk (a term that translates literally as "complete artwork" and which refers to an amalgamation of all the arts). He coined the term Bauhaus—an amalgamation of the words bauen (to build) and haus (house)—as a metaphor for his belief. Established with the aim of training artists for industrial production, the school was formed as the result of a merger between the Academy of Fine Art (Sächsische Hochschule für Bildende Kunst) and the School of Applied Arts (Sächsische Kunstgewerbeschule) in Weimar.

During its first phase, the Bauhaus school was greatly influenced by the artist Johannes Itten whose teaching strategies focused on "intuition and method" and "subjective experience and objective recognition." Along with two other artists, Lyonel Feininger (1871–1956) and Gerhard Marcks (1889–1981), Itten was responsible for the school's one-year foundation course, during which students were taught the basic principles of design and color theory.

Tutors at the school were referred to as Masters and students as Journeymen. After the preliminary course, students went on to train in at least one craft in the school's various workshops. However, Itten's involvement in the Mazdaznan sect (a Zoroastrian-styled movement based on principles of inner harmony, including meditation and vegetarianism) and his attempts to introduce spirituality into art and design did not sit well with Gropius.

In December 1922 Itten left the school, effectively ending the Bauhaus' expressionist period. His successors, Josef Albers and László Moholy-Nagy, opted for a more industrial approach, arranging student visits to factories as part of the curriculum.

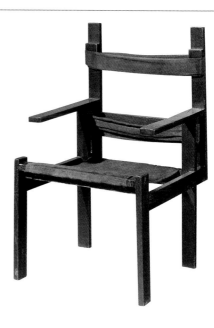

1924

Armchair: Marcel Breuer for the Bauhaus

Essentially a state-funded institution, the Bauhaus was the focus of much political opposition in Weimar. In 1923, in order to justify the state's continued support, a landmark exhibition was held. This featured work from the Bauhaus along with a number of **de Stijl** designs, including Gerrit Thomas Rietveld's Red/Blue chair. The exhibition saw the emergence of a new, overtly modern style of graphic design inspired by de Stijl and Russian **constructivism**. The exhibition did not fully achieve its aim; the school's grant was halved when Weimar became the first city in Germany to elect the National Socialist German Worker's Party. The Bauhaus' radical, and what many considered socialist ethos and esthetic was not liked by the local authorities. In 1925, following various political disagreements, the school was forced to move from Weimar to Dessau, a city still under the rule of the much more politically receptive Social Democrats. The move also brought much-needed financial support via the USA, where assistance loans were

being granted as part of the Dawes Plan. Funding was granted on the proviso that the school would part-fund itself through the production and retail of its own designs. The Staatliches Bauhaus moved into its new headquarters in Dessau in 1926. The building itself was designed by Gropius, with all the interiors, furniture, and furnishings designed by the school's students and staff.

The design of the new school signaled a new direction for the Bauhaus—that of industrial functionalism. The school began issuing its own diplomas, Masters were now referred to as Professors and the school cut all ties with the local crafts guilds. Bauhaus GmbH, a limited company through which Bauhaus products could be retailed, was formed in 1925. A catalog, designed by Herbert Bayer, was created, but sales were not good, largely because, although designed with a machine esthetic, many of the Bauhaus' products were not actually suitable for industrial production. When the various licensing agreements with external manufacturers failed to

bring in the necessary revenue, Gropius resigned, handing control over to Hans Meyer.

During his short directorship, from 1928–1930, Meyer increased the school's commercial success, licensing its designs to manufacturers and generally making the Bauhaus style available to a wider market. However, Meyer's Marxist principles were not popular; he sought to politicize the Bauhaus, introducing lectures on economics, psychology, and Marxism, and adopted a more scientific approach to design. Meyer believed form should be governed by function and cost in order to produce products that were both affordable and practical to working class consumers.

By 1930, Ludwig Mies van der Rohe had been persuaded to take control. Under pressure to depoliticize the school, he ordered its immediate closure on September 9, 1930. All students were forced to reapply for their places when the school reopened the following semester. During its closure a new curriculum was agreed upon, the original

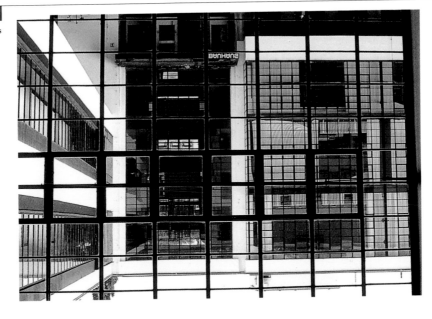

1925-1926

Staatliches Bauhaus (Bauhaus School), Dessau, Germany: Walter Gropius

preliminary course was made noncompulsory, and the study of architecture elevated to primary status. Applied arts were allowed to continue on the condition that only products that could be industrially manufactured were designed. The political situation, however, remained unstable and it wasn't long before the National Socialists won control of Dessau, forcing closure of the school within a year.

The Bauhaus was reestablished as a private school in Berlin, but before long the National Socialists seized that city too. The school was raided by the Gestapo who sealed the building, looking for communist literature, and it never reopened. On July 19, 1933, the Masters gathered and voted to dissolve the Bauhaus. Many of the school's Masters relocated to the US, often via Britain. Moholy-Nagy founded the New Bauhaus in Chicago in 1937, albeit with limited success; Gropius became professor of Architecture at Harvard University (1937–1952); and in 1938, a major retrospective celebrating the work of the Bauhaus was held at the Museum of Modern Art, New York, introducing the work of the Bauhaus to a new American audience.

The Bauhaus lasted just 14 years, and took in only 1,250 students during that time, but despite its short history, the progressive and experimental curriculum and innovative teaching practices that it developed had an enormous impact on design—one that continues to this day.

Bauhaus program and manifesto, 1919
- To establish architecture as the dominant design forum
- To elevate the status of craft skills to that of fine art
- The improvement of industrial products through the combined efforts of artists, industrialists, and craftsmen

1926

Offset Buch und Werbekunst (Offest Book and the Art of Advertising), No. 7 cover: Joost Schmidt

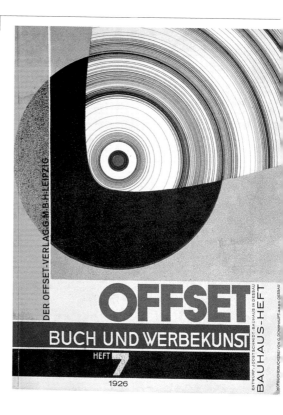

Twentieth century

Bauhaus design color lithograph.

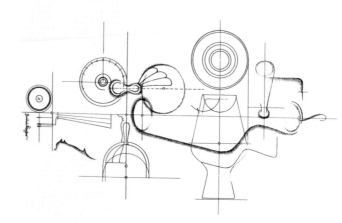

Barcelona chair,
Model MR 90:
Ludwig Mies van
der Rohe

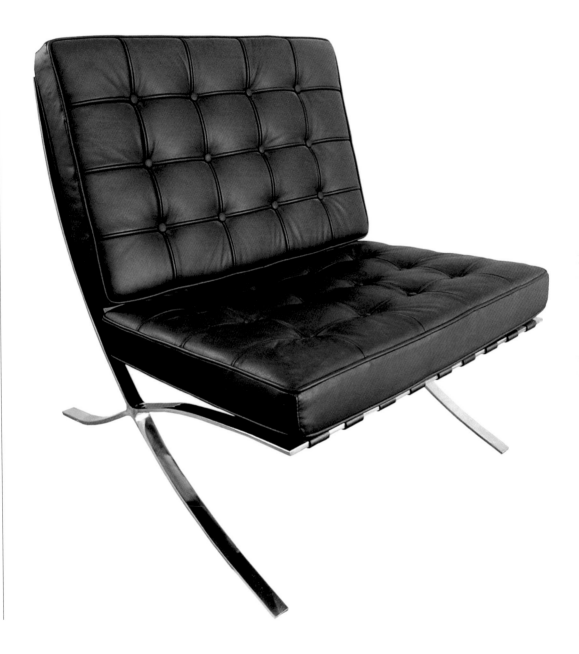

Edward Benguiat and Victor Caruso
This modern typeface is based on the prototype created in 1925 by Herbert Bayer.

abcdefghijklmnopqrstuvwxyz ﬀﬁ&@
ABCDEFGHIJKLMNOPQRSTUVWXYZ
1234567890
.,:;-–—'' ""'.‹›«»*%‰
!?¡¿()[]/†‡§\$£¢ ƒ

1997

Tykho radio: Marc Berthier
Berthier's designs are notable for their use of ordinary materials in unexpected ways. His Tykho radio is encased in splash- and shock-resistant synthetic rubber.

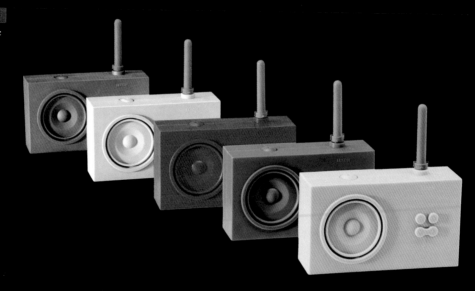

Key figures	Fields of work
Walter Gropius (1883–1969)	First Director of the Bauhaus (1919–1928)/Architect of the Bauhaus, Dessau
Marcel Breuer (1902–1971)	Student at Bauhaus, Weimar/Teacher at Bauhaus, Dessau
Ludwig Mies van der Rohe (1886–1969)	Director of the Bauhaus (1930–1933)
Hans Meyer (1831–1905)	Director of the Bauhaus (1928–1930)
László Moholy-Nagy (1895–1946)	Photographer/Artist/Graphic designer/Foundation Course leader at Bauhaus (1923–19
Marianne Brandt (1893–1983)	One of the few female Bauhaus members allowed in its Metal Workshops
Oskar Schlemmer (1888–1943)	Stage director/Master of Sculpture at the Bauhaus (1923–1929)

Apple iMac: Apple Industrial Group The original iMac, with its use of translucent plastic and bright colors, transformed the way we think about computers forever. This design approach can be traced back to that of the Bauhaus whose innovative, progressive curriculum and resulting work had an enormous impact on design.

LIFT 01 poster: Vince Frost The steel crane in Frost's poster for the London International Festival of Theatre is a graphic translation of the Bauhaus esthetic.

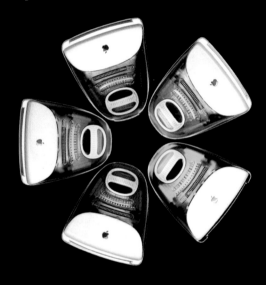

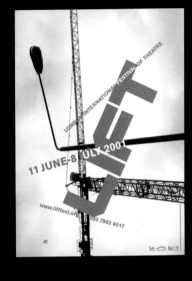

CD Player: Naoto Fukasawa This award-winning design avoids all superfluous decoration, yet remains a beautiful, functional object.

La Valise: Ronan and Erwan Bouroullec for Magis Valise is a filing system with a lid and handle. Its form is entirely dictated by its function.

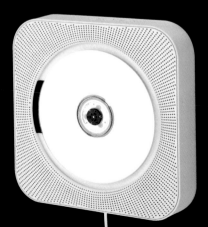

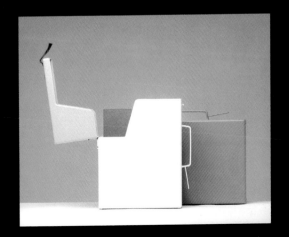

Moderne

Moderne is the name attributed to a form of **art deco** that existed during the 1920s and 1930s. Popular in Europe, moderne flourished in the USA where the chrome-and-glass sets of Hollywood films introduced this new style to a captive international audience. Taking inspiration from the **Wiener Werkstätte**, designers adopted strong, geometric forms in their work, and used chromium and aluminum to create gleaming surface finishes. The work of American interior and furniture designer Donald Deskey is often said to epitomize the moderne style.

Esthetically superficial, moderne was a decorative style that utilized the machine esthetic to conceal the inner workings of an object. It used the look of the machine ornamentally without necessarily possessing a functional relationship with it. In architecture, moderne figured most prominently in nonresidential buildings, from skyscrapers to movie theaters, advertising "the promise of a machine-made future." However, as the Depression deepened, fewer and fewer moderne buildings were constructed. Instead, the style was translated into consumer products and interiors. Not many homes were built in the moderne style, but with those that were, their decorative exteriors often belied the traditional floorplans and décor within.

Moderne also had many associations with the new; from materials to talent to technology. Bakelite and phenolic resins became extremely popular. Brick buildings were increasingly covered with concrete or plaster "skins" to provide a smooth, metal-like finish, thus reinforcing the machine esthetic. As the ocean liner was a physical manifestation of all that was new, it was no coincidence that these buildings began to resemble ships. With many designers working on private commissions from wealthy clients, the moderne style soon came to symbolize the American Dream. Many of the esthetic attributes associated with moderne were later revived through **postmodernism**.

Adjustable Table:
"E 1027" Eileen
Gray

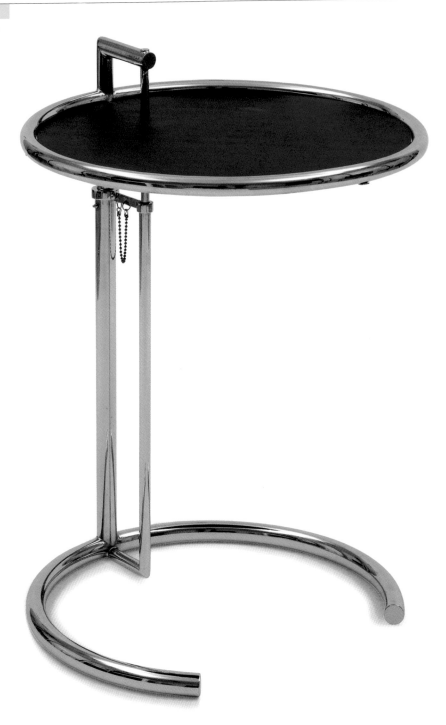

Later Applications

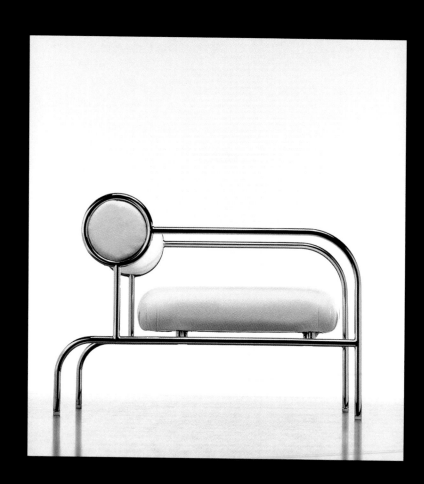

Key figures

Donald Deskey (1894–1989)

Karl Emanuel Martin (Kem) Weber (1889–1963)

Eileen Moray Gray (1879–1976)

Walter Dorwin Teague (1883–1960)

Raymond Fernand Loewy (1893–1986)

Fields of work

Designer (graphics, packaging, interiors, lighting,
furniture, exhibitions)

Designer

Architect/Designer

Industrial designer

Designer

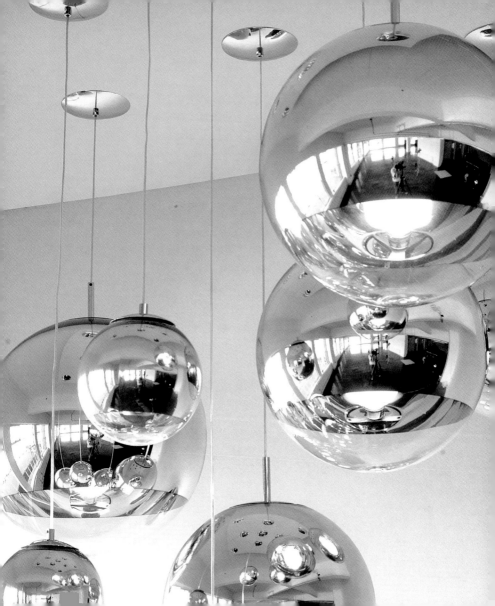

Constructivism

Also known as Soviet constructivism and Productivist School. Constructivism is the term used to describe an influential art movement instigated by the Soviet avant-garde following the Russian Revolution of 1917. Prior to this, and in tandem with the rest of Europe, designers in the Soviet Union had sought inspiration from modern European practices such as **Cubism** and **futurism**, but by 1917 the time had come for a new form of creative expression that echoed their desire for a new social and political order. Russian constructivists believed art and design should be absorbed into industrial production—as a result, they set about creating "production" art and architecture.

Constructivism was one of the first movements in art to adopt a purely nonobjective approach. Constructivists followed a geometric, precise, almost mathematical method in their work,

using rectangles, squares, and circles as the predominant shapes to construct carefully composed artworks that emphasized the dominance of machines over nature in the modern world. A number of Aleksandr Rodchenko's drawings were even created using a ruler and compass. Many of the constructivists had big ambitions, but the political and economic instability brought on by the Russian Revolution meant that few large-scale projects were ever undertaken. Instead, the constructivists turned their attentions to smaller projects, such as poster and exhibition design, typography and ceramics.

In 1920, Alexei Gan, Varvara Stepanova, and Rodchenko published a manifesto entitled *The Program of the Group of Constructivists*, in which they called for artists to stop creating idle esthetic forms and begin designing useful objects that could benefit the

1919

Beat the Whites
with the Red
Wedge: El Lissitzky

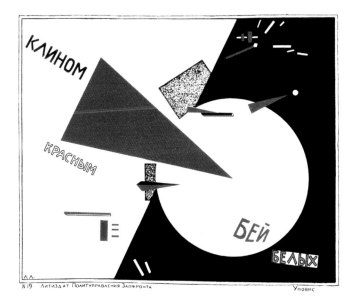

Soviet poster
celebrating the
emancipation
of women.

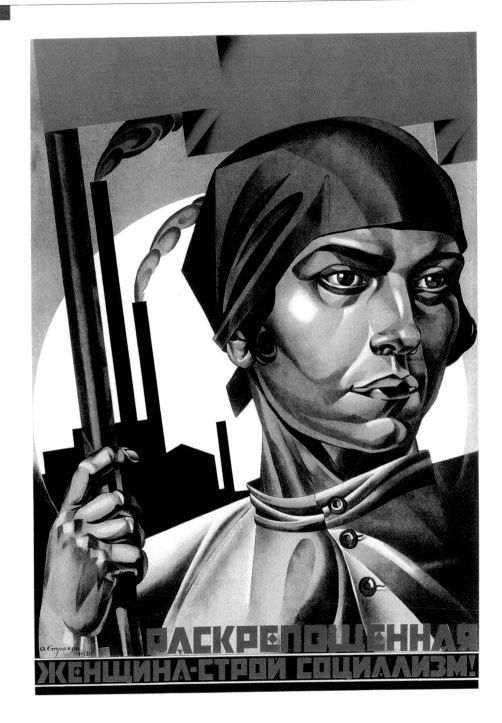

emerging Soviet state, maintaining that
the artist was a worker and responsible
for designing new objects. This new
emphasis on designing functional objects
did not sit well with Naum Gabo and
Antoine Pevsner, who published their
own Realistic manifesto the same year.
Gabo and Pevsner did not agree with the
Soviet constructivists' belief that all art
should be materialist and politically
Marxist. They believed that art, and
therefore constructivism, had an important role in the structure of life and was
an indispensable means of expressing
human experience. The two artists left
Russia in 1922 and 1923 respectively,
taking their concept of constructivism to
Europe. The remaining Soviet constructivists—Tatlin, Rodchenko, Stepanova,
and Popova—continued to design,
creating ceramics, furniture, textiles, and
interiors until Stalin outlawed the style
in 1932, introducing Soviet Realism as
the only permissible art form.

One of the leading figures in the
Soviet constructivist movement was
Kasimir Malevich, although he preferred
to describe his work not as constructivism,
but as suprematism. Perhaps best known
for his groundbreaking modernist
paintings, such as White on White and
Black Square, Malevich founded the
suprematist movement in 1913 with a
manifesto and exhibition entitled 0.10 The
Last Futurist Exhibition. Suprematists
sought to free art from the burden of the
object, promoting pure esthetic creativity
rather than a connection to anything
social or political. To Malevich, the
purest form was the square, although he
did use other elements such as rectangles,
circles, triangles, and crosses in his work.
In addition to painting, he also created
ceramics. He even dabbled in architecture
with his Architectron models.

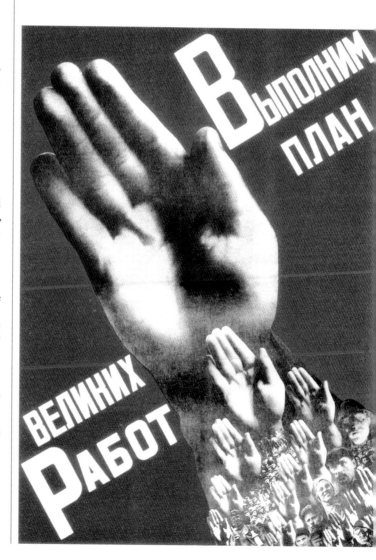

1930

Soviet poster
promoting the
Great Works
program.

International/European Constructivism

The constructivism that developed in Europe was not confined to a single group of artists, as it had been in Russia. Although the majority of constructivist activity outside the Soviet Union took place in Germany, constructivist ideas could also be found in art centers like Paris, London, and, eventually, the United States. International constructivism demonstrated that visual elements such as line, color, shape, and texture possess their own expressive qualities without the need for any reference to observable reality. Using everything from metal and wood to light and movement, devotees of the style experimented with complex visual relationships in a bid to expand their creative possibilities. In 1922, El Lissitzky organized an exhibition of Russian art in Berlin. This included pre-1920 works by Malevich, Tatlin, and Rodchenko. These early constructivist works immediately appealed to European artists, and constructivist philosophies were soon introduced into the teachings at the **Bauhaus**, and adopted by practitioners of **dada** and the Dutch **de Stijl** movement.

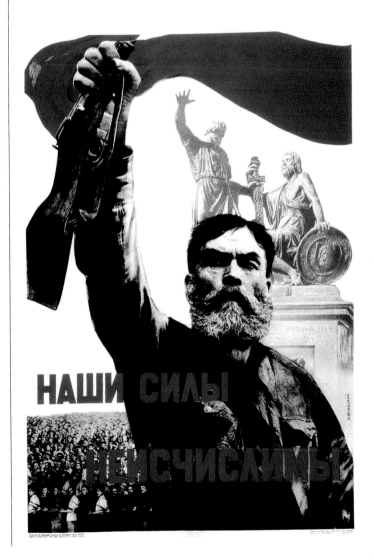

Soviet poster celebrating the limitless power of the people.

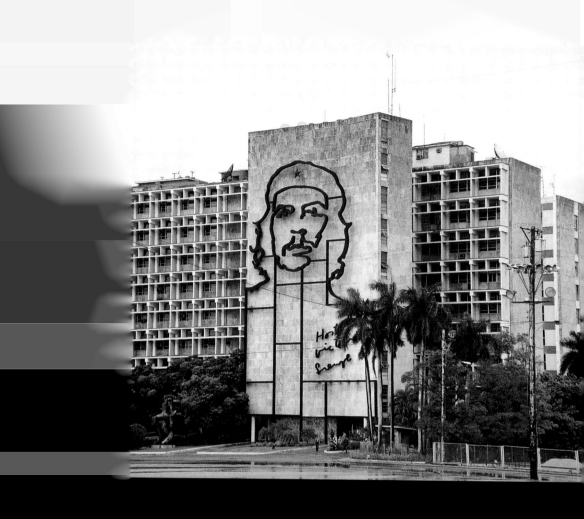

	Key figures	Fields of work
n	Aleksandr Rodchenko (1891–1956)	Painter/Designer/Graphic designer/Theater and cinema artist
	Varvara Fedorovna Stepanova (1894–1958)	Graphic designer/Theater set and costume designer
	El Lissitzky (1890–1941)	Artist/Architect
	Vladimir Evgrafovich Tatlin (1885–1953)	Artist
	Kasimir Severinovich Malevich (1878–1935)	Artist/Designer
tivism/ sm	Naum Gabo (1890–1977)	Sculptor
	Antoine Pevsner (1884–1962)	Sculptor/Painter

ABCDEFGHIJKLMNOPQRSTU
UXYZ ßE
ABCDEFGHIJKLMNOPQRSTU
UXYZ
2345678Q0
;;-—"''"".‹›«»★%
?¿£()[]/†‡§$£¢ƒ

2000

3-D objects made
with strata studio
pro 1.75: Dextro

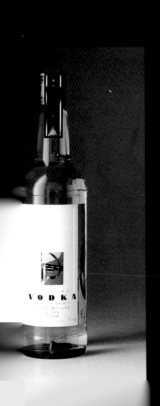

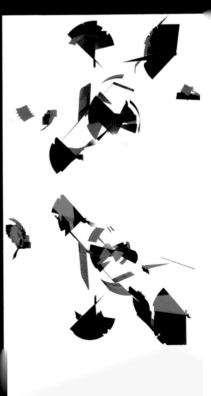

Surrealism

Origin

France

Key characteristics

Dreamlike depictions

Deliberate construction of strange combinations using found objects

Key facts

Evolved from the nihilistic ideas of dadaism, which it replaced

Inspired by the theories of Sigmund Freud; founded on the belief that the subconscious be expressed free from esthetic or moral preoccupations

Politics was an inherent part of the movement

See also

Dadaism p 104

A term first coined in 1917 by the poet Guillame Apollinaire (1880–1918), surrealism is the name of the twentieth-century art movement that evolved from the nihilistic ideas of **dadaism**, which it replaced. Inspired by the theories of Sigmund Freud (1856–1939), the pioneer of psychoanalysis, the surrealist movement was led by the French writer and poet André Breton. He wrote three manifestos about surrealism in 1924, 1930, and 1934. Founded on the belief that the subconscious be expressed either as imagery or poetry, "free from the exercise of reason and every esthetic or moral preoccupation," the beliefs of the surrealists were best manifested in the dreamlike creations of Salvador Dali and the "deliberate construction of strange conjunctions of found objects" of Marcel Duchamp's dada-influenced works. In his 1924 *Manifeste du Surréalisme*, Breton defined surrealism as "pure psychic automatism, by which it is intended to express … the real process of thought."

Although primarily an art movement, surrealism did infiltrate the world of graphic design. Examples of surrealist design can be seen in a number of advertisements created by British artists during the 1930s, such as Paul Nash's landscapes for the Shell Oil Company and Man Ray's posters for the London Underground. Works such as Dali's Mae West sofa served to challenge perceptions of what art and design should be, and indeed could be, often blurring the boundaries between the two.

As with a number of twentieth-century design movements, politics was an inherent part, with a number of surrealists becoming actively involved with the Communist Party.

1923

Metronome
(Object to be
Destroyed):
Man Ray

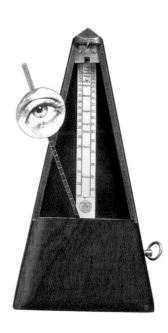

**Keep London
Going poster:
Man Ray** Man Ray
was one of several
famous artists who
created posters for
the London
Underground. More
than advertising,
posters such as this
were public art, free
and available to all
who rode the "tube."

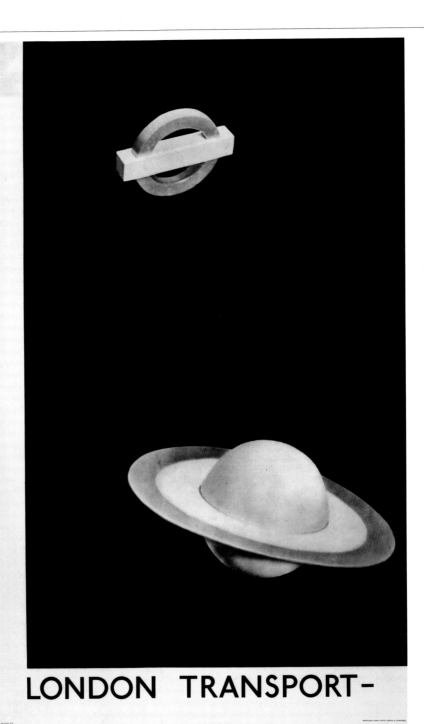

Shortly Before
Dawn: Herbert
Bayer

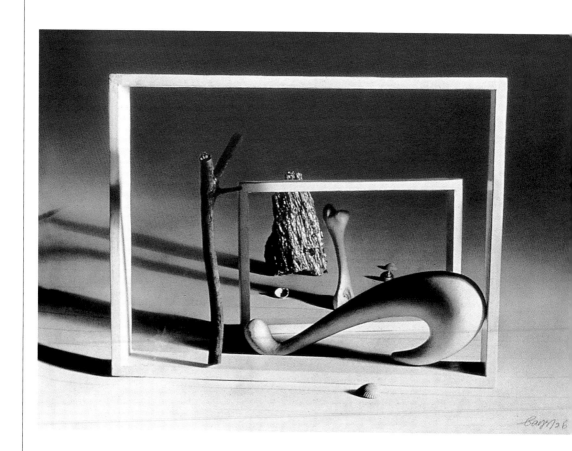

Mae West Lips
sofa: Salvador Dali

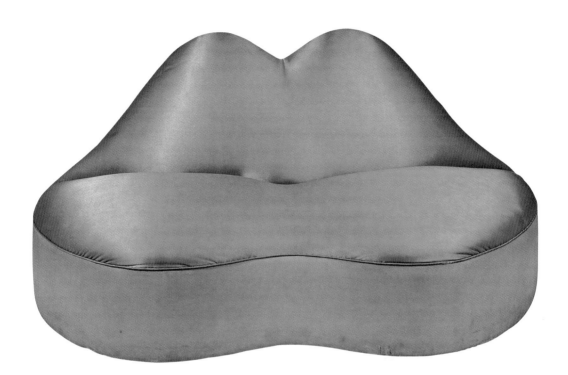

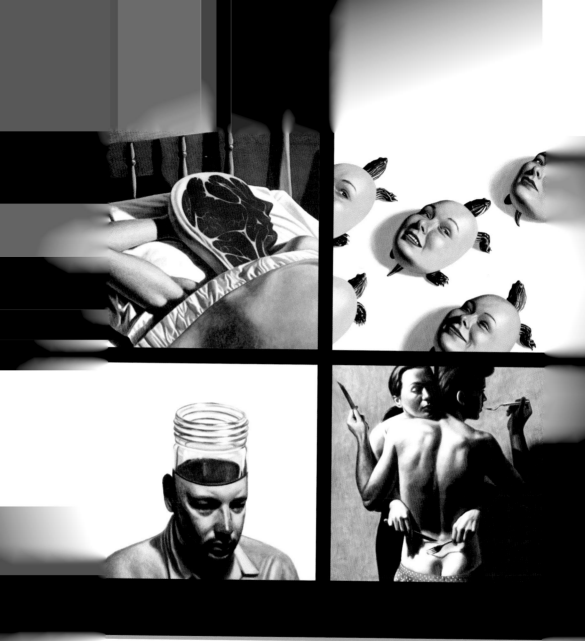

	Fields of work
...naire (1880–1939)	Poet
...96–1966)	Writer/Poet
...04–1988)	Painter/Sculptor/Engraver/Designer/Book illustrator/
...946)	Painter/Designer
...976)	Photographer/Painter/Sculptor/Filmmaker

**Autumn Intrusion
window display,
Harvey Nichols
department store:
Thomas
Heatherwick**
This display was
mounted for
London Fashion
Week at London's
most fashionable
department store.

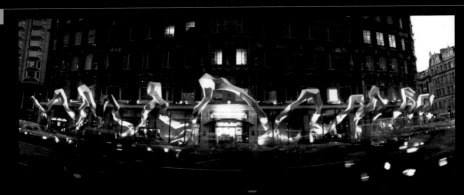

**Can Can
can opener:
Stefano Giovanni
and Paul Van Iersel
Harry for Alessi**

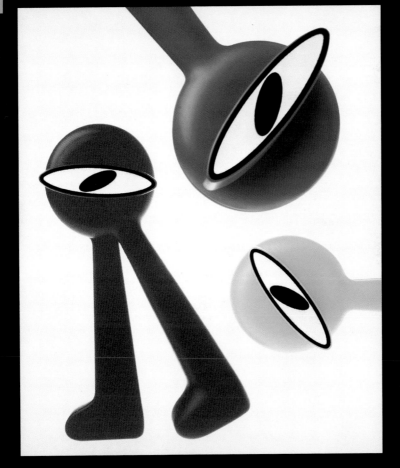

Rationalism

Origin

Italy

Key characteristics

Severe geometric forms

State-of-the-art materials, such as chromed
tubular metal

Key facts

A logical, functionalist approach to architecture,
devoid of any unnecessary decoration

Embraced simplicity as a symbol of the new Italy

Conceived a unique architectural element by
incorporating landscape windows in a building

See also

Futurism p 80

The Italian rationalist movement was founded in 1926 in Milan by a group of seven architectural students, known as Gruppe Sette (Group of Seven), who believed that there was a new, fresh artistic spirit in Europe, and that Italy had the power to develop it. Primarily an architectural movement, rationalism was characterized by a logical, functionalist approach to architecture, devoid of any unnecessary decoration. The movement was brought to the public's attention—and effectively launched—when in 1926, the Group published a four-part manifesto in the magazine *Rassegna*.

Strongly opposed to **futurism**, rationalists celebrated advances in technology through the use of state-of-the-art materials, such as chromed met and severe geometric forms, embracing simplicity as a symbol of the new Italy.

The 1929 apartment complex Palazz Gualino, by Giuseppe Pagano and Gin Levi-Montalcini, exemplified the rationalist style. The uniform surface texture of the building's facade was initially painted yellow-green to create the illusion of identical levels stacked one on top of the other. The architects also added a new, and at that time

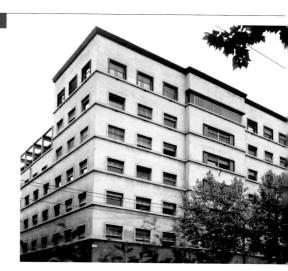

1929

Palazzo Gualino,
Turin, Italy:
Guiseppe Pagano
and Gino Levi-
Montalcini

Key figures	Fields of work
Giuseppe Terragni (1904–1943)	Architect
Gino Pollini (1903–1991)	Architect
Luigi Figini (1903–1984)	Architect
Adalberto Libera (1903–1963)	Architect
Carlo Enrico Rava (1904–1943)	Architect
Sebastiano Larco	Architect
Guido Frette	Architect

unique architectural element to the building by incorporating landscape windows. Another rationalist architect of the time, Dullio Torres, redesigned the facade of the Italia pavilion at the Venice Biennale in 1932. Torres immediately disposed of the neo-classical decoration that had adorned the building's facade since 1914, replacing it with an all-new, simple, linear style. This new approach to design was very different from the overly ornate architectural style that characterized traditional Italian art forms of the time.

Date not known

These buildings in Berlin demonstrate the functionalist approach to design that is characteristic of rationalism.

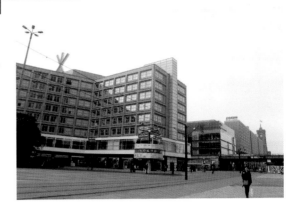

Later Applications

1999

Air Chair: Jasper Morrison
Jasper Morrison has succeeded in revitalizing rationalist design with his inventive approach to material and form, as seen in the simple design and single-piece construction of the Air Chair, created using advanced air molding techniques.

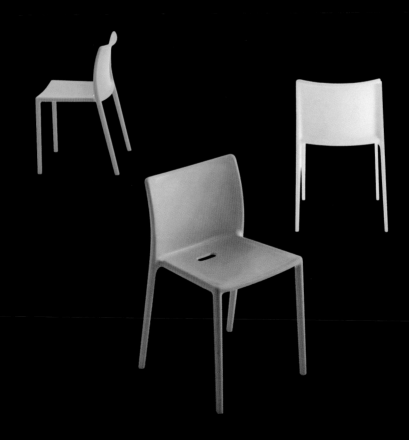

Streamlining

Origin

United States

Key characteristics

Aerodynamic appearance

Rounded edges, smoothly finished forms

Teardrop-shapes

Key facts

Where functionalism sought to break things down, streamlining championed the seamless whole

The approach captured the public's imagination as a symbol of progress

Had a major impact on the American manufacturing industries where annual restyling programs encouraged limited stylistic durability

See also

Moderne p 122

International Style p 154

One interpretation of the machine esthetic that often clashed with the functional ideals of the **International Style** was that of streamlining. Where functionalism sought to break things down and reassemble them as a series of connected parts, streamlining championed the seamless whole, an efficient and integrated sleek silhouette— albeit designed with functionality in mind—at the time when the need for mass transportation, such as the design of planes, trains, and boats was becoming increasingly urgent. Exponents of streamlining regarded speed as "the essence of the modern age." Accordingly, the shape most conducive to speed was the ovoid, or teardrop. This approach to design also captured the public's imagination as a symbol of progress.

The result of streamlining was not only the appearance of speed in all manner of objects. It also diverted attention from the item's actual inner workings. Like **moderne**, streamlining concealed all—the good, the bad, and the ugly. Bakelite, a thermoset plastic particularly suited to the characteristic molding of streamlined forms, became the material of choice for many designers during this period.

By the late 1930s, streamlining was no longer being used purely for functional reasons but also for formal ones. Increasingly employed to restyle rather than redesign, designers such as Norman Bel Geddes and Raymond Loewy were unconcerned that an object's esthetic did not derive from its purpose, so long as it did not explicitly contradict it. As a result everything from toasters to trailer were streamlined. The style also had a major impact on the American manufacturing industries. Annual restyling programs encouraged limited stylistic durability as consumers found themselves unwittingly sucked into the perpetually changing cycle of fashion and fashionability; and while functional obsolescence remained a necessary part of technological evolution, stylistic obsolescence had no such moral alibi. Even children's toys could not escape the streamline treatment. As one critic noted "streamlining is legitimate in the tricycle because the younger generation expects the latest modernity in its playthings."

**Cisitalia 202 GT car:
Pinin Farina**
Simple, elegant,
and beautifully
proportioned, the
Cisitalia 202
represented a new
era in automotive
styling. The car was
selected for the Museum
of Modern Art's 8
Automobiles exhibition.
The catalog stated:
"The Cisitalia's body is
slipped over its chassis
like a dustcover over
a book."

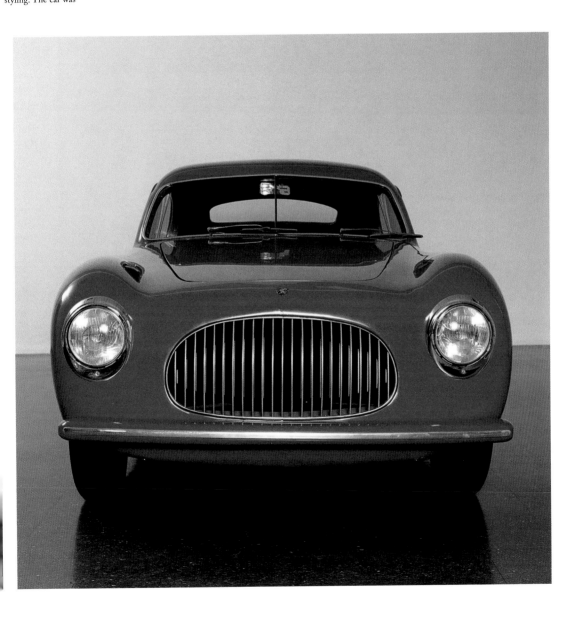

Later Applications

Lama prototype
scooter: Philippe
Starck for Aprilia

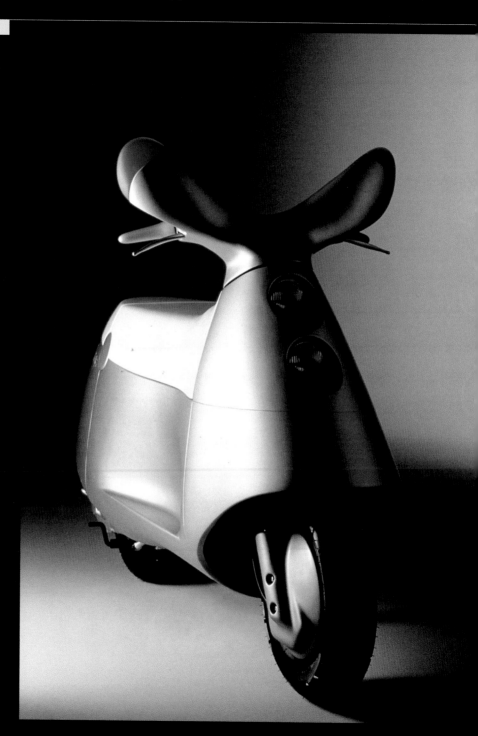

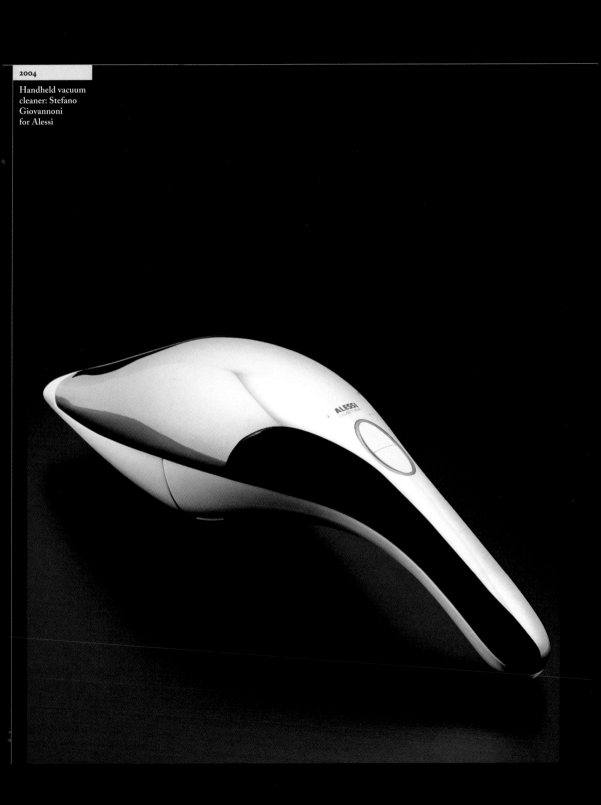

Handheld vacuum
cleaner: Stefano
Giovannoni
for Alessi

2004

Kelvin 40 concept jet: Marc Newson for the Fondation Cartier pour l'Art Contemporain Unmistakably Newson, it is the seamless integration of engineering and technology that places this objèt d'art so comfortably between the two opposing realms of fantasy and reality.

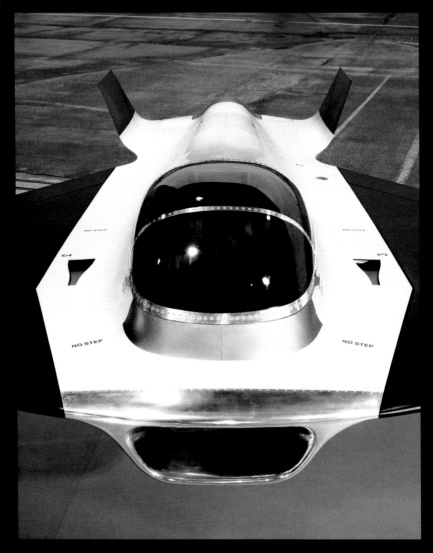

Key figures	**Fields of work**
Raymond Fernand Loewy (1893–1986)	Designer
Norman Bel Geddes (1893–1958)	Industrial and theatrical designer
Henry Dreyfuss (1904–1972)	Industrial designer
Walter Dorwin Teague (1883–1960)	Industrial designer

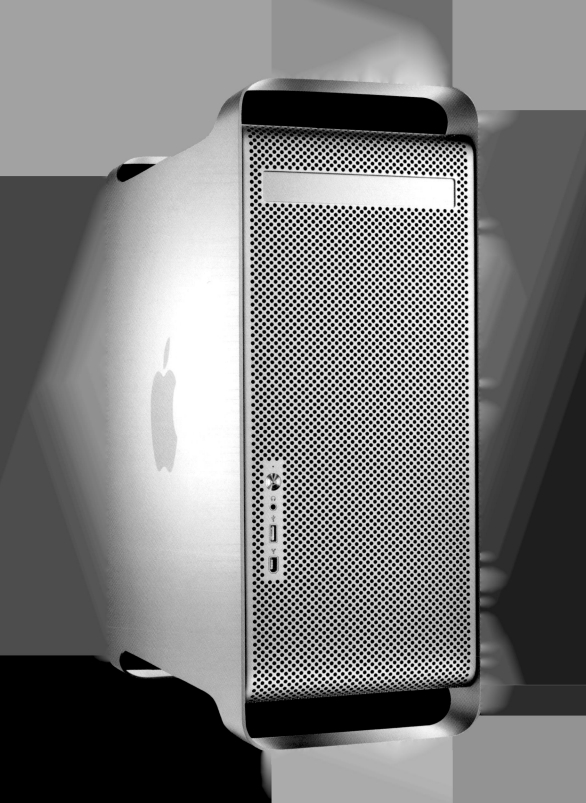

Organic design

Origin

United States

Europe

Key characteristics

Soft, flowing lines and sculptural forms

Holistically conceived designs that relate to their surrounding environment

Use of both natural materials and synthetics, such as plastic, that can be easily molded into organic forms

Key facts

Believed that individual elements, such as furniture, should connect visually and functionally with both their interior surroundings and the building as a whole

Inspired by new manufacturing processes, new materials, and advancements in computer-aided design

Seeks the subtlety of form

See also

Art nouveau p 42

Organic design takes its roots from the concept of organic architecture, originally developed by Frank Lloyd Wright and Charles Rennie Mackintosh toward the end of the nineteenth century. Central to their approach was the belief that individual elements, such as furniture, should connect visually and functionally with both their interior surroundings and the building as a whole. Moreover, they felt that buildings should also express a special relationship with their immediate surroundings, whether through their structure, use of materials, or color.

Although the notion of integration and nature was inherent in this approach, it was not necessarily expressed esthetically, and the use of organic forms was not commonplace at this time. It was not until the idea of organicism was applied to design that the flowing, ergonomic lines that have come to define organic design as we know it today were first introduced.

One of the founding fathers of organic design was Finnish architect Alvar Aalto, whose design philosophy was integral to the work of designers such as Charles and Ray Eames in later years. Aalto firmly believed in the use of natural materials as a means of addressing both the functional and psychological needs of the user. In 1940, the Museum of Modern Art (MoMA) in New York held an exhibition and competition entitled Organic Design for Home Furnishings, curated by Eliot Fette Noyes. The aim was to showcase furniture and furnishings whose design approach or materials were of an organic nature. It was this competition that saw Charles Eames and Eero Saarinen join forces to create the ergonomically formed, molded plywood armchair that won the Seating for a Living Room category. Saarinen's organic approach to design is also evident in his architecture, in particular his TWA Terminal at New York's John F. Kennedy Airport.

More recently, the resurgence of organic design in the 1990s saw the opening of the London Design Museum. 1991 exhibition, entitled simply, Organic Design. New manufacturing processes, the development of new materials—especially plastics—and advancements in computer-aided design have all contributed to the evolution of this design style. In the twenty-first century, one of the greatest advocates of organic design is Ross Lovegrove. Describing his approach as "organic essentialism," Lovegrove combines ergonomic, almost sculptural forms with state-of-the-art materials and manufacturing processes to create modern-day masterpieces such as his Go chair, created from high-pressure, injection-molded magnesium. For Lovegrove, it is the subtlety of form that emerges when a sensual organic correspondence occurs between an animate and an inanimate situation that really fascinates.

LCW (Lounge Chair Wood): Charles and Ray Eames

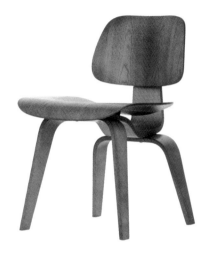

"La Chaise": Charles and Ray Eames
The formal approach to organic design is evident in Charles and Ray Eames' La

Chaise, designed for MoMA's International Competition for Low-Cost Furniture Design, held in 1948.

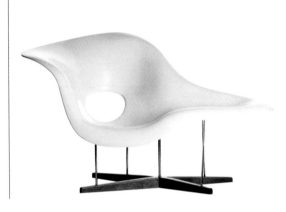

The Atomic stovetop coffeemaker was designed in Milan.

Tulip Armchair: Eero Saarinen
An immediate classic on its introduction in the 1950s but a design

in progress since Saarinen's work with Charles Eames in the 1940 MoMA Organic Design contest. "The

undercarriage of chairs and tables makes an ugly, confusing, unrestful world," said Saarinen of the design.

"I wanted to clean up the slum of legs and make the chair all one thing again."

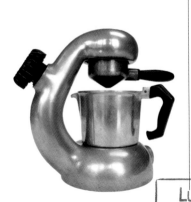

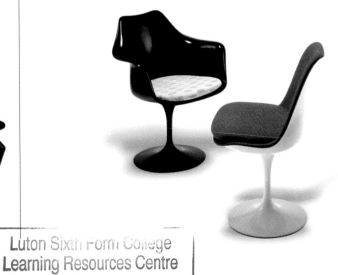

Sails of the Sydney Opera House: Jorn Utzon The Sydney Opera House makes no reference to classical architectural forms. The organic shape creates a synergy between the building and its environment.

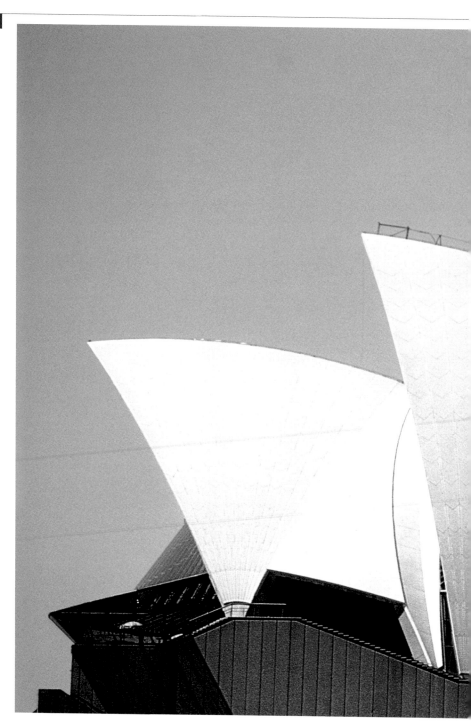

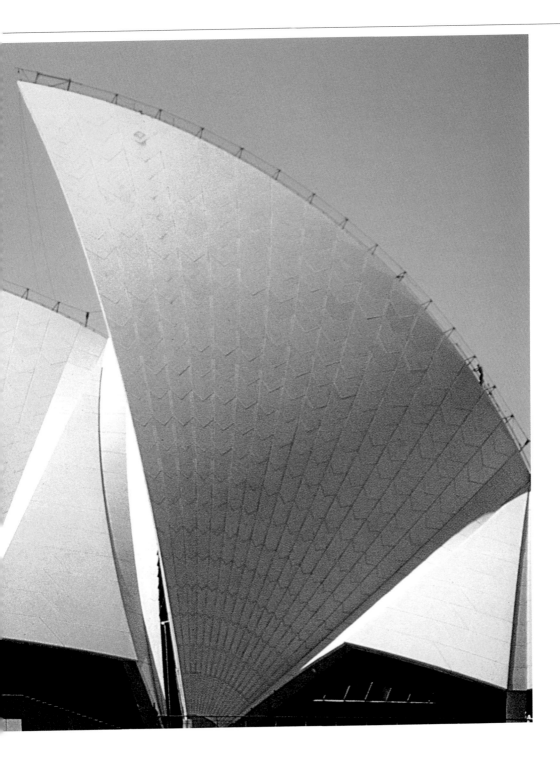

1957–1973

Side view of the
Sydney Opera
House.

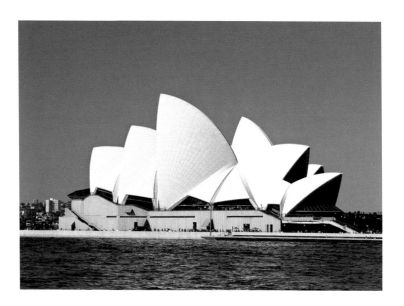

1961

Staircase in the
Berliner Congress
Center: Hermann
Henselmann

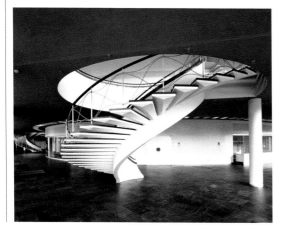

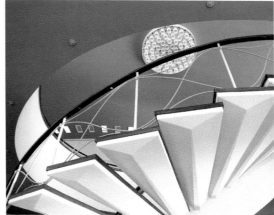

1962

Maquette for
Reclining
Connected Forms:
Henry Spencer
Moore

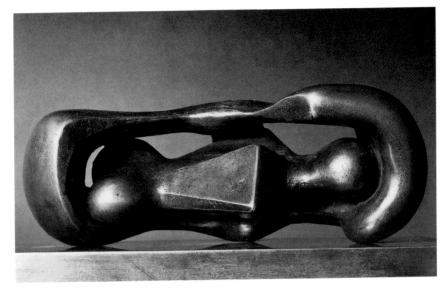

1993

Orgone Stretch
Lounge: Marc
Newson

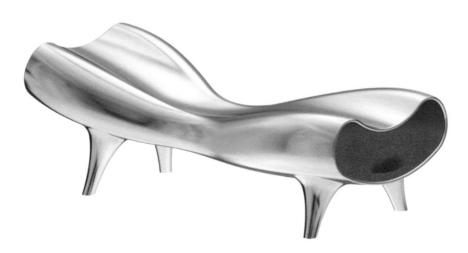

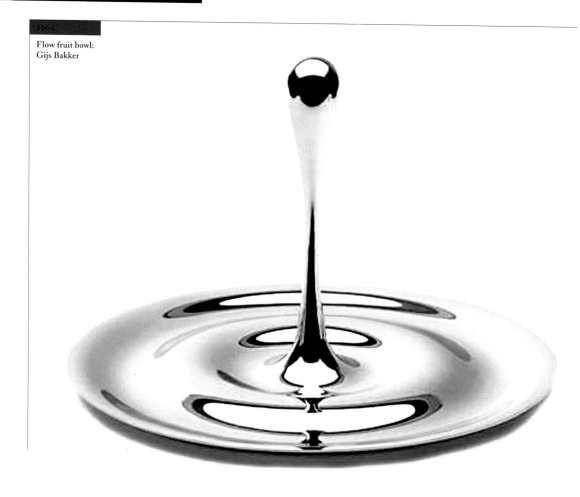

2000

Flow fruit bowl:
Gijs Bakker

Key figures	Fields of work	Works
Charles Rennie Mackintosh (1868–1928)	Architect/Designer	Glasgow School of Art (1896–1909)
Frank Lloyd Wright (1867–1959)	Architect/Designer/Theorist	Prairie Houses (1900–1911)
Alvar Aalto (1898–1976)	Architect/Town planner/Designer (furniture, textiles, lighting, glass)	Model No. 43 chaise longue for Artek (1936)
Eero Saarinen (1910–1961)	Architect	TWA Terminal, John F. Kennedy Airport, New York (1956–1962)
Charles Eames (1907–1978)	Architect/Designer	La Chaise (1948)
Ray Eames (1912–1988),	Designer	La Chaise (1948)
Pierre Paulin (b. 1927)	Designer	Tongue chaise for Antifort (1967)
Ross Lovegrove (b. 1958)	Designer	Go chair for Bernhardt Design (2001) Ty Nant Mineral Water Bottle (2002)

Kareames chairs: Karim Rashid for Magis The influence of Charles and Ray Eames' LCW (Lounge Chair Wood) is obvious in Karim Rashid's Kareames chairs, designed for Magis more than 50 years after the original.

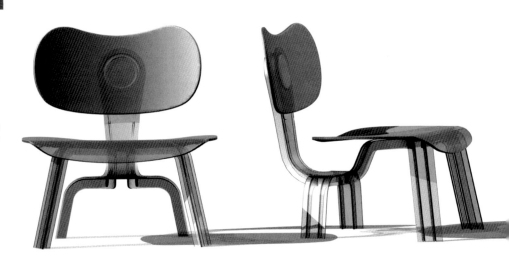

Mineral water bottle: Ross Lovegrove for Ty Nant At one with nature, the shape of Lovegrove's mineral water bottle emulates the flow patterns that water makes when it is poured.

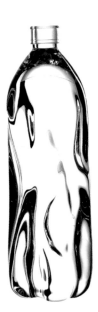

Tea and coffee set: UN Studio for Alessi The inherent organic shape of this tea and coffee set, created for Alessi's Tea and Coffee Towers project, carries organic design confidently to the twenty-first century.

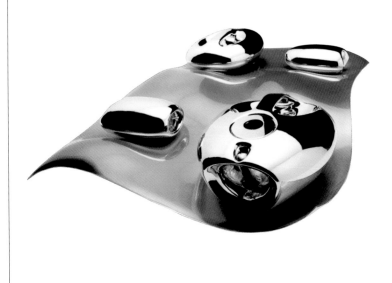

International Style

When the **Bauhaus** was dissolved in 1933, Walter Gropius, Ludwig Mies van der Rohe, and a number of other Bauhaus professors emigrated to the United States, many via Britain, where they continued to spread the Bauhaus philosophy through exhibitions, architectural commissions, and, in the case of Gropius and van der Rohe, by taking up high-profile teaching positions following the war. International Style was the name given to the less utilitarian form of **modernism** that emerged in the USA as a result. The style was named by Alfred H. Barr Jr., then Director of the Museum of Modern Art (MoMA), New York, after the catalog—International Style: Architecture Since 1922—created to accompany the 1932 exhibition of Russell Hitchcock and Philip Johnson's work which was held at the museum.

In addition to relating to the specific type of **modernism** advocated by the likes of Gropius and van der Rohe, the

term International Style has also been attributed to the esthetics of modernism that occurred as a result of its functionalist approach to design, purely on a stylistic level. Characterized by the use of industrial materials, such as steel and glass, and the utilitarian, undecorated approach to architecture and interior design, the International Style reached its peak during the 1960s. As the style evolved, some designers, including Eero Saarinen and Charles Eames, sought to humanize it by contrasting geometric forms with organic shapes, while others, such as Kenzo Tange, took it to the other extreme by dehumanizing materials and surfaces in the brutalist style.

A term almost synonymous with International Style was "good design," a concept that emerged in northern Europe and the USA immediately following WWII, whereby products were designed "in accordance with the formal, technical, and esthetic principles" of

1940

Cabinet with four drawers: Charles Eames

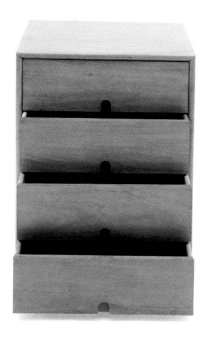

Seagram Building,
New York: Ludwig
Mies van der Rohe
with Philip
Johnson (interiors)

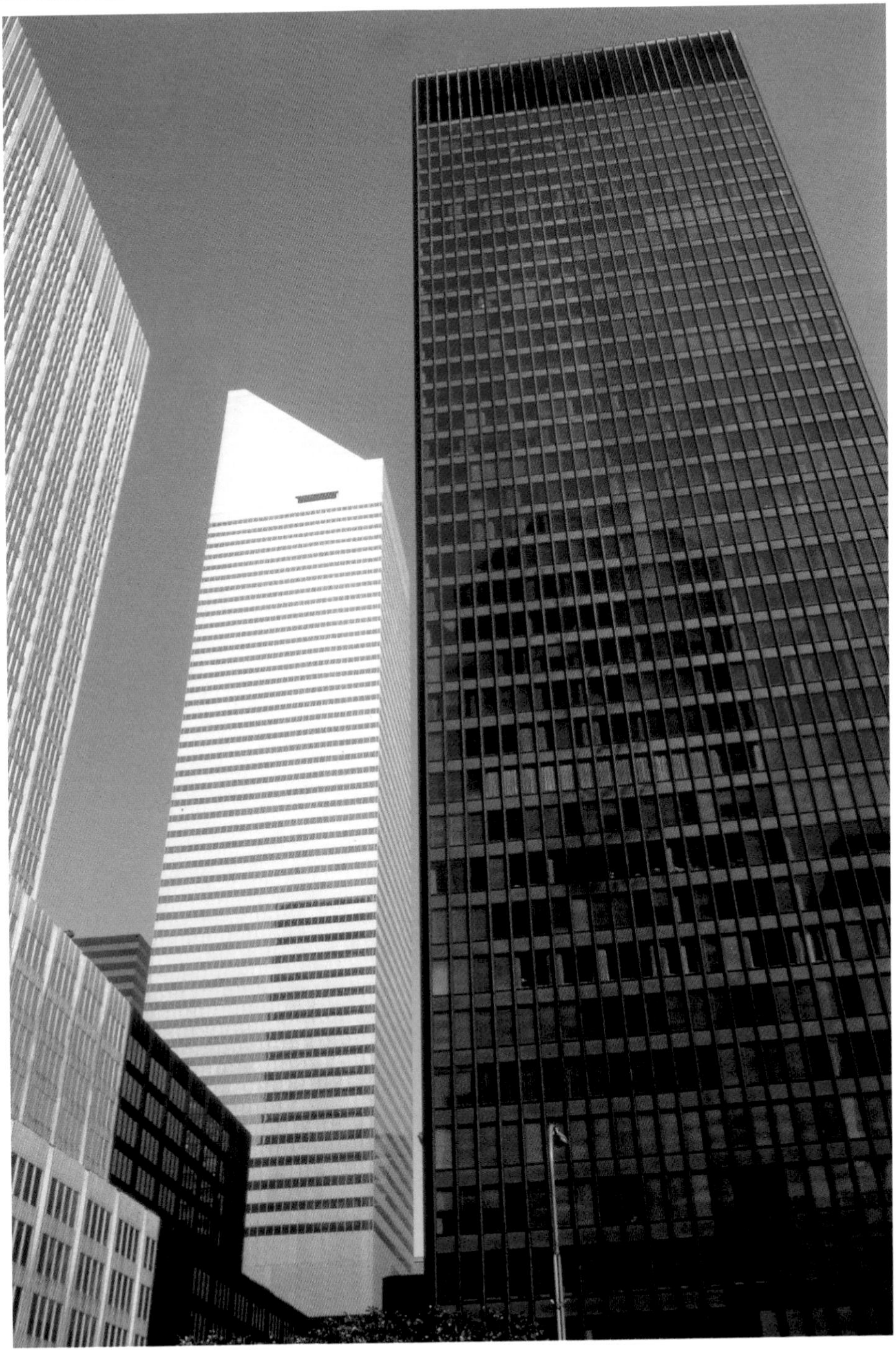

modernism. The Design Council, London, and MoMA, New York, both sought to promote good design through exhibitions, lectures, and journals. In London, products were given the official seal of approval courtesy of the Design Council's good design "kitemark," while in Germany Max Bill, keen to uphold the ideals of the Bauhaus where he himself had trained, cofounded the Hochschule für Gestaltung (The Ulm School of Design) to promote good design. At the first Good Design exhibition, held at MoMA in 1950, a number of designs were promoted and sold sporting the Good Design label. Good design, and in turn International Style, were exemplified in the simple, functionalist house-style developed by Dieter Rams at Braun.

1950s

Roberts Radio R550.

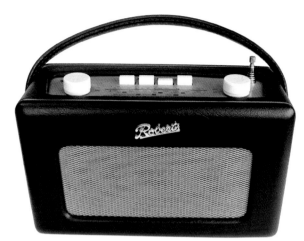

1957

Multipurpose kitchen machine: Braun AG

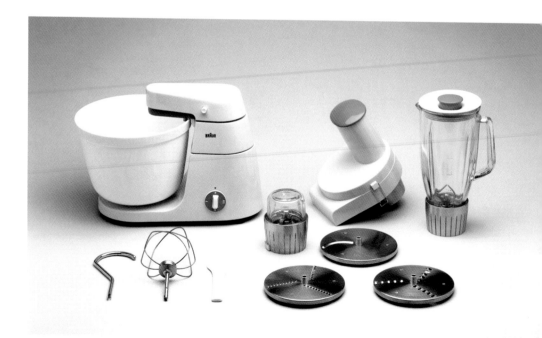

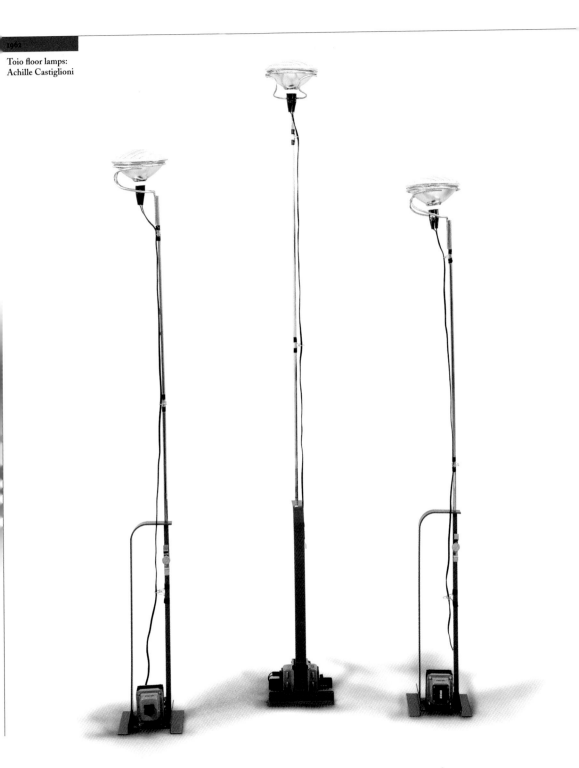

1962

Toio floor lamps:
Achille Castiglioni

Simple, utilitarian
buildings in Berlin.

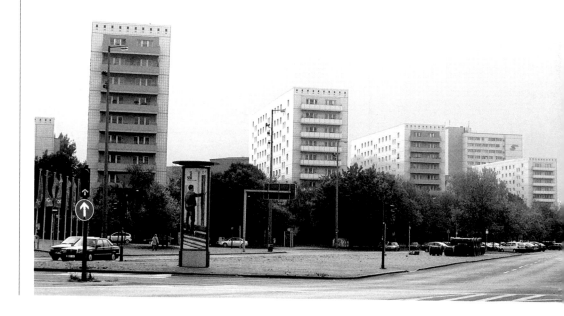

Key figures	Fields of work
Ludwig Mies van der Rohe (1886–1969)	Architect/Designer
Charles Eames (1907–1978)	Architect/Designer
Ray Eames (1912–1988)	Designer
Jacobus Johannes Pieter Oud (1890–1963)	Architect/Town planner/Designer
Walter Adolph Gropius (1883–1969)	Architect
Philip Cortelyou Johnson (1906–2005)	Architect
Alfred H. Barr Jr. (1902–1981)	Founding Director, Museum of Modern Art, New York

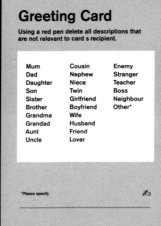

Birthday Card

Before giving card, tick box or specify which birthday is being celebrated.

- First
- Eighteenth
- Twenty-first
- Fortieth
- Fiftieth
- Sixtieth
- Hundredth
- Other*

*Please specify
....

Greeting Card

Using a red pen delete all descriptions that are not relevant to card s recipient.

Mum
Dad
Daughter
Son
Sister
Brother
Grandma
Grandad
Aunt
Uncle

Cousin
Nephew
Niece
Twin
Girlfriend
Boyfriend
Wife
Husband
Friend
Lover

Enemy
Stranger
Teacher
Boss
Neighbour
Other*

*Please specify
....

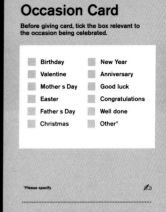

Occasion Card

Before giving card, tick the box relevant to the occasion being celebrated.

- Birthday
- Valentine
- Mother s Day
- Easter
- Father s Day
- Christmas
- New Year
- Anniversary
- Good luck
- Congratulations
- Well done
- Other*

*Please specify
....

004

udioside storage
stem: Jonas
indvall for
e Nord

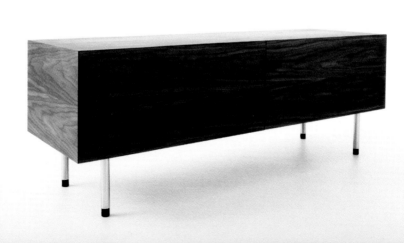

Biomorphism

Also known as zoomorphism and neo-organicism. Characterized through its use of natural forms, implemented purely for decorative purposes, the biomorphic esthetic "dislocated the machine from primary image to enabler." Sympathetic to the forms of nature and the human body, this new stylistic development, with its swirling tendril-like motifs and elongated vegetal forms, first emerged at the turn of the twentieth century and was adopted by a number of **art nouveau** designers. Later, however, new machine technologies and materials such as plastics paved the way for many of the formal aspects of biomorphism. As a result the style is often regarded as an integral part of the machine esthetic in terms of production and manufacturing techniques, as opposed to esthetic values. The seamless combination of flowing natural forms with new, high-tech materials resulted in everything from steel stairways that resembled a strand of DNA to biomorphic buildings that looked like skeletal remains.

The vogue for biomorphic design faded as **art deco** and **modernism** rose to prominence during the 1920s and 1930s, but the style reemerged in the 1940s. Under the direction of its first President, the Finnish architect Eero Saarinen, the Cranbrook Academy of Art was a major center of biomorphism at this time, and the biomorphic furniture designs of Italian designer Carlo Mollino also championed the style. Mollino's landmark authentic plywood furniture designs adopted dramatic zoomorphous shapes, while Saarinen, and particularly Charles and Ray Eames, pioneered the style through the use of plastic materials in furniture manufacturing.

In terms of domestic architecture, the biomorphic label could also be attributed to the work of Frank Lloyd Wright, who consistently argued for the use of natural materials and form, and Lewis Mumford whose visual esthetic may have been more aligned to that of the **International Style**, but whose sympathies for regional ecology and promotion of greenbelt towns also suggested a biomorphic ethic.

DAR chair
(Dining Armchair
Rod) (top); RAR
(Rocking Armchair
Rod) (right); LAR
(Lounge and
Armchair Rod)
(bottom); DAX
(Dining and Desk
Chair) (left):
Charles and
Ray Eames

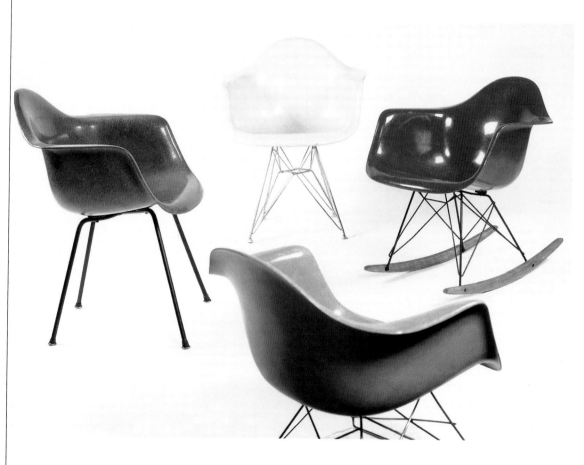

Later Applications

30 St Mary Axe, the "Gherkin": Foster and Partners
London's first environmental tall building, the building's shape, structure, and ventilation scheme all find a parallel in the class of sea creatures known as glass sponges.

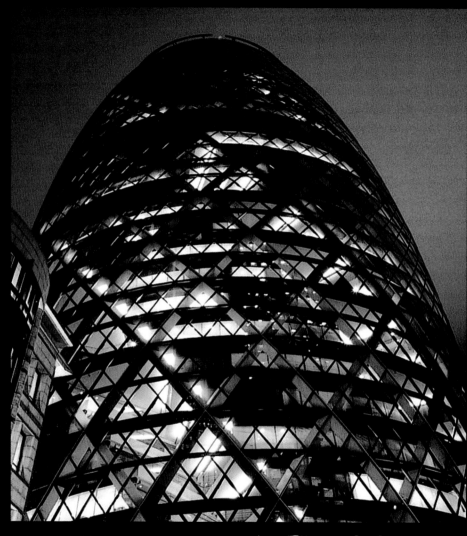

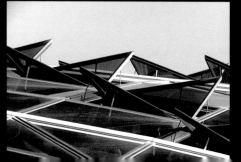

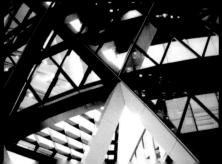

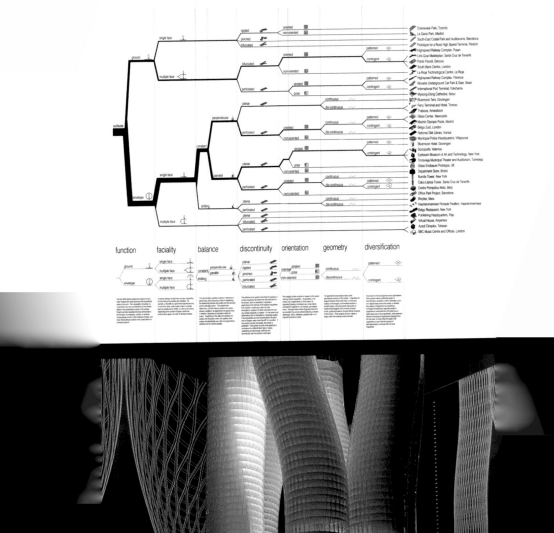

Later Applications

Due for completion in 2007

Centre Pompidou-Metz, Metz, France: Shigeru Ban in association with Jean de Gastines and Philip Gumuchdijan The first decentralized branch of the Centre national d'art et de culture Georges Pompidou, the building is designed to reflect the idea of the human body by changing as a person does, according to different climates and occasions.

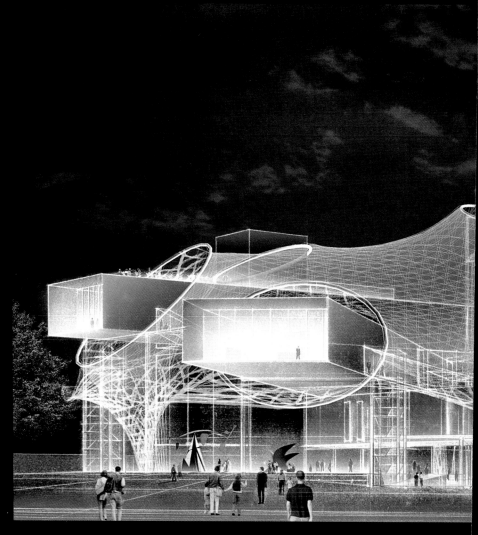

Key figures

Le Corbusier (born Charles Edouard Jeanneret) (1887–1965)

Carlo Mollino (1905–1973)

Eero Saarinen (1910–1961)

Florence Schust-Knoll (b. 1917)

Harry Bertoia (1915–1978)

Fields of work

Architect

Architect/Designer

Architect

Designer (interiors, furniture, textiles)/Architect/Entrepreneur

Sculptor/Printmaker/Designer (furniture, jewelry)

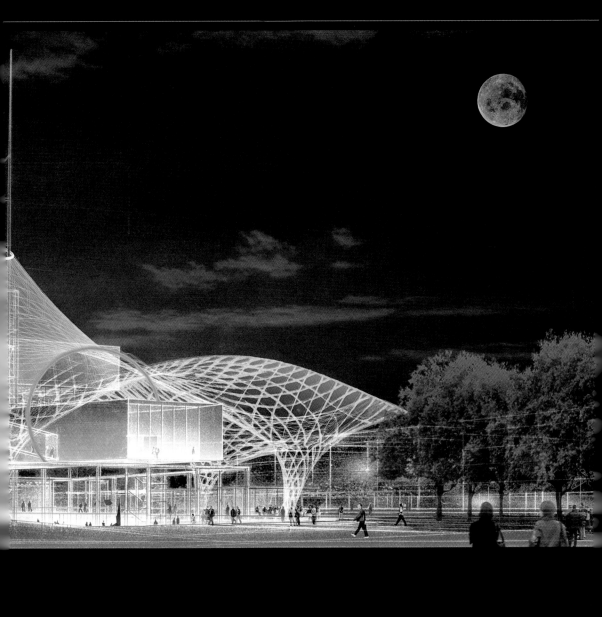

Scandinavian modern

See also

Art nouveau p 42

Modernism p 50

Origin

Denmark

Finland

Key characteristics

Blonde wood

Clean lines

Simple, sculptural forms

Key facts

Continues to this day as a dominant domestic design style in Scandinavia and around the world

Ongoing commitment and respect for natural materials such as wood—especially birch, beech, and teak—and leather

Older and more adventurous Finnish designers excelled in the areas of textiles and furniture, using strong, screen-printed patterns and colors

Also known as Swedish modern and Danish modern. Scandinavian modern is the name of a stylistic development that evolved within **modernism** during the 1930s. Characterized by blonde wood furniture with a specific emphasis on line, shape, and form, the look is often punctuated with bursts of color, albeit in small doses, and continues to this day as a dominant domestic design style, both in Scandinavia and around the world.

Swedish modern

By 1900, Sweden, Denmark, and Finland had each developed their own variation of **art nouveau** and, in turn, applied it to the traditional craft areas of furniture, ceramics, glass, and textiles, all of which were popular in Scandinavia. It was Sweden, however, that led the field in creating its own twentieth-century design movement and style, no doubt spurred on by the activities of its leading design organization, Sjlödforeningen, which had been teaming up arts and crafts men since the 1900s. The ceramics firms Gustavsberg and Rorstrand and glass company Orrefors were the first to take advantage of this innovation. As a

result, during the 1920s and 1930s, their employees became pioneers of the Swedish modern style. Distinguished b simplicity and natural imagery, Swedis modern was seen to incorporate the democratic ideal and as such, achieved international acclaim during the post-war period.

An exhibition held in Stockholm in 1930 may have seen a number of the country's architects temporarily distracte by the harsher, more functional esthetic that had developed in Germany by the middle of the decade, but its furniture designers were not so easily distracted. With their ongoing commitment to an championing of natural materials such as wood and leather, the likes of Bruno Mathsson, G. A. Berg, and Josef Frank had begun to reassert the values, tradition, and imagery associated with Swedish design. By 1939, the Swedish exhibit at New York's World Fair marked Scandinavian modern as an internationally recognized style synony-mous with elegance and good living. Stores across the globe adopted Swedis names, such as Svenska and Form, whil glossy magazines filled their pages with

1931–1932

Armchair 41:
Alvar Aalto

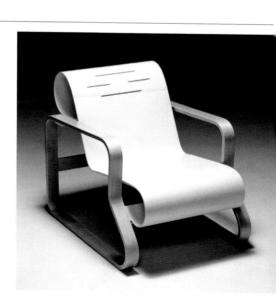

1932

Glasses: Aino
Aalto

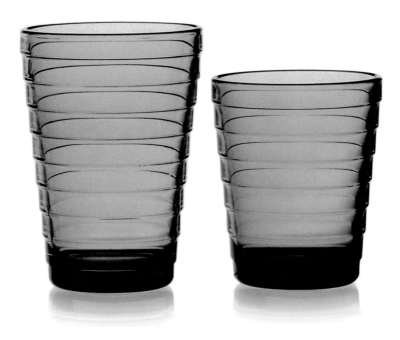

1936

Aalto vase: Alvar
Aalto The unique
shape of this vase
has become one of
the major icons of
glass design.

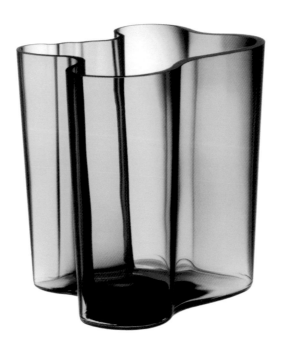

Swedish interiors, promoting Scandinavian modern as "a style to live with, not just look at!"

Danish modern

Although it emerged a little later, by the 1950s Danish modern had achieved equal popularity and visibility within the design world. The new Danish style, developed by the likes of Arne Jacobsen, Verner Panton, and Poul Kjaerholm, established a sense of respect for natural materials, especially birch, beech, and teak, while at the same time creating an interest in revived chair types, such as the stick-back chair, deck chair, and safari chair, all of which affected the mass market furniture produced during this period.

Mogensen's African-inspired chair designs in wood and leather, and the expressive, sculptural chairs designed by his younger colleague Finn Juhl during the 1940s and 1950s, are characteristic of the primitivism that became a major feature of Danish furniture design in the 1950s. In metalwork, the simple elegance first seen in the work of Georg Jensen at the turn of the century, and later by Kay Bojesen, continued thanks to the work of Henning Koppel. One of the most outstanding—and defining—features of Danish design at this time was its ability to create timeless objects that remain as fresh today as the day they were designed.

Finnish modern

It wasn't until the Milan Triennales of 1951 and 1954 that Finland took its position as a leading light in the world of contemporary design. This was thanks largely to the unique glass designs exhibited by Iittala. Tapio Wirkkala and Timo Sarpaneva had never previously worked with glass, but won a competition held by Iittala before going on to earn international reputations for their expressive, sculptural approach to the material during the 1950s.

Older and more adventurous than their Scandinavian counterparts, in stylistic terms, Finnish designers excelled in the areas of textiles and furniture. Textiles featured strong, screen-printed patterns and colors, characterized by the application of bold, abstract motifs on monochrome backgrounds. The work being produced by Marimmekko was also outstanding, which continues to this day. The Finnish approach to design was less committed to traditional craft principles than that of its neighbors, relying instead on stimuli from the world of contemporary design at large. That said, however, the bent plywood furniture of Finland's great designer Alvar Aalto exudes tradition and craftsmanship. They were kept in production after the war as classic pieces of modern design.

1952

Ant chair: Arne Jacobsen for Fritz Hansen

1956

Egg chair (left); Swan chair (right): Arne Jacobsen

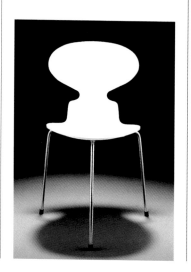

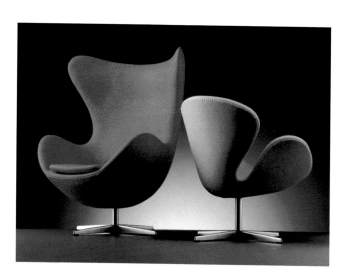

1956

PK20 chair: Poul Kjaerholm for Fritz Hansen

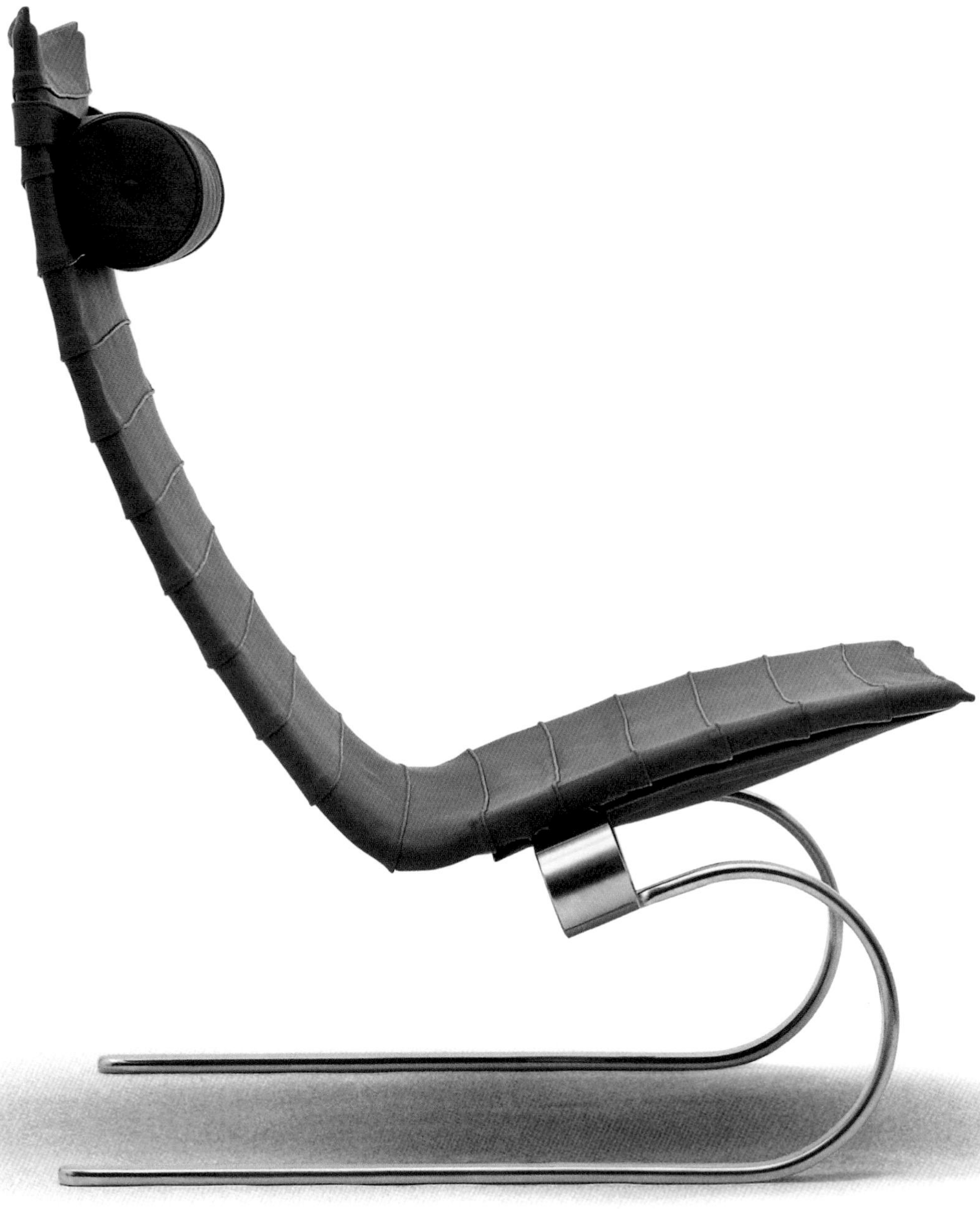

1959

Candlesticks: Arne
Jacobsen

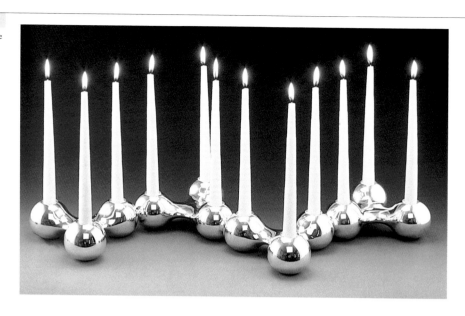

1959

AJ lamp: Arne
Jacobsen

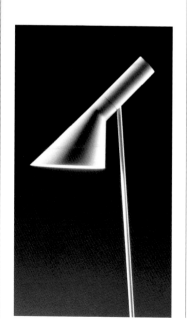

1965

Unikko (Poppy)
textile: Maija Isola
for Marimekko

1999

**Low Pad chair:
Jasper Morrison
for Cappellini**
Inspired by one of
his favorite mid-
twentieth-century

chairs, Jasper
Morrison's Low Pad
chair was based on
the 1956 steel-and-
leather chair by
Finnish designer

Poul Kjaerholm,
but used a new
method of condensed
upholstery to create a
comfortable, durable,
padded leather seat.

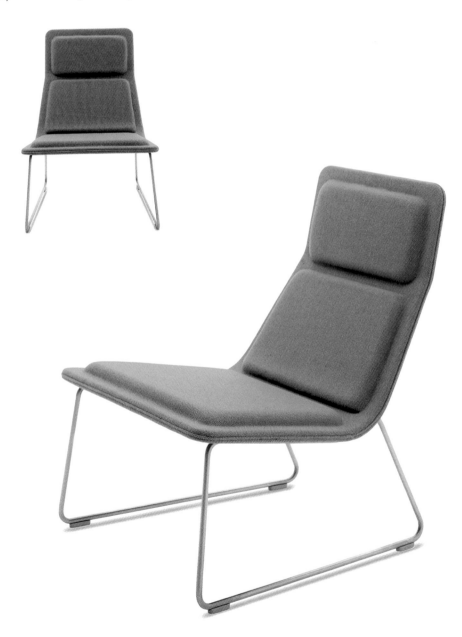

2002

Papermaster
magazine table:
Norway Says for
Swedese

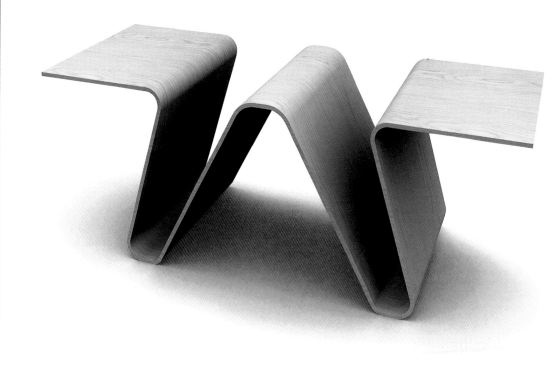

Regional variations	Key figures	Fields of work
Swedish modern	Bruno Mathsson (1907–1988)	Designer/Architect
	G. A. Berg (1891–1971)	Designer
	Josef Frank (1885–1967)	Designer
Danish modern	Arne Jacobsen (1902–1971)	Designer
	Verner Panton (1926–1998)	Architect/Designer
	Henning Koppel (1918–1981)	Architect/Designer
	Borge Mogensen (1914–1972)	Furniture Designer
	Hans Jorgen Wegner (b. 1914)	Designer
Finnish modern	Alvar Aalto (1898–1976)	Architect/Town planner/Designer (furniture, textiles, lighting, glass)
	Tapio Veli Ilmari Wirkkala (1915–1985)	Designer (glassware, wood, metalwork, exhibitions)/Metalworker
	Timo Sarpaneva (b. 1926)	Designer

Benjamin stool:
Lisa Norinder;
and Buskbo coffee
table: Ehlén
Johansson, both
for IKEA

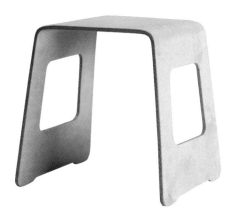

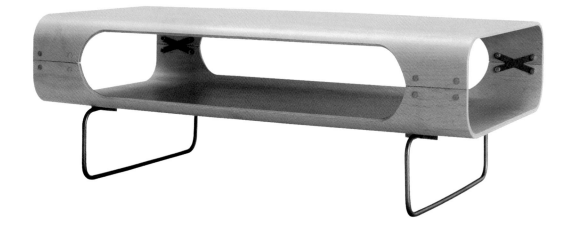

Contemporary style

Origin

United Kingdom

Key characteristics

Organic shapes

Spiky forms

Bright colors

Key facts

A style of design, art, and architecture that emerged in Britain after WWII

Light, expressive furniture, often characterized by thin metal rods and pale timber

3-D science models epitomize the style

See also

Modernism p 50

Also known as Festival style, South Bank style, and New English style. Contemporary style refers to a movement in design, art, and architecture that emerged in the UK after WWII. Popularized by the Festival of Britain in 1951, exponents of the style used a combination of organic shapes and bright colors in their work. They also capitalized on technological advances in striving to make their designs as democratically accessible as possible. The furniture produced during this period was lighter and more expressive than that which had emerged as a result of **modernism** prior to the war and was often characterized by the use of thin metal rods and pale timber. Two-dimensional patterns and geometric designs featured in upholstery, textiles, and wallpaper. The 3-D models used to represent molecular structures in science labs epitomize the contemporary style.

Date not known

Red and Black on a
Blue Background:
Joan Miró

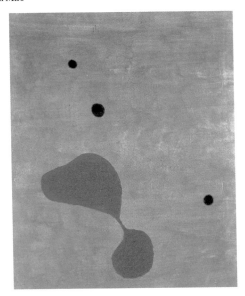

1945

Cross Patch textile:
Charles and Ray
Eames

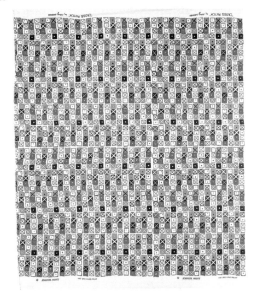

Ball clock: George
Nelson

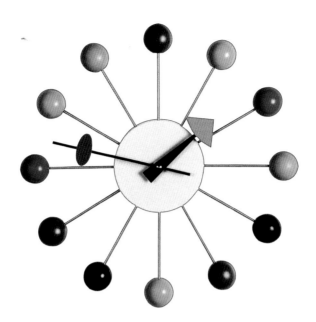

Hang-It-All:
Charles and Ray
Eames, originally
for Tigrett
Enterprises

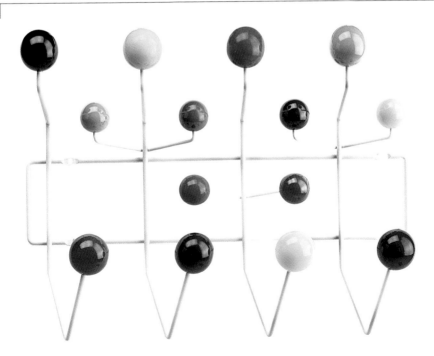

Jason chair:
Carl Jacobs

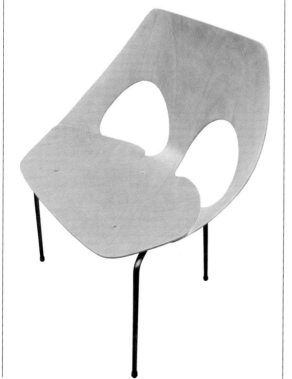

Microgramma/
Eurostile typeface:
Aldo Novarese and
Alessandro Butti
Reflecting the
spirit of the 1950s

and 1960s with its
big, squarish form
and rounded corners
reminiscent of the
television sets of the
time. Fifty years on,

this font is still
widely used by
*Wallpaper** magazine
to name just one
example.

abcdefghijklmnop
qrstuvwxyz fiflß&
ABCDEFGHIJKL
MNOPQRSTUVW
XYZ
1234567890
.,:;-–—
'' ""' .⟨⟩《》 * %‰
!?¡¿()[]/†‡§$£¢ƒ

Key figures	Fields of work
Barbara Hepworth (1903–1975)	Sculptor/Designer
Joan Miró (1893–1983)	Artist
Charles Eames (1907–1978)	Architect/Designer

2003

**Alto writing desk:
Norway Says**
This example is
laminated plywood
with lacquered
steel legs.

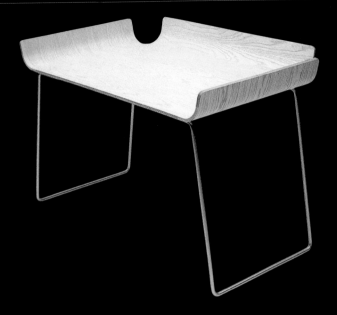

2004

**Prototype chair:
Egg Designs**
Stainless steel and
maple/panga-panga,
silk-screened with
copper printing ink.

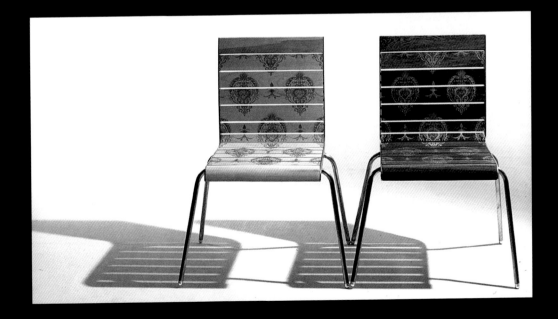

Swiss school

Origin

Switzerland

Germany

Key characteristics

Use of photomontage

Sans-serif typography

Use of "white space"

Objective photography (realistic images)

Key facts

Asymmetrical design constructed on grids to give a visual unity

Information presented in a clear and factual manner, clarity and order being the ultimate goal

Design regarded as a socially useful and important activity, with personal expression and eccentric solutions rejected in favor of a more universal and scientific approach

Believed the solution to the design problem should emerge from its content

See also

During the 1950s a design movement emerged from Switzerland and Germany called the Swiss school or, perhaps more appropriately, the International Typographic Style. A major force for over two decades, the objective clarity of this design movement attracted attention throughout the world, and its influence continues to this day. The characteristics of this international style include a visual unity of design, achieved through the asymmetrical organization of the design elements on a mathematically constructed grid, objective photography, and copy that presents visual and verbal information in a clear and factual manner. Achieving clarity and order was the ultimate goal of the Swiss school.

Sans-serif typography conveyed the progressive spirit of the time, while mathematical grids provided the most legible and harmonious means for structuring information. Another vital aspect of this style was the attitude of its early pioneers to their profession. By defining design as a socially useful and important activity, personal expression and eccentric solutions were rejected in favor of a more universal and scientific approach to design problem-solving.

The roots of the Swiss school grew from **de Stijl**, **Bauhaus**, and the new typography of the 1920s and 1930s. Two Swiss designers who studied at the **Bauhaus**, Théo Ballmer (1902–1965) and Max Bill (1908–1994) provide the vital links between earlier **constructivist**

1954

Schematic diagram of the twenty-one Univers fonts: Adrian Frutiger

Helvetica typeface:
Max Miedinger

ABCDEFGHIJ

KLMNOPQRS

TUVWXYZ

abcdefghijklmn

opqrstuvwxyz

@$%&(.,:;#!?)

and 1970s, as the style began to gain momentum around the world. The movement began in Switzerland and Germany, but soon outgrew its native boundaries to become a truly international style with numerous devotees across the globe. The Swiss school's international rise in popularity came about, in part, from the harmony and order that characterized the style. This methodology was of particular value in countries such as Canada and Switzerland where bi- and even trilingual communications were the norm. In cases such as this, the style of the Swiss school enabled designers to design large amounts of information—such as signage—as a unified, coherent whole.

Largely responsible for the quality of discipline for which the Swiss school movement became renowned, Ernst Keller (1891–1968) believed the solution to the design problem should emerge from its content. During the 1950s the influence of the style was spread through *New Graphic Design*, a journal launched in 1959, while graphics produced by the Swiss School were exhibited at the 1939 Swiss National Exhibition.

Entertainment
Visible grids, boxed information panels, and bold sans-serif typefaces characterized the *Trainspotting* poster and spawned numerous imitations.

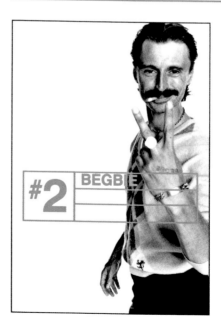

Trainspotting 18

THIS FIL
EXPECT
ARRIVE.

23:02:96

From the team that brought you

#2 BEGBIE

IS
TO

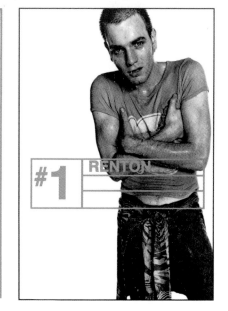

#1 RENTON

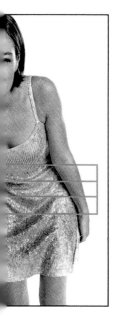

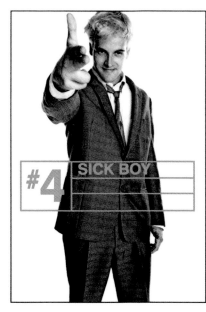

#4 SICK BOY

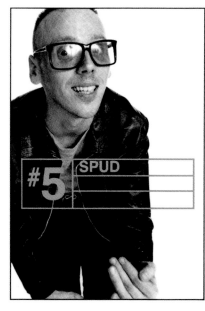

#5 SPUD

Later Applications

2001

Restart: New Systems in Graphic Design: Christian Küsters, Emily King

Throughout, the book is set in Univers according to the grid system illustrated in Adrian Frutiger's

diagrammatic display of the typeface, developed in 1957.

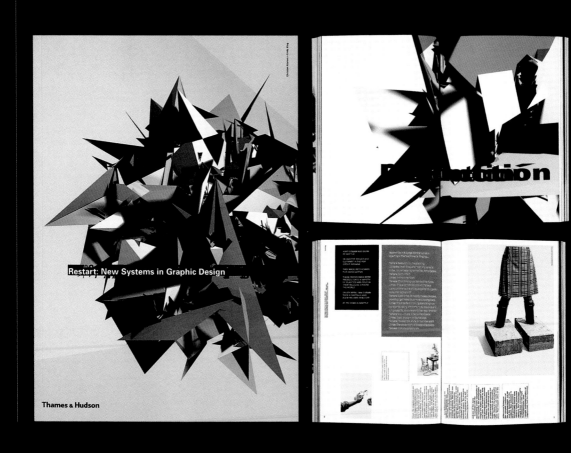

Key figures	Fields of work
Ernst Keller (1891–1968)	Graphic designer/Typographer
Théo Ballmer (1902–1965)	Graphic designer
Adrian Frutiger (b. 1928)	Typographer/Graphic designer (lettering, signage, book design, symbols)
Max Miedinger (1910–1980)	Typographer
Walter Herdeg (b. 1908)	Graphic designer/Editor/Founder of *Graphis*

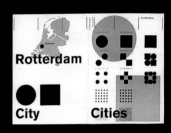

Rotterdam

City **Cities**

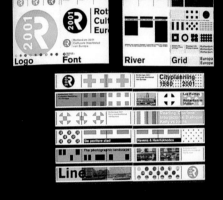

Logo Font River Grid Europa
Europe

Line up

Rotterdam
2001
Culturele
Hoofdstad
van
Europa

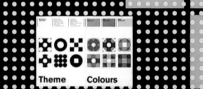

Theme Colours

Pop art

An abbreviation of "popular art," the pop art movement occurred primarily in the USA and UK as a reaction to abstract painting, which pop artists considered too sophisticated and elite. They preferred to utilize images of objects taken from everyday life, as exemplified by Andy Warhol's soup cans and Roy Lichtenstein's comic strips, cartoon-like bulbous typefaces, and fluorescent, gaudy colors. Warhol's use of serigraphy, a photo-realistic, mass-production technique of printmaking, was typical of the pop art movement. Inspired by mass consumerism and popular culture, proponents of the style openly questioned the precepts of good design, rejecting **modernism** and its values and replacing them with its own—fun, change, variety, irreverence, and disposability. Destroying the traditional boundaries between the fine and commercial arts, pop intruded on the media and advertising voluntarily, a point exemplified by the album covers created in the 1960s, such as Peter Blake and Jann Howarth's 1967 design for The Beatles' *Sgt. Pepper's Lonely Hearts Club Band*. Drawing inspiration from "low art" advertising, packaging, comics, and television, artists such as Warhol and David Hockney, with their references to mass culture, crossed over into interiors, murals, wallpaper, and posters, opening up a whole new world of fun and frivolity in art and design.

1959–1960

"Panton" stacking side chair: Verner Panton

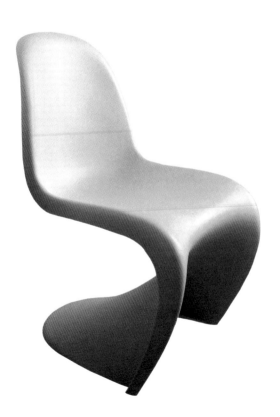

Founded in London in 1952, the Independent Group was the first to explore the growth of popular consumer culture in the US. Targeting a new breed of design-conscious young professionals, designers suddenly realized they needed a younger, alternative approach to that promulgated by the Good Design of the 1950s; pop design provided the perfect solution. As Terence Conran pointed out at the time, "there was a strange moment around the mid 1960s when people stopped needing and need changed to want... Designers became more important in producing 'want' products rather than 'need' products." Product styling became de rigueur, fueling the throwaway culture we now accept as the

norm. Plastics were the material of choice for most as designers used bright colors and bold forms to attract the youth market. As a result products were cheap and often poor quality, but disposability soon became part of the attraction as creator and consumer alike opted for expendability over durability, the antithesis of all that **modernism** stood for.

Disposability was a key characteristic of many pop designs, including Peter Murdoch's polka dot Spotty child's chair (1963), De Pas, D'urbino, Lomazzi, and Scolari's PVC Blow chair (1967), and the many gimmicks that appeared at the time, such as paper clothes, the epitome of 1960s throwaway culture. Inspired by

everything from **art nouveau** and **art deco** to **futurism**, **surrealism**, **op art**, psychedelia, kitsch, and **space age**, pop design had a major impact on the worlds of art and design, but it wasn't to last. The oil crisis of the early 1970s eventually called for a more rational approach to design as pop art itself was disposed of in favor of the craft revival.

1963

Crak! poster:
Roy Lichtenstein
Designed for the
Roy Lichtenstein
exhibition at The
Leo Castelli Gallery,
New York, this
poster epitomizes
the pop art esthetic.

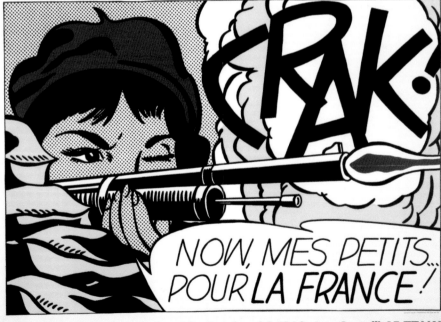

Roy Lichtenstein · September 28 - October 24, 1963 · Leo Castelli 4 E. 77 N.Y.

Totem coffee pot:
**Portmeirion
Potteries** The
Totem range uses
primitive, abstract
symbols in true
pop art style.

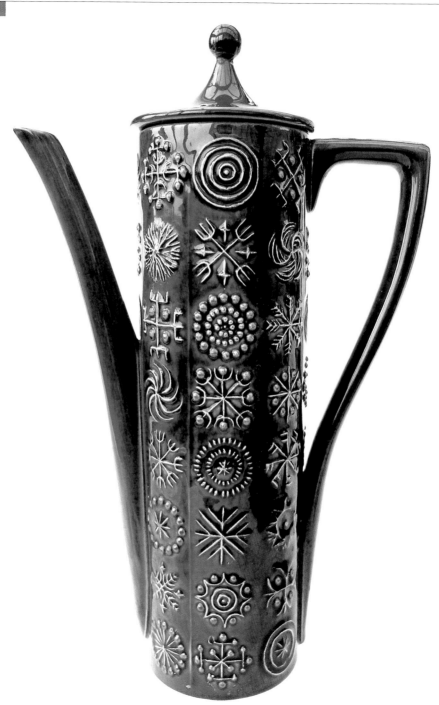

The Beatles' *Sgt Pepper's Lonely Hearts Club Band*: **Peter Blake and Jann Howarth** Released by EMI Records in 1967, this is arguably the most famous album sleeve of all time. The

image on the album cover is composed of a collage of celebrities totaling 88 figures, including the band members themselves. Pop artist Peter Blake and his wife Jann Haworth conceived and constructed the

set, including all the life-sized cutouts of historical figures. The set was then photographed, with the Beatles standing in the center, by Michael Cooper.

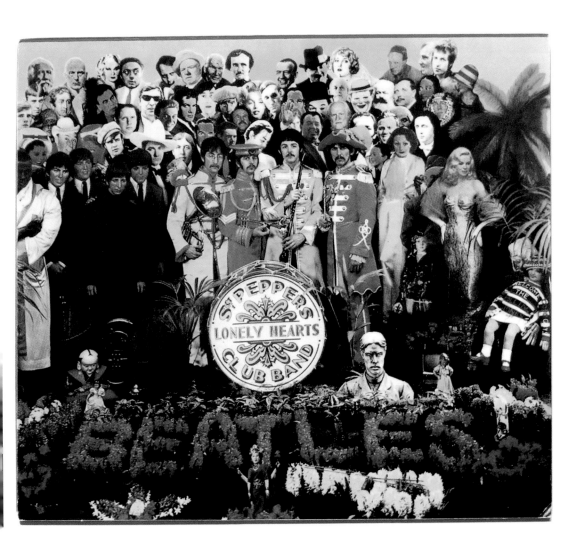

Later Applications

Campbell's Soup:
Andy Warhol

Pop Art Comic
typeface: Richard
Kegler and
Desmond Poirier
(above); Pop Art

Three D typeface:
Richard Kegler
(below) These
typefaces are inspired
by comic books,

magazines, advertising,
and films of the 1950s
and 1960s.

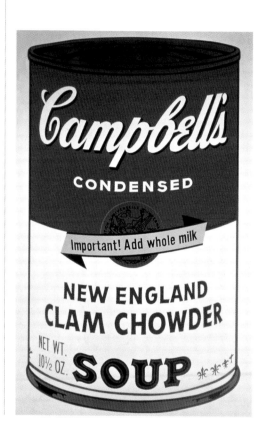

ABCDEFGHIJKLMNOPQR
STUVWXYZ FLFLß&
ABCDEFGHIJKLMNOPQR
STUVWXYZ
1234567890
.,:;---_''"".‹›«»*%%
/?\¿()[]/†‡§$£¢ƒ

ABCDEFGHIJKLMN
OPQRSTUVWXYZ
ABCDEFGHIJKLMN
OPQRSTUVWXYZ
1234567890
○¸¸⁀¨⌐○¸!?

Regional variations	Key figures	Fields of work
UK	Peter Murdoch (b. 1940)	Designer (furniture, interiors, graphics, industrial)
USA	Roy Lichtenstein (1923–1998)	Artist/Filmmaker
	Andy Warhol (1928–1987)	Artist/Filmmaker
	Jasper Johns (b. 1930)	Artist/Sculptor
	Tom Wesselmann (b. 1931)	Artist
	Robert Rauschenberg (b. 1925)	Artist
Denmark	Verner Panton (1926–1998)	Architect/Designer

Don't Go With Strangers T-shirt logo for Tak2 clothing company: Büro Für Form

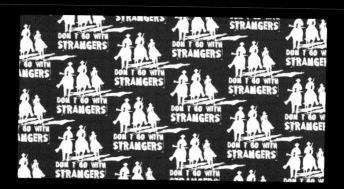

San Francisco 2012: Morla Design
Promotional poster for the Bay Area sports organizing committee. The radiating lines, bright colors, and posterized dot screens are a modern take on San Francisco music posters from the 1960s.

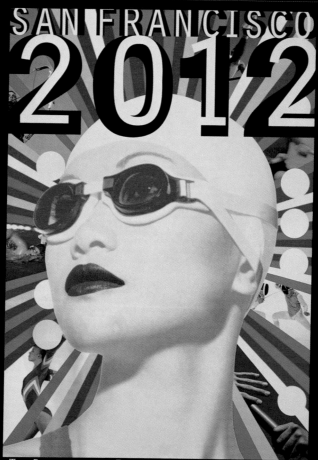

SAN FRANCISCO
2012

THE BRIDGE TO THE FUTURE
San Francisco   U.S. Bid City   2012 Olympic Games

Space age

Origin

United States

Key characteristics

Use of white and silver

Reflective surfaces

Pod shapes and futuristic forms

Key facts

The epitome of design that is about style as well as about function and reliability

A reaction to the excitement of the space race between the USSR and the USA

By the beginning of the 1960s, design was no longer just about function and reliability. Another factor had entered the equation—style. This was the decade of change and, more importantly, progress. A young John F. Kennedy ignited the dream during his infamous speech of May 25, 1961, during which he stated, "I believe that this nation should commit itself to achieving the goal, before this decade is out, of landing a man on the moon and returning him safely to the Earth. No single space project in this period will be more impressive to mankind, or more important for the long-range exploration of space; and none will be so difficult or expensive to accomplish."

Referencing time, space, and travel, in 1962, *Vogue* called for "space-age clothes that can be launched to cram into suitcases, crush into narrow spaces for long journeys, and emerge at the end laboratory fresh." In 1964, Courrèges presented a space-age series of clothes that proved influential in establishing white and silver as the colors of the season, a point echoed by *Queen* the

following year. "Silver clothing that fits into current fashion like an astronaut into his capsule," noted the magazine.

Released at the height of the space race between the USSR and the USA, Stanley Kubrick's landmark, science fiction classic *2001: A Space Odyssey* (1968), depicted a world where mankind ventured deep into outer space in amazing vehicles, designed by Harry Lange and Frederick Ordway. With less than 40 minutes of dialog in the entire film, viewers were inspired by its story of a man dwarfed by technology and space, as were many designers. Olivier Mourgue's infamous Djinn chairs also featured in the film.

In industrial design white and silver again dominated. Rounded, continuous shapes, reflective surfaces, and what were deemed to be space-age, futuristic forms featured in everything from television sets to textiles, lighting to kettles. Marco Zanuso and Richard Sapper's Algol television, designed in the late 1960s, showed just how influential the space age was on the design of everyday consumer products.

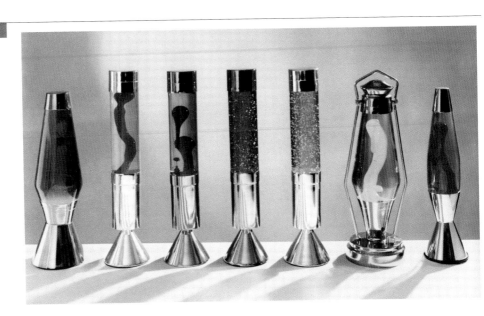

Two Capsule Line
felt helmets—dots
and moons:
Edward Mann

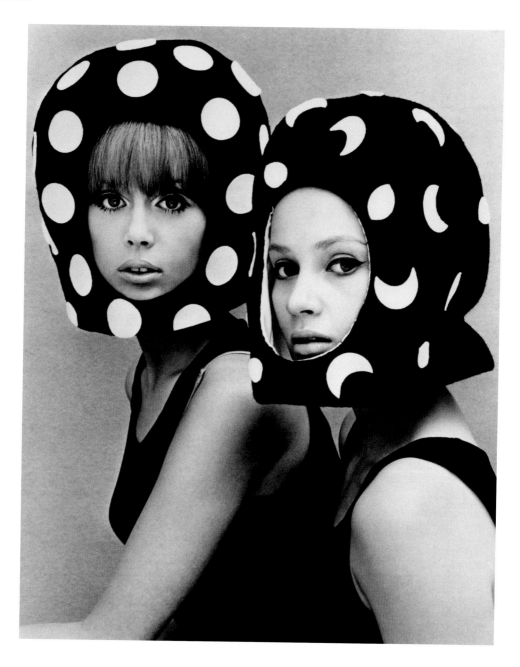

1968

OCR-B: Adrian Frutiger
OCR stands for Optical Character Recognition. This font, intended for use on products to be both scanned by electronic devices and read by humans, was made a world standard in 1973. Its distinctive technical appearance also made it a hit with graphic designers.

abcdefghijklmnopqrst
uvwxyz ß&
ABCDEFGHIJKLMNOPQRST
UVWXYZ
1234567890
.,:;–'''""._*%
!?()[]/†§$£

1968

Still from Stanley Kubrick's science fiction classic *2001: A Space Odyssey*

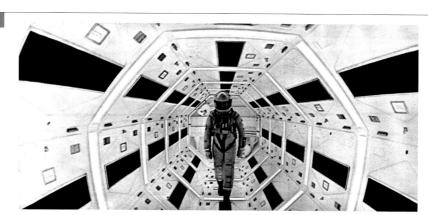

Key figures	Fields of work
Eero Aarnio (b. 1932)	Designer (interiors, industrial)
Olivier Mourgue (b. 1939)	Designer
Richard Sapper (b. 1932)	Designer
Marco Zanuso Sr. (1916–2001)	Architect/Designer

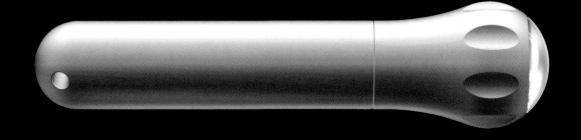

Yotel room:
Priestman Goode
Inspired by British
Airways first-class
and Japanese
capsule hotels, each
Yotel room is just 12
square yards (10m²)
and features rotating
beds and techno
walls. All windows
are internal and look
onto corridors. The
rooms are naturally
lit through reflective
mechanisms and
channelling of light.

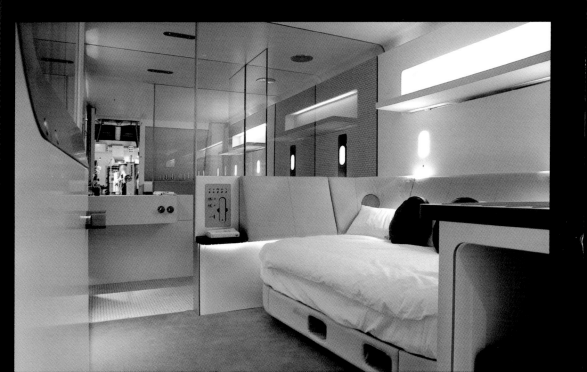

Op art

Origin

United States

Europe

Key characteristics

Moiré patterns

Black and white used in contrast

Concentric circles

Key facts

Use of reduced geometric forms to simulate movement

In competition with pop art, op art had a strong influence in graphic and interior design during the 1960s, finding its way onto everything from furniture to wallpaper

See also

Pop art p 184

Op art is the term used to describe a style of abstract art and graphics that emerged first in Europe and later in the US in the 1960s. Op art expressed itself through the use of reduced geometric forms to simulate movement. Short for "optical art" the style, derived from the abstract expressionist movement, used a variety of visual effects to create illusions of movement and vibration. Vibrating colors, concentric circles, and moiré patterns were characteristic of works by the likes of Victor Vasarely, Richard Anusziewicz, Joseph Albers, Bridget Riley, Ad Reinhardt, Kenneth Noland, and Larry Poons. Often seen as being in competition with **pop art**, op art had a strong influence in graphic and interior design during the 1960s, finding its way onto everything from furniture to wallpaper. Its abstract visual effects were easily translatable to both advertising designs and interior treatments, such as the large, colorful wall hangings known as Supergraphics. However, op art never succeeded in becoming the popular mass-movement of art and design that pop art was.

1965

Impact furnishing fabric: Evelyn Brooks for Heals Fabrics London
Brooks' screen-printed cotton design uses monochrome colors and geometric forms to simulate movement.

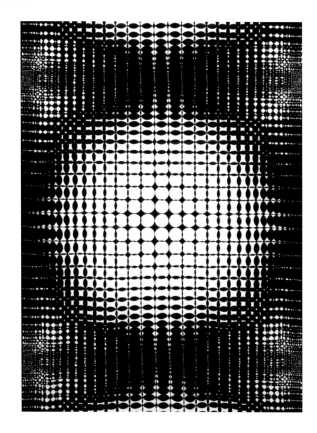

1966

Untitled (winged
curve): Bridget
Riley

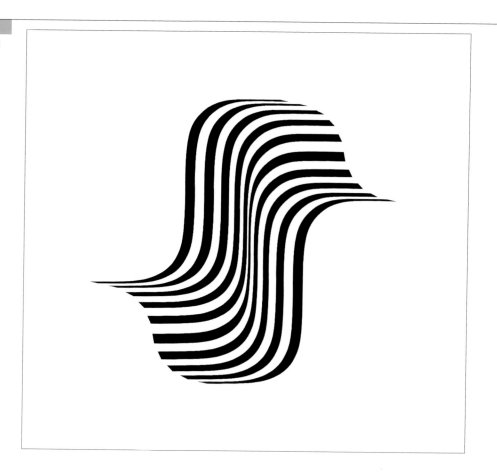

1968

Logo for the Mexico
City Olympic
Games, 1968:
Lance Wyman

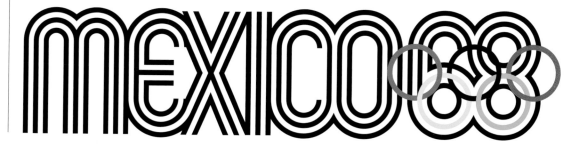

n
ent:
ondon

nent

From a distance the
poster reveals
a face; up close all
that can be seen are
the PlayStation
symbols.

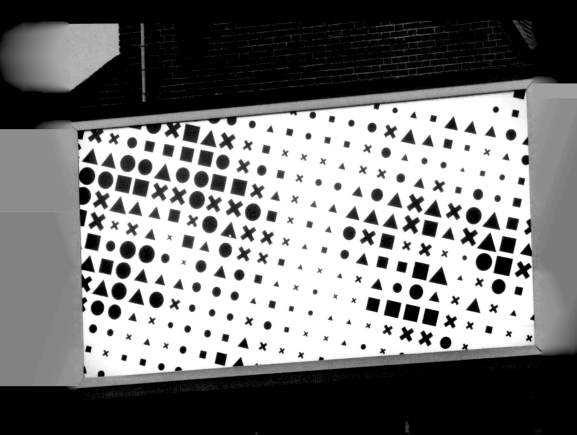

	Fields of work
ey (b. 1931)	Artist
rely (1908–1997)	Artist
nszkiewicz (b. 1930)	Artist
s (b. 1937)	Artist

Tile: Barber
Osgerby/Universal
Design Studio for
the Stella
McCartney store,
New York

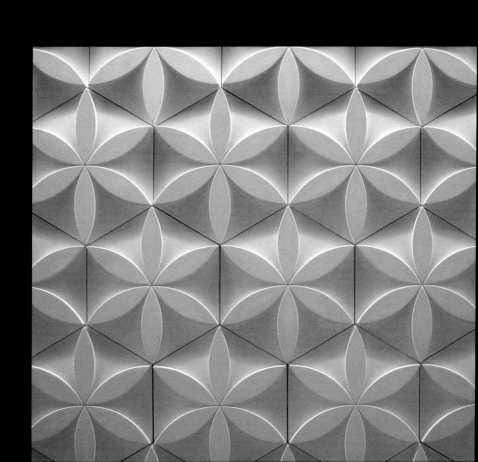

Antidesign

Origin

Italy

Key characteristics

Strong colors

Distortions of scale

Use of irony and kitsch to undermine the functionality of an object

Key facts

A concern for the total environment rather than the individual object

Rejected formalist values of Italian neomodernism and sought to renew the cultural and political role of design

Questioned the concepts of taste and good design by undermining the functionality of design

See also

Modernism p 50

Postmodernism p 216

Memphis p 224

Also known as radical design. By the 1960s, a growing number of avant-garde designers had begun to rebel against the stylized elegance of **modernism**. At the heart of the architectural and design avant-garde, radical designers began to form their own groups, such as Archizoom and Superstudio, both of which formed in Florence in 1966. These collectives became think tanks for design, creating prototypes and organizing installations and events that illustrated their concern for the total environment rather than the individual object. By the latter half of the decade, following Ettore Sottsass' 1966 exhibition of furniture in Milan, these groups had become a significant force in the world of design and were known as the Radical or antidesign movement. Rejecting the formalist values of Italian neomodernism, the antidesign

1972

Cactus coat rack: Guido Drocco and Franco Mello of Studio 65 (painted polyurethane foam); Bocca sofa: Studio 65; and Gherpe Shrimp light: Superstudio (plastic)

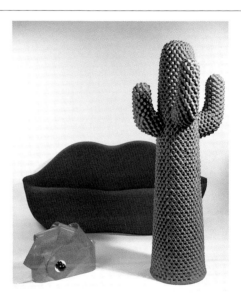

Key figures	Fields of work
Alessandro Mendini (b. 1931)	Designer
Michele de Lucchi (b. 1951)	Architect/Designer
Ettore Sottsass Jr. (b. 1917)	Designer

Antidesign groups	Fields of work
Archizoom (1966–1978)	Italian design studio
Superstudio (1966–1982)	Italian architecture and design cooperative
Gruppo Strum (est. 1963)	Italian architecture and design organization

movement sought to renew the cultural and political role of design, believing that the original aims of **modernism** had, by this time, become nothing more than a cheap marketing tool. In contrast, proponents of antidesign sought to undermine the "good taste" and elite esthetic values of modernism by employing all the design values it so vehemently rejected. The antidesign movement embraced ephemerality, irony, kitsch, strong colors, and distortions of scale to undermine the purely functional value of an object and question concepts of taste and good design.

Led by its chief spokesman Alessandro Mendini, the Milan-based Studio Alchimia was founded in 1976. Its aim was to promote the transformation of everyday consumer goods into objects of esthetic contemplation. The group also included Ettore Sottsass Jr., Paola Navone, Andrea Branzi and Michele de Lucchi. With Sottsass as its driving force, the movement's activities were carried out in individual groups but eventually consolidated as the **Memphis** collective in the early 1980s. As Memphis began to emerge in Italy, antidesign, with its slogan of "liberation of decoration for its own sake," evolved into the internationally recognized style known as **postmodernism**.

Later Applications

2000

"VIP Chair":
Marcel Wanders
for Moooi

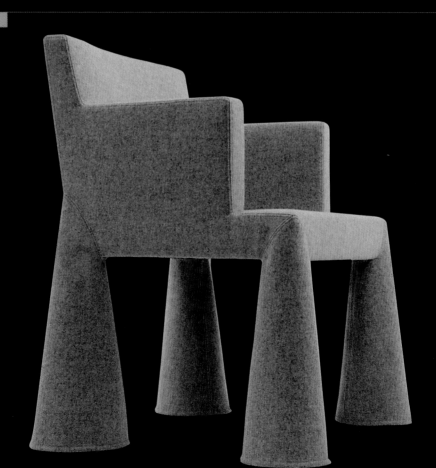

Minimalism

Origin

New York

Key characteristics

Art–geometric forms, rigid planes of color, grid-based compositions

Architecture–extreme simplicity, formal cleanliness, use of light

Key facts

Nonhierarchical relationships among component parts

Centered on a reduction in expressive media and the value of empty space

Architecture explored the fundamentals of space, light, and materials while avoiding stylistic mannerisms

The term minimalism first appeared in the mid-1960s when it was used primarily to describe the stripped-down sculptures of artists such as Robert Morris, Dan Flavin, and Donald Judd. Today, however, the term is used to describe everything from fashion and music to design and architecture.

Employing only commercial fluorescent lights in his work, Flavin's embrace of the unadorned fluorescent fixture as an esthetic object placed him at the forefront of a generation of artists whose use of industrial materials, emphasis on elementary forms, and nonhierarchical relationships among component parts became the key characteristics of minimalism.

In its architectural form the word minimalism has been used to describe the work of architects from profoundly different origins and cultural backgrounds, whose work centers on a reduction in expressive media, the rediscovery of the value of empty space, extreme simplicity, and formal cleanliness. Famous for his rigorously minimal designs, the work of John Pawson exemplifies the style. Pawson's distinctive approach to modern architecture explores the fundamentals of space, light, and materials while avoiding stylistic mannerisms. Other minimalist architects include Luis Barragán, A. G. Fronzoni, Claudio Silvestrin, Peter Zumthor, and Tadao Ando.

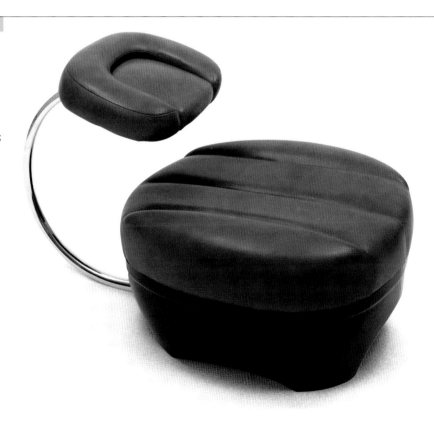

1970

Primate kneeling stool: Achille Castiglioni Combining minimalism with his newfound appreciation for Japanese simplicity and efficiency, Primate is a seating compromise for western guests at formal Japanese dinner parties.

Later Applications

1994

Kissing salt and
pepper shakers:
Karim Rashid

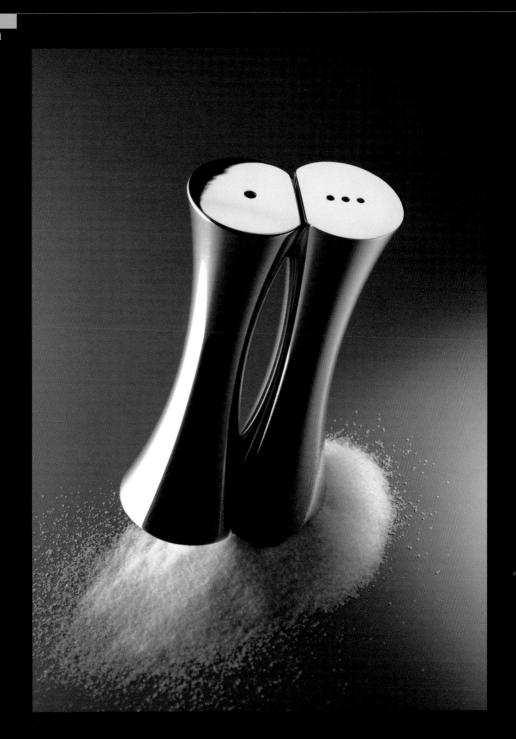

Later Applications

UMBRA Garbino
trashcans: Karim
Rashid

Bend chair:
Mårten Claesson
for Swedese

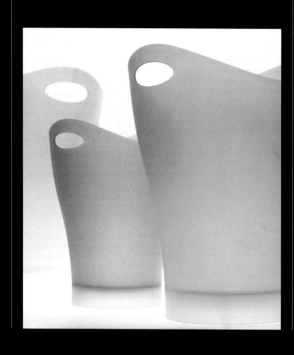

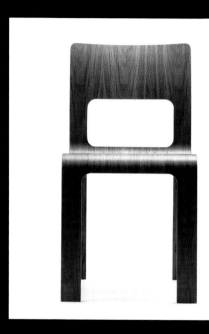

Key figures	Fields of work
Carl Andre (b. 1935)	Sculptor
Dan Flavin (1933–1996)	Installation Artist
Donald Judd (1928–1994)	Sculptor/Designer
Tadao Ando (b. 1941)	Architect
Luis Barragán (1902–1988)	Architect
AG Fronzoni (1929–2001)	Architect
John Pawson (b. 1949)	Architect/Designer
Claudio Silvestrin (b. 1954)	Architect
Peter Zumthor (b. 1943)	Architect

2001

Teatro Armani, Giorgio Armani Headquarters, Milan: Tadao Ando Architect & Associates

Interior view showing entrance corridor with its minimal, concrete, square columns.

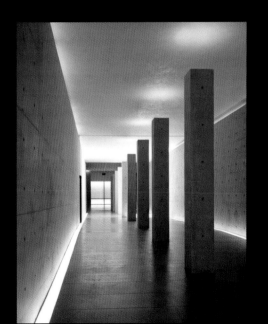

2005

Apple iPod Shuffle: Apple Industrial Group Stripping back the iPod to the bare essentials, Apple's iPod Shuffle is the epitome of minimalist design.

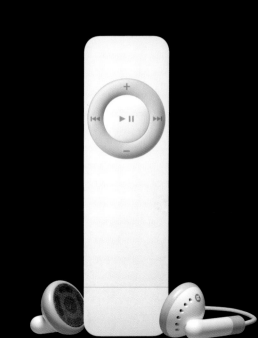

High-tech

Also known as Industrial Style and Matt Black. High-tech refers to a design style that emerged as part of the language of postmodernist design, initially in architecture, in the early 1970s. Inspired by modern technology, the style was characterized by visual simplicity and elegance, and the use of industrial materials, or those made available through technological advances, in nonindustrial settings. For example, industrial carpet and rubber flooring from hospital and factory catalogs, office supplies, and industrial lighting devices were all characteristic of the high-tech style. The term has also been used to refer to a stylistic development within **modernism** in which designers began using new materials such as glass bricks, metals, and plastics in favor of traditional materials such as wood.

High-tech was pioneered by British architects, such as Norman Foster and Richard Rogers, both of whom incorporated industrial elements into their buildings. The idea was not to hide the construction but to make significant design elements out of constructional necessities according to L. H. Sullivan's "form follows function"

1960

606 Universal
Shelving System:
Dieter Rams
for Vitsoe

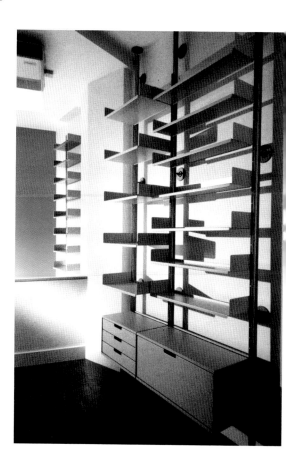

Lloyds of London,
London: Richard
Rogers

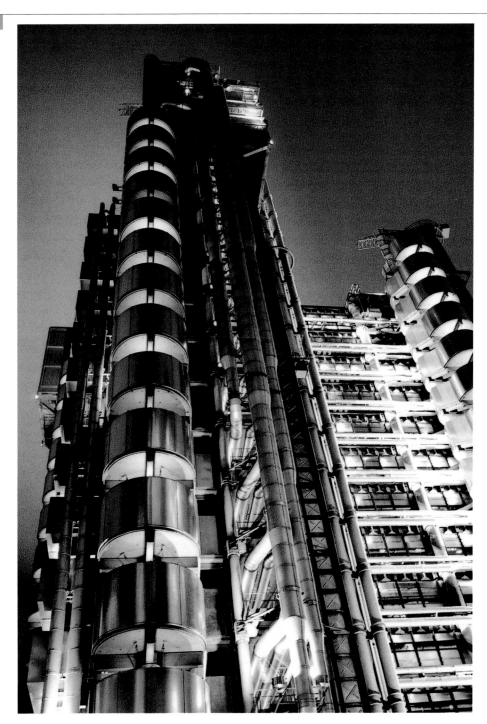

1992

Aeron chair:
Donald T.
Chadwick

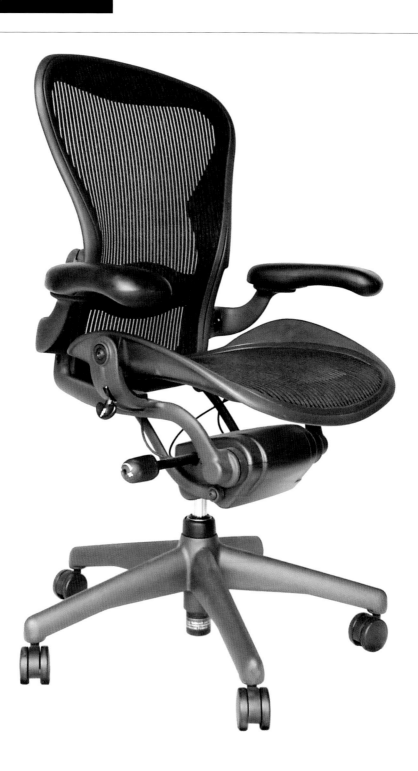

dictum. Classic examples of high-tech architecture include the Center Pompidou, Paris, designed by Richard Rogers and Renzo Piano (1971–1977), and Sir Norman Foster's Hong Kong and Shanghai Bank (1979–1988), as well as the interior designs of Peter Andes, Paul Haigh, and Joseph Paul D'Urso.

In designing the Center Pompidou, Rogers and Renzo decided to place all the technology required outside of the actual glass facade, thus making the building equipment the real visual esthetic, while stairways, cables, and a steel skeleton of colored tubes were deliberately positioned in the visitors' line of vision. Where steel constructions such as this had always been deliberately concealed behind classic facades, the arrival of high-tech saw designers actively breaking with tradition in favor of this new and unique approach. The Center Pompidou was built early on in the high-tech period, but its construction still marked a turning point for the style as the maximal dependency between form and function was reached. High-tech architecture continued to exist after this, but not necessarily for the right reasons. Architectural designs became increasingly focused on esthetics, to the point where many constructions were made a lot more complex than was required in a bid solely to create buildings that looked even more futuristic and complex. High-tech buildings still exist though today the pure high-tech style is often mixed with more classic design elements.

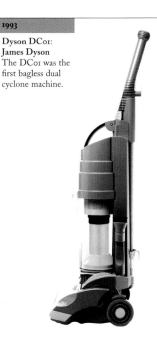

1993

Dyson DC01: James Dyson
The DC01 was the first bagless dual cyclone machine.

1999

Peckham Library and Media Centre, London: Alsop Architects
With a huge, multicolored glass facade that covers the entire back of the building, and unusual use of copper (three elevations are clad in prepatinated copper sheet), this uncompromising design was awarded the prestigious Stirling Prize for the best new building in Britain in 2000.

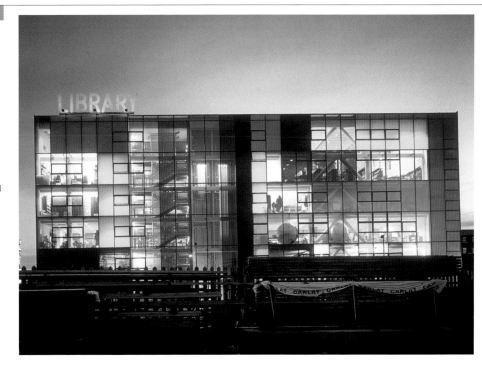

Later Applications

Apple Pro Mouse: Apple Industrial Group Housed in a crystal-clear enclosure, the high-performance optical sensor ensures extreme precision and eliminates skipping and sticking.

You Can Find Inspiration In Everything: book design, Aboud·Sodano; magnifying glass and polystyrene cover: Jonathan Ive

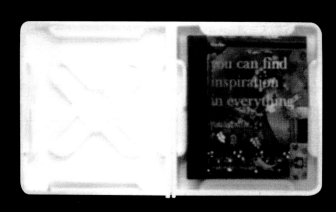

Logo for D&AD's Rewind exhibition: johnson banks

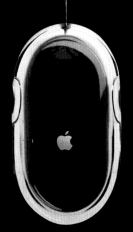

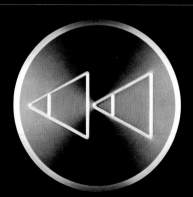

Country	Key figures	Fields of work
UK	Norman Foster (b. 1935)	Architect/Designer
	Richard Rogers (b. 1933)	Architect
	Michael Hopkins (b. 1935)	Architect
	Paul Haigh (b. 1949)	Interior designer
USA	Joseph Paul D'Urso (b. 1943)	Interior designer
	Ward Bennett (1917–2003)	Artist/Sculptor/Designer (textiles, jewelry, interiors)

Blow Up citrus basket: Fratelli Campana for Alessi

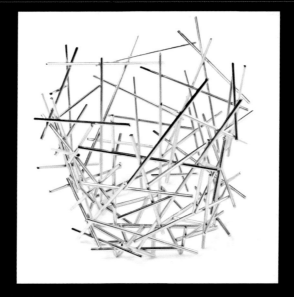

Rolling Bridge: Thomas Heatherwick Studio

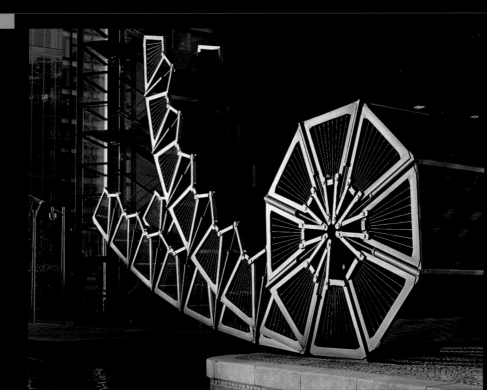

Postindustrialism

Postindustrialism refers to a **postmodern** approach to design that emerged in the UK following the end of Fordism (manufacturing by production line) and the mass manufacturing that characterized the 1960s and 1970s. The arrival of postindustrialism represented a significant shift for the design industry from an industrial to a service-based economy, producing goods for pre-determined sectors or individuals in batch production as designers began creating products in limited editions or as unique one-off pieces. No longer restricted by the confines of industrial process, designers approached their work in a completely new way, revelling in their newfound creative freedom.

The early work of designers such as Ron Arad and Tom Dixon epitomized the style as they distanced themselves from the standardization of industrial manufacture by producing one-off, unfinished pieces, such as Arad's Concrete hi-fi (1984). Dixon's early work saw the designer reuse found objects as he began making and selling limited editions of welded furniture—such as the S-Chair and Pylon Chair—unique designs that were unafraid to reference and indeed celebrate their industrial past.

Many postindustrialist designs succeeded in communicating the "postmodern design rhetoric" that designers found themselves hankering after in opposition to the souless order and organisation of **modernism**. Experimental and often ironic, postindustrialism signified the arrival of the "usable artwork" and, as a result, enabled a whole new approach and genre for design practice.

1986

Well Tempered
chair: Ron Arad

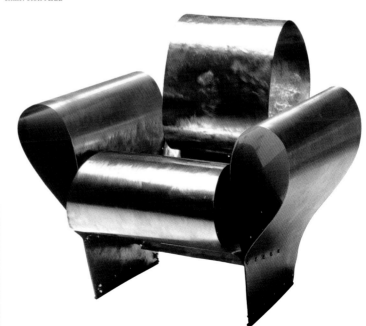

Speaking coffee
maker: Elbert
Draisma/Droog
Design

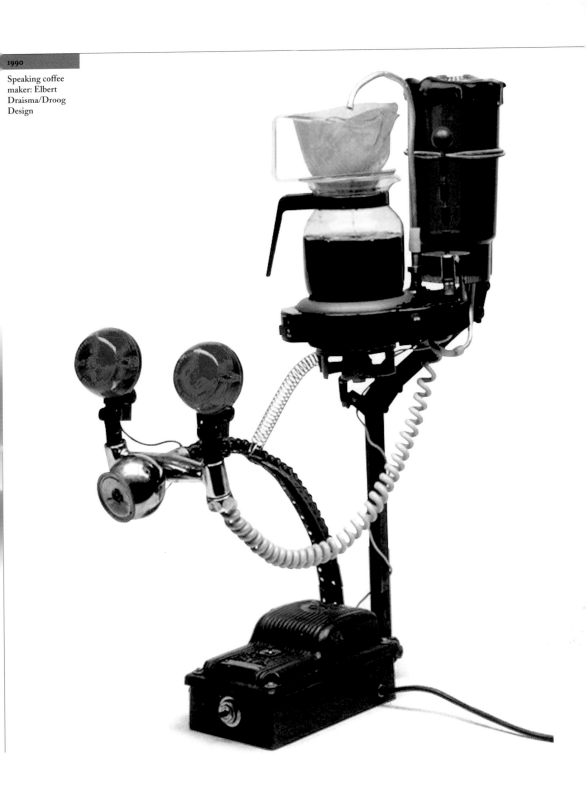

**Pylon Chair:
Tom Dixon for
Cappellini**
Tom Dixon's
Pylon Chair is
constructed from
iron wire varnished
with natural
aluminum.

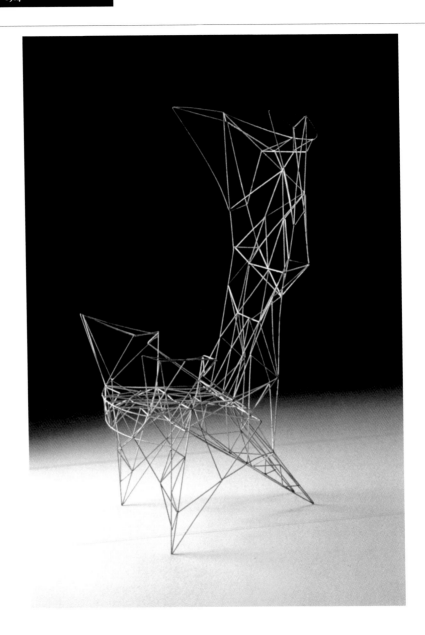

Key figures	Fields of work
Tom Dixon (b. 1959)	Designer
Ron Arad (b. 1951)	Designer

2002

**Nuage (Cloud):
Ronan and Erwan
Bouroullec for
Cappellini**
Storage system
constructed from
polystyrene.

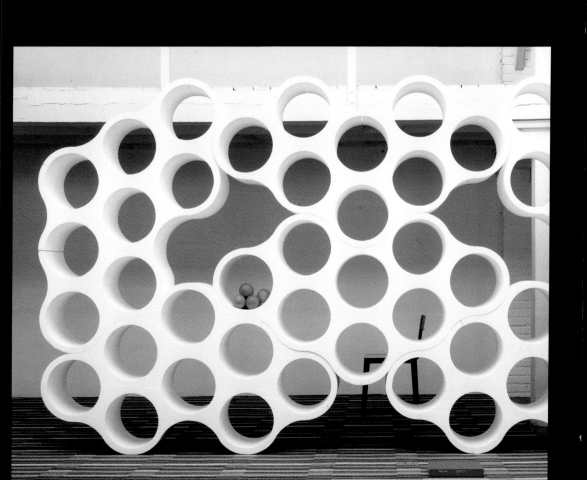

Later Applications

**Concrete record
stack and speakers:
Solid Soul**

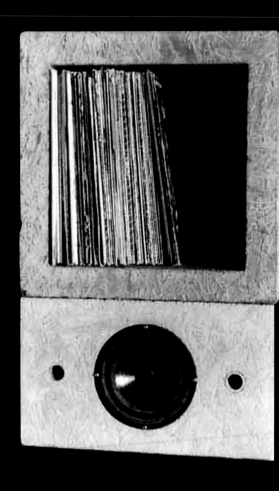

**The Locker:
Egg Designs**
Mild steel laser-
profiled flower
motif based on
African desert
succulent, epoxy
powder coated.

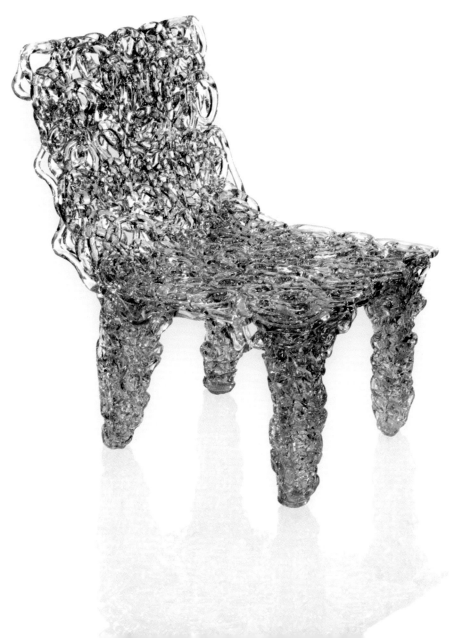

Postmodernism

Postmodernism is the term that has come to describe the stylistic developments that emerged in response to the rationalism of modernist design. The move toward postmodernism was initiated in the 1960s, before coming into its own in the early 1980s. Postmodernists believed that the efforts of **modernism** had resulted in the creation of incomprehensible books and works of art, soulless objects, and unwanted buildings that people could not bear to live with. In his 1966 book, *Complexity and Contradiction in Architecture*, Robert Venturi questioned the validity of the emphasis modernists placed on logic, simplicity, and order, suggesting that ambiguity and contradiction also had a valid place. Venturi argued that modern architecture was essentially meaningless. Early postmodernists regarded the lack of ornament and geometric abstraction championed by the modernists as

dehumanising architecture, and, as a result, alienating it. In 1972, the English translation of Roland Barthes *Mythologies* (1957) created widespread interest in his theories on semiotics, fueling the belief that if buildings and objects incorporated symbolism, consumers would be more likely to relate to them on a psychological level.

In response, postmodernism advocated the merging of fine art and mass culture, highbrow and populist art. Surface decoration was once again admired, and other styles were drawn upon freely. By the mid-1970s, American architects such as Michael Graves had begun to introduce decorative, and often ironic motifs into their work. These regularly referenced past decorative styles, such as **art deco**, **constructivism**, and **de Stijl**. The introduction of color, decoration, texture, references to historical styles, and the eccentric elements characterized

1975

I love NY logo: Milton Glaser
In the aftermath of September 11, 2001, Glaser updated his

design by adding a smudge to the lower corner of the heart and the words "more than ever."

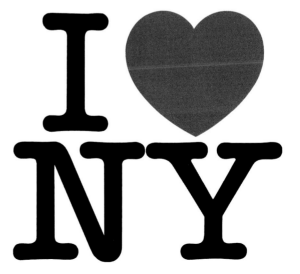

by the work of Ettore Sottsass, **Memphis**, and Studio Alchimia quickly became integral to the postmodern style. Bright, bold designs were applied to everything; ceramics, textiles, jewelry, silverware, furniture, and lighting were all batch produced in limited editions by companies such as Alessi, Artemide, Cassina, and Formica. Often referred to as the "ultimate fruit salad" of style, the **Memphis** group produced a number of smaller objects and furniture pieces that displayed postmodern characteristics. Playful and humorous in their approach, postmodernists loved decoration and color as much as modernists hated it, and with their irreverent, audacious approach to design, played by their own rules.

Architecturally speaking, Philip Johnson's AT&T Building in New York (1978–1983) exemplified the postmodern esthetic, while at the same time offending the architectural establishment through its use of decoration, not to mention the quotation from a "lesser" design form: furniture. Built in the **International Style**, this otherwise sleek skyscraper was adorned with a baroque pediment that was scornfully described as the Chippendale top. This use of a visual idea out of its normal context is a **deconstructivist** tactic, an approach that moved from literature into the arts during the 1970s and 1980s.

Criticized by many for being too cold and formal, the **Swiss school** had begun to lose its energy by the late 1970s and early 1980s. While modernists rejected historicism, decoration, and the vernacular, postmodern designers drew upon these resources to expand their range of design possibilities. Layered imagery, collage, and photomontage inspired by **Cubism** and **dada**, and the assimilation of the vernacular all contributed to postmodern design of the late 1970s and early 1980s as designers, sensing that the modern esthetic no longer held relevance in postindustrial society, began to broaden their visual vocabulary by breaking established rules

Svincolo' standard lamp: Ettore Sottsass, 1979; Tindouf tambour fronted cabinet:

Paolo Navone, 1979, both for the Bauhaus Collection (Studio Alchimia)

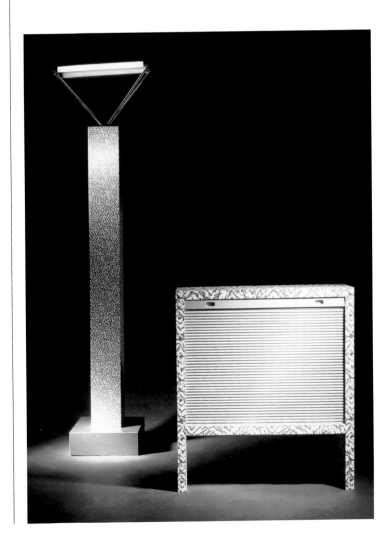

and exploring different periods, styles, and cultures. The postmodern revolt was led by Wolfgang Weingart whose experimental approach to design resulted in a series of posters that appeared at once complex and chaotic, playful and spontaneous. Another notable designer of the late twentieth century is Milton Glaser, creator of the famous "I Love NY" ad campaign (1973) and cofounder of Pushpin studios, whose humorous decorative qualities led to postmodernism.

The antirational approach to design flourished during the decadent 1980s as the style became increasingly diverse, encompassing **deconstructivism**, **high-tech**, and **postindustrialism**. However, by the early 1990s, as the recession loomed, designers began looking for a more rational approach. The postmodern ethos, however, remains as even to this day we find ourselves constantly reassessing what is essential in design.

1948–1950/1958

Palatino and Optima typefaces: Hermann Zapf Zapf has designed some of the twentieth century's most important fonts.

abcdefghijklmnopqrst
uvwxyz fiflß&
ABCDEFGHIJKLMNO
PQRSTUVWXYZ
1234567890
.,.:;-–—'' ""‚.‹›«»*%‰
!?¡¿()[]/†‡§$£¢ƒ

abcdefghijklmnopqrstu
vwxyz fiflß&
ABCDEFGHIJKLMNOP
QRSTUVWXYZ
1234567890
.,.:;-–—'' ""‚.‹›«»*%‰
!?¡¿()[]/†‡§$£¢ƒ

1985

Bird kettle: Michael
Graves for Alessi

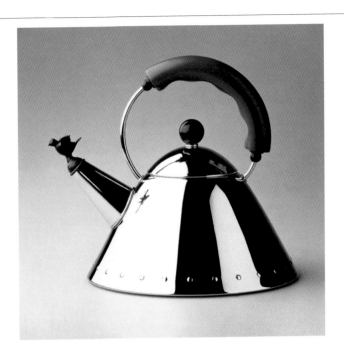

1989

Museumsinsel
Groningen,
The Netherlands:
Alessandro Mendini

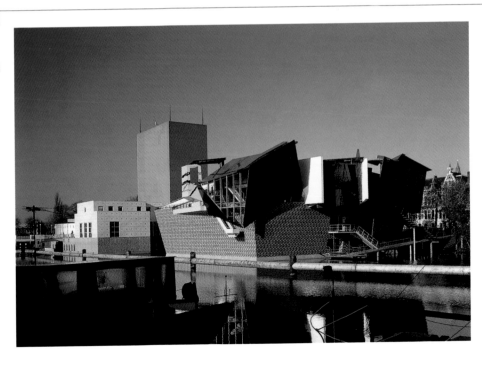

2001

I love NY more
than ever: Milton
Glaser

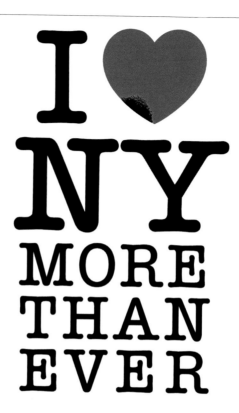

Key figures	Fields of work
Mario Botta (b. 1943)	Architect/Designer
Andrea Branzi (b. 1938)	Designer
Michele de Lucchi (b. 1951)	Architect/Designer
Nathalie du Pasquier (b. 1957)	Artist
Aldo Rossi (1931–1997)	Architect
Matteo Thun (b. 1952)	Ceramicist/Designer
Shiro Kuramata (1934–1991)	Designer (furniture, interiors)
Michael Graves (b. 1934)	Architect/Designer
Alessandro Mendini (b. 1931)	Designer
Ettore Sottsass Jr. (b. 1917)	Designer
Philip Cortelyou Johnson (b. 1906)	Architect
Paula Scher (b. 1948)	Graphic designer
April Greiman (b. 1948)	Graphic designer
Wolfgang Weingart (b. 1941)	Graphic designer

Tea Urn with Feet:
Virginia Graham

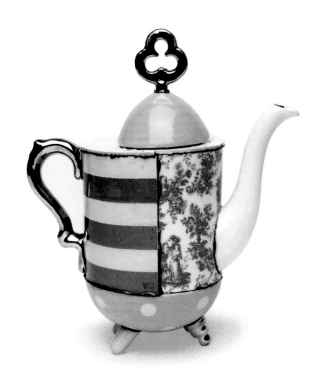

Kila work lamp:
Harry Allen for
IKEA

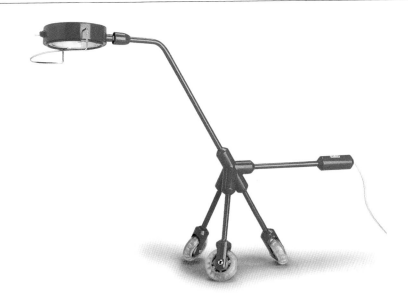

California new wave

California new wave is the name attributed to a postmodern style of graphic design that emerged in the late 1970s. Drawing inspiration from past cultural references such as art, photography, film, and advertising, new-wave designs retained some elements characteristic of the **Swiss school**, while also subverting the "holy grid of **modernism**."

Inspired by new forms of electronic media, California new wave incorporated deconstructed compositions so as to create a sense of messages being filtered through layers. Designers used Apple Macintosh software to create a language of hybrid energy with encoded messages, while the seemingly random placing of collage-like images gave refreshing edge to their work. Key exponents of the style included April Greiman and Jan van Toorn. In 1982 the launch of *Émigré* magazine could not have been better placed as the magazine took it upon itself to disseminate the ideas behind the California new wave graphic style, opening it up to a whole new, international audience.

Postmodernism would eventually replace much that the new-wave style initially stood for, representing a whole host of graphic styles all characterized by innovative design, layered compositions, and often indecipherable meanings.

1978

Identity and business cards for Vertigo (design accessories and retail shop): April Greiman

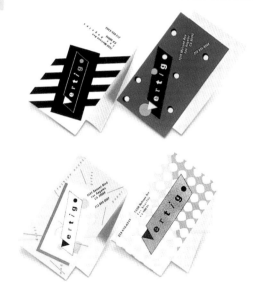

Key figures

April Greiman (b. 1948)

Kenneth Hiebert (b. 1930)

Paula Scher (b. 1948)

Jan van Toorn (b. 1932)

Fields of work

Graphic designer

Graphic designer

Graphic designer

Graphic designer

Cal Arts View:
April Greiman for
California Institute
of the Arts

China Club
restaurant and
lounge identity:
April Greiman

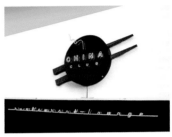

Cal Arts catalog:
April Greiman for
California Institute
of the Arts
(photography
Jayme Odgers)

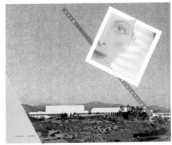

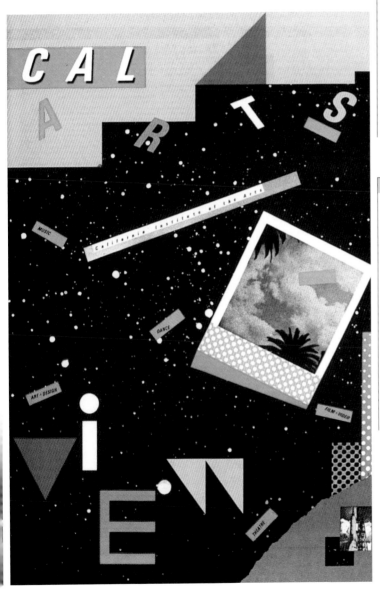

Memphis

Memphis was the name of the Milan-based collective of furniture and product designers whose work dominated the design scene in the early 1980s. Led by Ettore Sottsass, the group made its debut at the 1981 Milan Furniture Fair, shocking the design fraternity with its brightly colored plastic laminates emblazoned with kitsch geometric and leopard-skin patterns. One of the aims of the group was to further develop the experimental approach to design that Sottsass and de Lucchi had begun as members of the Italian Radical design group, Studio Alchimia in the late 1970s.

On December 11, 1980, Sottsass had invited a group of designers/friends to his house to discuss a new approach to design. Michele de Lucchi, Aldo Cibic Matteo Thun, Marco Zanini, and Martine Bedine all attended the meeting, at which the group decided to call themselves Memphis after the Bob Dylan song they were listening to, *Stuck Inside of Mobile,* became stuck on the words "with the Memphis blues again" on Sottsass' record player. When the group met again the following February, with the addition of Nathalie du Pasquier and George Sowden, they were armed with more than 100 colorful, bold designs drawing influences from past and present. They were soon sourcing manufacturers willing to batch produce their designs, and creating promotional material. Ernesto Gismondi became the president of Memphis and on September 18, 1981, the group presented its first collection at the Arc '74 showroom in Milan. It included furniture, lighting, clocks, and ceramics designed by a score of international architects and designers. Within the design industry, Memphis was either loved or hated, while to those outside the style was seen as being perfectly in tune with the post-punk popular culture of the early 1980s, "a clearly defined manifestation of the often obscure postmodernist theories" then so influential in art and architecture. Classic Memphis designs include

Sottsass' Beverly cabinet (1981) with its yellow "snakeskin" laminate doors, angled tortoiseshell bookshelves, and red light bulb; the red upholstery and bright yellow legs of Sowden's Oberoi armchairs (1981); and Martine Bedine's Super lamp with its uncompromising array of multicolored bulbs.

In contrast with what was seen as the soulless "good taste" that had come to dominate modernist design, Memphis' new, postmodern vocabulary of design was soon splashed across the covers of magazines around the world. The group also published a book, *Memphis: The New International Style,* as a means of promoting its work, as well as holding exhibitions in London, Edinburgh, Paris, Montreal, Stockholm, Geneva, Hannover, Chicago, Düsseldorf, Los Angeles, New York, and Tokyo, organized by Barbara Radice, the group Art Director from 1981–1988. There was never any pretence that Memphis was anything more than a passing phase. In 1988, when its popularity began to wane, Sottsass dissolved the group. However, despite its short life span, Memphis played a central role in the internationalization of **postmodernism** and many of its exponents continue to push the boundaries of design to this day.

Casablanca
sideboard:
Ettore Sottsass

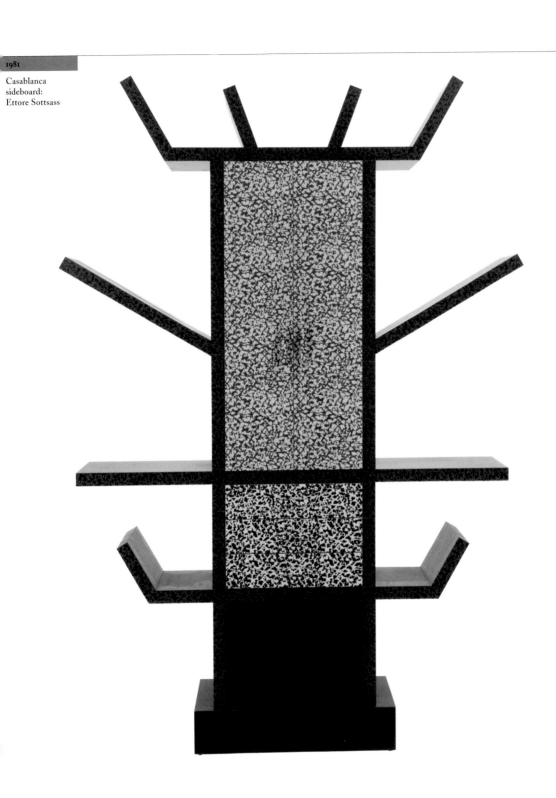

Kariba fruit bowl:
Memphis

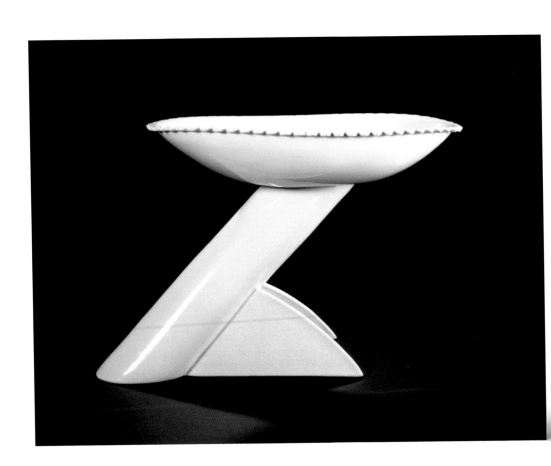

Installation in the
Coop Himmelblau
pavilion: Roy
Lichtenstein and
Michele de Lucchi

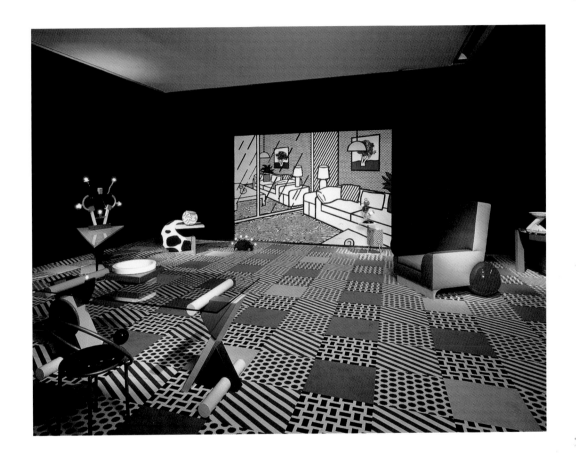

Later Applications

Kozmos Blocks: Karim Rashid for Bozart Toys
These colorful blocks come in a range of virtuoso shapes, colors, graphics, and sizes reminiscent of the Memphis style.

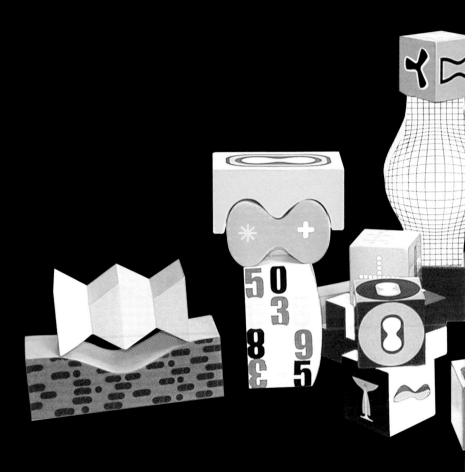

Key figures	Fields of work
Ettore Sottsass Jr. (b. 1917)	Designer
Matteo Thun (b. 1952)	Ceramicist/Designer
Michele de Lucchi (b. 1951)	Architect/Designer
Barbara Radice (b. 1943)	Art/Design director/Writer
Martine Bedine (b. 1957)	Designer

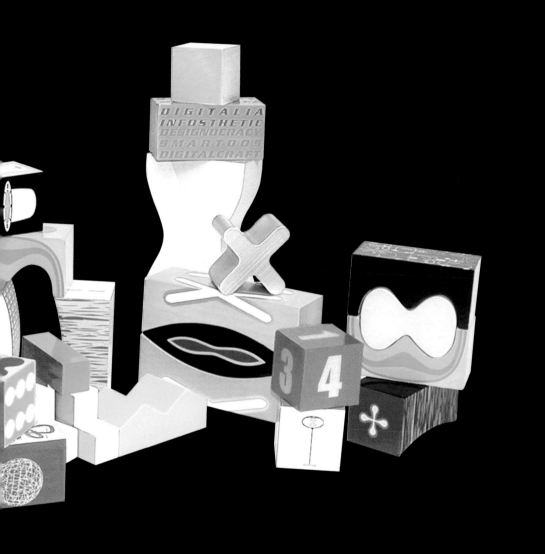

Deconstructivism

A term coined in the late 1980s, deconstructivism was not so much a design movement as a common direction in architecture and interior design. The style was characterized by the use of broken and jagged forms, warped and overlapped planes, and at times, "disturbing" shapes, in contrast to the logic and order dictated by **modernism**. The concept of deconstructivism was derived from that of deconstruction, a method of literary criticism developed by Jacques Derrida in the late 1960s. Derrida believed a text could have multiple interpretations and, therefore, could never exactly mean what it says or say what it means. Deconstruction aimed to extract the meaninglessness of the text by destabilizing its intellectual foundation. In the 1970s Derrida's methodology was translated into a style of architecture and interior design—deconstructivism—which aimed to challenge ideas of rational order

and expose hidden workings. In 1988 Philip Johnson organized an exhibition at the Museum ofMofdern Art, New York, in which he identified the style through the work of seven architects— among them Peter Eisenman, Zaha Hadid, Frank Gehry, and Bernard Tschumi. The exhibition featured models and drawings of fantasy architecture tha aimed to challenge what were, by this time, considered to be the rather sedate conventions of **modernism**. Only a smal number of deconstructivist designs have ever been realized, among them Tschumi follies in the Parc de la Vilette in Paris.

By centering their exhibition around a new "ism," Johnson identified and celebrated the elements of this new style characterized by twisted geometries, centerless plans, and shards of glass and metal, stylistic features that were soon translated from architecture to graphic design, providing graphic designers with

1981

Radio in a Bag:
Daniel Weil

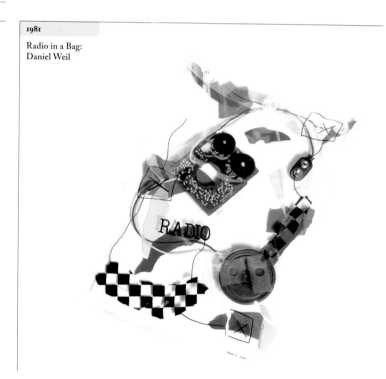

a ready-to-use formal vocabulary that could be broadly adopted. A number of designers associated with the Cranbrook Academy of Art, including Katherine McCoy and Lucille Tenazas, applied deconstructivist ideologies to their work through the use of multilayering, of both type and image, to suggest multiple interpretations of the message being communicated, while in industrial design Daniel Weil's radios, encased in plastic bags to reveal their workings, reinterpreted the accepted form of this everyday product. The fragmented forms of many deconstructivist designs bear similarities to **constructivism**. The style has also been allied to **postmodernism**.

1990

Dead History typeface: P. Scott Makela According to the designer, Dead History signals the end of an era of traditionally produced fonts. It personifies a new attitude in type creation marked by the design of hybrid typefaces, which are largely the result of the computer's capabilities to function as the perfect assembling tool.

AaBbCcDdEeFfGgH

1997

Hammerhead typeface: Felix Braden

abcdefghijklmnopqrstu

vwxyz fifl&&

ABCDEFGHIJKLMNOPQR

STUVWXYZ

1234567890

..,.-—— '‚ "„ .‹›«» * % ‰

..,,

!?¡¿()[]/†‡§$£¢ƒ

The Jewish
Museum, Berlin:
Daniel Libeskind

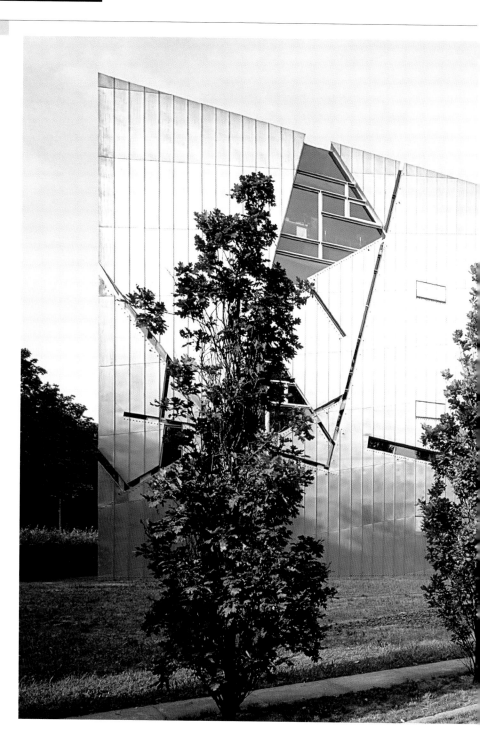

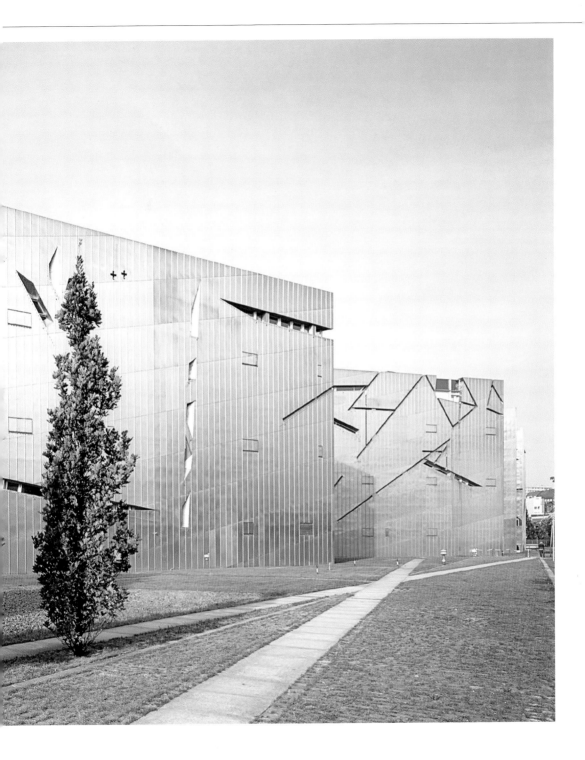

2003

Richard B. Fisher
Center for the
Performing Arts
at Bard College,
New York:
Frank Gehry

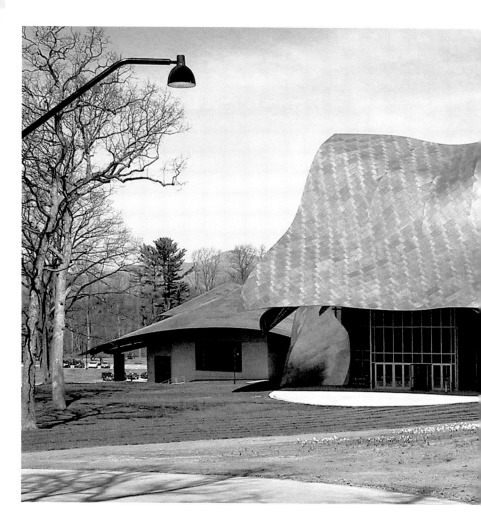

Key figures

Frank Owen Gehry (b. 1929)

Zaha Hadid (b. 1950)

Peter Eisenman (b. 1932)

Bernard Tschumi (b. 1944)

Katherine McCoy (b. 1945)

Daniel Weil (b. 1953)

Fields of work

Architect/Designer/Artist

Architect

Architect/Teacher

Architect

Graphic designer/Lecturer

Architect/Designer

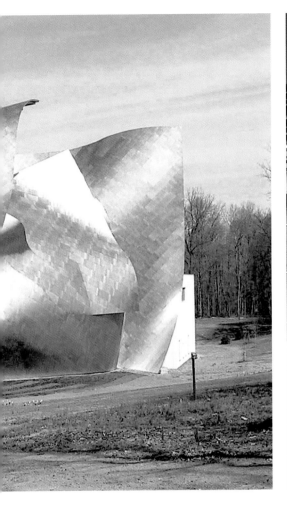
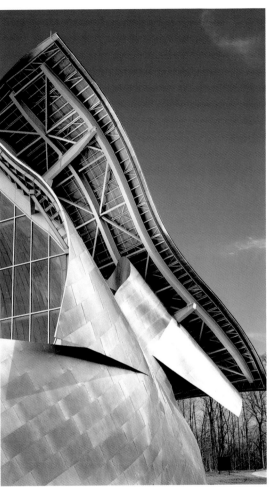

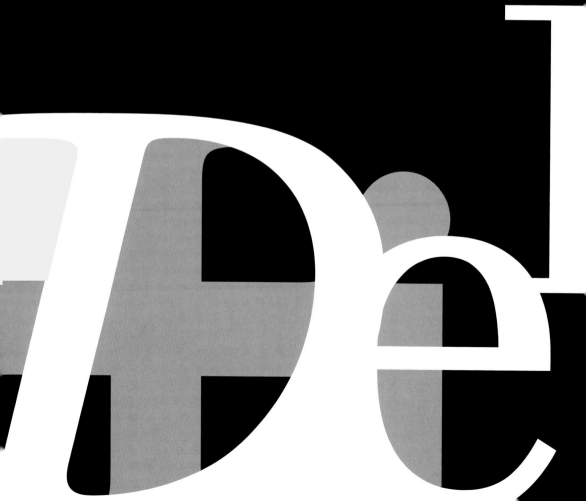

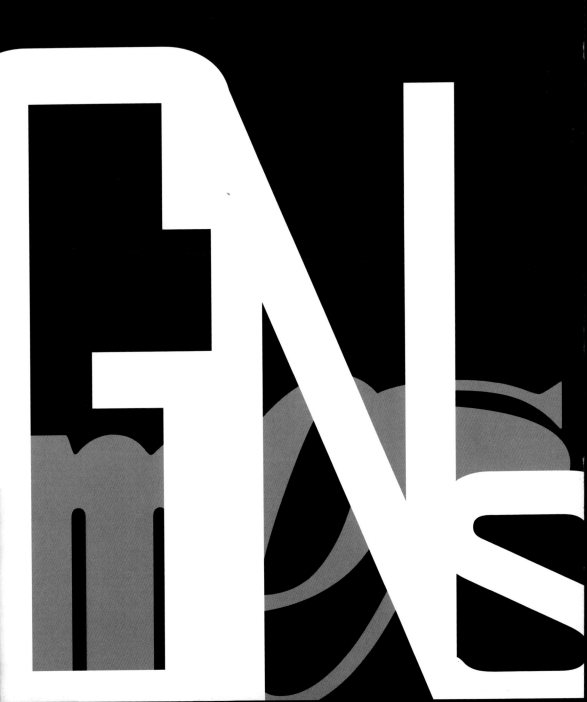

Where to see

Antidesign

Michele De Lucchi
www.produzioneprivata.it

Michele De Lucchi's workshop in Milan, Italy, produces handblown glass ceramic lamps, vases, and wooden folding chairs. The workshop is often open for special exhibitions.

via Giorgio Pallavicino 31
20145 Milano
Italy

The Museum of Modern Art, USA
www.moma.org

The collection includes work by Ettore Sottsass.

11 West 53 Street
New York
New York 10019-5497
USA

Art deco

The Museum of Modern Art, USA
www.moma.org

The collection includes work by A. M. Cassandre.

11 West 53 Street
New York
New York 10019-5497
USA

The National Art Library at The Victoria and Albert Museum, UK
www.vam.ac.uk

The National Art Library holds a large collection of art deco material including beautifully bound and illustrated books, books of designs, and fashion illustrations. The library also holds exhibition and sales catalogs, as well as publications on the major artists and designers of the period.

Other art deco at the V&A includes:
Twentieth Century Study Gallery
A range of furniture and small objects including several art deco items.

Twentieth Century Gallery
Includes ceramics, graphic art, glass, silverware, sculpture, furniture, textiles, photography, and radios.

Frank Lloyd Wright Gallery
The complete office —desk, chairs, wall paneling, and lights—by America's greatest architect and designer, Frank Lloyd Wright.

Cromwell Road
South Kensington
London SW7 2RL
UK

Buildings in New York, USA
www.greatbuildings.com/buildings/Chrysler_Building.html
The Chrysler Building, William Van Alen

www.greatbuildings.com/buildings/Empire_State_Building.html
The Empire State Building, Shreve, Lamb, and Harmon

The Rijksmuseum, the Netherlands
www.rijksmuseum.nl

The collection includes pieces by Rene Lalique, including *Hairpin*.

Jan Luijkenstraat 1
1070 DN
Amsterdam
The Netherlands

Art nouveau

Aberdeen Art Gallery and Museums, UK
www.aagm.co.uk

The collection includes original sketches by Charles Rennie Mackintosh.

Aberdeen Art Gallery
Schoolhill
Aberdeen AB10 1FQ
UK

Buildings designed by Antoni Gaudí
www.greatbuildings.com/architects/Antonio_Gaudi.html

Casa Batllo, Barcelona, Spain
Parc Guell, Barcelona, Spain
The Sagrada Familia, Barcelona, Spain

The Horta Museum, Belgium
www.hortamuseum.be

The museum is housed in the Horta House, the former home and studio of Victor Horta.

25 rue Américaine
1060 Brussels
Belguim

Buildings designed by Charles Rennie Mackintosh
www.greatbuildings.com/architects/Charles_Rennie_Mackintosh.html

Glasgow School of Art, Glasgow, UK
Hill House, Helensburgh, UK
The Willow Tea Rooms, Glasgow, UK

The Mucha Museum, Czech Republic
www.mucha.cz

Dedicated to the life and work of Alphonse Mucha, the museum houses paintings, photographs, drawings, and lithographs by the famous poster designer.

Kaunicky palác
Panská 7
110 00 Prague 1
Czech Republic

The National Gallery of Art, USA
www.nga.gov

The gallery has a collection of decorative arts featuring art nouveau pieces by Antoni Gaudí, Charles Rennie Mackintosh, Emile Galle, and Victor Horta.

National Mall
Between Third and Seventh Streets at Constitution Avenue, NW
Washington, DC
USA

Arts and Crafts movement

Liberty, UK
www.liberty.co.uk

The famous London store opened in 1875, selling ornaments, fabrics, and artworks from Japan and the East. Liberty was instrumental in the development of the Arts and Crafts movement, the esthetic movement, japonisme, and art nouveau. The store continues to sell original Arts and Crafts pieces, as well as contemporary design.

Regent Street
London W1B 5AH
UK

The Victoria and Albert Museum, UK
www.vam.ac.uk

This museum has one of the most wide-ranging and comprehensive collections of Arts and Crafts in the world. Highlights include the William Morris collection and objects in every media by leading Arts and Crafts designers from the UK, the USA, Germany, Austria, Norway, Russia, and Japan. The museum building itself has outstanding Arts and Crafts features.

Cromwell Road
South Kensington
London SW7 2RL
UK

William Morris Gallery, UK
www.lbwf.gov.uk/wmg

The only public museum devoted to the UK's best-known and most versatile designer. The gallery is located in what was Morris' family home from 1848–1856, the former Water House, a substantial Georgian dwelling set in its own extensive grounds.

Lloyd Park
Forest Road
London E17 4PP
UK

Bauhaus

The Bauhaus Archive / Museum of Design, Germany
www.bauhaus.de

Concerned with the research and presentation of the history and impact of the Bauhaus, this is the most complete existing collection focused on the history of the school and all aspects of its work. The collection is housed in a building drafted by Walter Gropius.

Klingelhöferstraße 14
D-10785 Berlin
Germany

The Gropius House, USA
www.spnea.org

Walter Gropius designed this house as his family home in 1937, when he came to teach at Harvard's Graduate School of Design. The house contains an important collection of furniture designed by Marcel Breuer and made for the Gropius family in the Bauhaus workshops.

68 Baker Bridge Road
Lincoln
Massachussets 01773
USA

The Guggenheim Museum, USA
www.guggenheim.org

The collection includes many Bauhaus paintings by artists such as Paul Klee, Vasily Kandinsky, and Laszlo Moholy-Nagy.

Smithsonian Cooper-Hewitt, National Design Museum, USA
ndm.si.edu

The collection includes a prototype of the Barcelona chair by Ludwig Mies van der Rohe.

2 East 91st Street
New York
New York 10128
USA

The Victoria and Albert Museum, UK
www.vam.ac.uk

The collection includes many examples of furniture and product design from Bauhaus artists, such as William Wagenfeld, Walter Gropius, Adolf Meyer, and Marcel Breuer.

Cromwell Road
South Kensington
London SW7 2RL
UK

Beaux-arts

Buildings designed by Raymond Hood
www.greatbuildings.com/architects/Raymond_Hood.html

Daily News Building, New York, USA
McGraw-Hill Building, New York, USA
Rockefeller Center, New York, USA

Buildings designed by McKim, Mead, and White
www.greatbuildings.com/architects/McKim_Mead_and_White.html

American Academy in Rome, Italy
Boston Public Library, Boston, Massachusetts, USA
Isaac Bell House, Newport, Rhode Island, USA
Morgan Library, New York, USA
New York Herald Building, New York, USA
New York Racquet Club, New York, USA
Newport Casino, Newport, Rhode Island, USA
Pennsylvania Station, New York, USA
Rhode Island State Capitol, Providence, Rhode Island, USA
University Club, New York, USA
W. G. Low House, Bristol, Rhode Island, USA

Buildings designed by John Russell Pope
www.greatbuildings.com/buildings/Temple_of_the_Scottish_Ri.html

The Temple of the Scottish Rite, Washington, DC, USA

Biomorphism

Buildings designed by Foster and Partners
www.fosterandpartners.com

30 St Mary Axe, London, UK

Buildings designed by Eero Saarinen
www.greatbuildings.com/architects/Eero_Saarinen.html

Dulles Airport, Chantilly, Virginia, USA
Yale Hockey Rink, New Haven, Connecticut, USA
Gateway Arch, St. Louis, Missouri, USA
John Deere and Company, Moline, Illinois, USA
Kresge Auditorium, Cambridge, Massachusetts, USA
TWA, New York, USA

California new wave

George Ayars Cress Gallery of Art, University of Tennessee, USA
www.utc.edu

The collection includes work by April Greiman.

615 McCallie Avenue
Chattanooga
Tennessee 37403
USA

Constructivism

The Penny Guggenheim Collection, Italy
www.guggenheim-venice.it

Houses works by El Lissitzky, Kasimir Malevich, and Antoine Pevsner.

Palazzo Venier dei Leoni
701 Dorsoduro
30123 Venice
Italy

Tate Modern, UK
www.tate.org.uk/modern

Houses sculptures by Nuam Gabo including *Head No. 2*, *Red Cavern*, and *Linear Construction No.1*.

Bankside
London SE1 9TG
UK

Tate St Ives, UK
www.tate.org.uk/stives

The collection includes *Construction in Space with Crystalline Centre* by Naum Gabo.

Porthmeor Beach
St Ives
Cornwall TR26 1TG
UK

Smithsonian Cooper-Hewitt, National Design Museum, USA
ndm.si.edu

Includes *Half Teacup* by Ilia Grigorevich Chasnik and Kazimir Severinovich Malevich.

2 East 91st Street
New York
New York 10128
USA

Contemporary style

Fundació Joan Miró
www.bcn.fjmiro.es

The collection consists of paintings, sculptures, textiles, ceramics, and graphic works by Miró.

Parc de Montjuïc
08038 Barcelona
Spain

Tate Britain, UK
www.tate.org.uk/britain

The collection includes many works by Barbara Hepworth and Joan Miró.

Millbank
London SW1P 4RG
UK

Czech Cubism

Museu Picasso, Spain
www.museupicasso.bcn.es

Houses one of the most extensive collections of Picasso's work.

Montcada Street, 15–23
08003 Barcelona
Spain

The National Gallery in Prague, Czech Republic
www.ngprague.cz

The Cubist collection includes works of applied art, commercial graphics, photographs, architecture, period technology, and stage design.

Veletrzni Palace
Praha 7–Holesovice
Dukelskych hrdinu 47
Prague
Czech Republic

The National Technical Museum, Czech Republic
www.ntm.cz

Features the personal archives of distinguished Czech architects, covering the period from the mid-nineteenth century to the present. Materials include sketches, drawings and plans, photographs and negatives, and architectonic models. Includes Cubist works by Pavel Janak and Josef Gocar.

Národní technické muzeum
Kostelní 42
170 78 Praha 7
Czech Republic

Dadaism

Museum of Modern Art, USA
www.moma.org

The collection includes many works by Kurt Schwitters, including the cover of *Die Kathedrale*. Also included are paintings by Marcel Duchamp.

11 West 53 Street
New York
New York 10019-5497
USA

The Pompidou Centre, France
www.cnac-gp.fr

The collection includes paintings and sketches by Marcel Janco, paintings and poetry by Marcel Duchamp, *Collage A* by Johannes Baader, and paintings by Raoul Hausmann, Kurt Schwitters, and Max Ernst.

Place Georges Pompidou
75004 Paris
France

Tate Modern, UK
www.tate.org.uk/modern

The collection includes the sculptures *Fountain* and *Why Not Sneeze Rose Sélavy?* by Marcel Duchamp, and the painting *Les hommes n'en sauront rien* (*Men shall know nothing of this*) by Max Ernst.

Bankside
London SE1 9TG
UK

Deconstructivism

Buildings designed by Frank Gehry
www.greatbuildings.com/architects/Frank_Gehry.html

Experience Music Project, Seattle, Washington, USA
Gehry House, Santa Monica, California, USA
Guggenheim Museum Bilbao, Spain
Venice Beach House, at Venice, California, USA
Vitra Design Museum, Weil-am-Rhein, Germany

Buildings designed by Zaha Hadid
www.greatbuildings.com/architects/Zaha_Hadid.html

Hafenstrasse Building, Hamburg, Germany
Rosenthal Center for Contemporary Art, Cincinnati, USA
Tokio Cultural Center, Tokyo, Japan

Buildings designed by Bernard Tschumi
www.greatbuildings.com/architects/Bernard_Tschumi.html

Parc de la Villette, Paris, France
Vacheron Constantin Headquarters, Geneva, Switzerland

Deutsche Werkbund

Buildings designed by Walter Adolph Gropius
www.greatbuildings.com/architects/Walter_Gropius.html

Bauhaus, Dessau, Germany
Fagus Works, Alfred an der Leine, Germany
Gropius House, Lincoln, Massachusetts, USA
Harvard Graduate Center, Cambridge, Massachusetts, USA

The Museum of Modern Art, USA
www.moma.org

The collection includes work by Peter Behrens and Henri Van de Velde.

11 West 53 Street
New York
New York 10019-5497
USA

Buildings designed by Josef Franz Maria Olbrich
www.greatbuildings.com/architects/J._M._Olbrich.html

The Secession House, Vienna, Austria

Weissenhof Siedlung, Germany
www.weissenhofsiedlung.de

The housing estate designed by Deutsche Werkbund architects now receives 30,000 visitors per year.

Am Weissenhof 20
D-70191 Stuttgart
Germany

Esthetic movement

Alessi, Italy
www.alessi.com

Manufactures the designs of Christopher Dresser, and the works of many twentieth-century and contemporary designers.

The Charles Hosmer Morse Museum of American Art, USA
www.morsemuseum.org

Houses the most comprehensive collection of the works of Louis Comfort Tiffany in the world, a major collection of American art pottery, and representative collections of late nineteenth- and early twentieth-century American paintings, graphics, and the decorative arts.

445 North Park Avenue
Winter Park, Florida 32789
USA

The Fine Art Society, UK
www.victorianweb.org

Founded in 1876, the Society quickly established itself as one of London's leading art dealers. The front of its New Bond Street building was remodeled in 1881 by E. W. Godwin, and the interior by Faulkner Armitage.

148 New Bond Street
London W1S 2JT
UK

Memorial Art Gallery of the University of Rochester, USA
www.magart.rochester.edu

The collection includes many candlesticks, vases, and stained glass windows by Louis Comfort Tiffany.

500 University Avenue
Rochester
New York 14607-1415
USA

Futurism

The Estorick Collection, UK
www.estorickcollection.com

The Estorick Collection is Britain's only gallery devoted to modern Italian art. It is perhaps best known for its outstanding core of Futurist works. The collection includes many futurist paintings, drawings, and sculptures by various artists including Umberto Boccioni and Giacomo Balla.

39a Canonbury Square
London N1 2AN
UK

The Guggenhiem Museum, USA
www.guggenheim.org

The collection includes sculptures by Umberto Boccioni.

1071 Fifth Avenue at 89th Street
New York
New York 10128-0173
USA

Tate Liverpool, UK
www.tate.org.uk/liverpool

The collection includes the futurist painting *Abstract Speed – The Car has Passed* by Giacomo Balla.

Albert Dock
Liverpool
L3 4BB
UK

Tate Modern, UK
www.tate.org.uk/modern

The collection includes the futurist sculpture *Unique Forms of Continuity in Space* by Umberto Boccioni.

Bankside
London SE1 9TG
UK

High-tech

Buildings designed by Michael Hopkins
www.greatbuildings.com/architects/Michael_Hopkins.html

Bracken House, London, UK
Glyndebourne Opera House, East Sussex, UK
Hopkins House, London, UK
The Mound Stand, Lord's Cricket Ground, London, UK
Schlumberger Centre, Cambridge, UK

Buildings designed by Richard Rogers
www.greatbuildings.com/architects/Richard_Rogers.html

88 Wood Street, London, UK
Centre Pompidou, Paris, France
Lloyds Building, London, UK
Millenium Dome, London, UK
NMOS Factory, Newport, UK
PA Technology Center, Princeton, New Jersey, USA
PA Technology Center UK, Hertfordshire, UK
Palais des Droits de l'Homme, Strasbourg, France

International Style

Buildings designed by Charles Eames
www.greatbuildings.com/architects/Charles_Eames.html

Eames House, Pacific Palisades, California, USA

Buildings designed by Philip Cortelyou Johnson
www.greatbuildings.com/buildings/Johnson_House.html

Johnson House and The Glass House, New Caanan, Connecticut, USA

The Museum of Modern Art, USA
www.moma.org

The collection includes work by Ludwig Mies Van der Rohe and Charles Eames.

11 West 53 Street
New York
New York 10019-5497
USA

Japonisme

The Louvre Museum, France
www.louvre.fr

The collection features work by Henri de Toulouse-Lautrec.

34 quai Louvre
75001 Paris
France

The National Gallery, UK
www.nationalgallery.org.uk

The collection features many paintings by Henri de Toulouse-Lautrec.

Trafalgar Square
London WC2N 5DN
UK

Jugendstil

The Museum of Modern Art, USA
www.moma.org

The collection features designs by August Endell, Richard Riemerschmid, and Henri Van de Velde.

11 West 53 Street
New York
New York 10019-5497
USA

Buildings designed by Henri Van De Velde
www.greatbuildings.com/architects/Henry_van_
de_Velde.html

Bloemenwerf House, Uccle, near Brussels,
  Belgium
Werkbund Theater, Cologne, Germany

Memphis

The Design Museum, UK
www.designmuseum.org

The collection includes many designs by the
Memphis group.

Shad Thames
London
SE1 2YD
UK

The Pompidou Centre, France
www.cnac-gp.fr

Houses a large collection of designs by Michele
de Lucchi.

Place Georges Pompidou
75004 Paris
France

Minimalism

Buildings designed by Tadao Ando
www.greatbuildings.com/architects/Tadao_
Ando.html

Azuma House, Osaka, Japan
Children's Museum, Himeji, Hyogo, Japan
Modern Art Museum of Fort Worth,
  Texas, USA
Naoshima Contemporary Art Museum,
  Naoshima, Japan
Pulitzer Foundation for the Arts, St. Louis,
  Missouri, USA
Rokko Housing One, Rokko, Kobe, Japan
Rokko Housing Two, Rokko, Kobe, Japan

The Chinati Foundation, USA
www.chinati.org

Contemporary art museum based upon the
ideas of its founder, Donald Judd. Includes the
work of Donald Judd and Carl Andre.

Marfa
Texas
USA

Buildings designed by John Pawson
www.eyestorm.com/artist/John_Pawson_
biography.aspx

Pawson House, London, UK
Calvin Klein flagship store, New York, USA
Cathay Pacific first-class lounge, Chek Lap Kok
  airport, Hong Kong

The designs of Karim Rashid, USA
www.karimrashid.com

357 West 17th Street
New York
New York 10011
USA

Tate Modern, UK
www.tate.org.uk/modern

The collection features sculptures by Carl
Andre and Dan Flavin, and an original sketch
by Donald Judd.

Bankside
London SE1 9TG
UK

Mission style

**Buildings designed by Greene and Greene
(Charles Sumner and Henry Mather)**
www.greatbuildings.com/architects/Greene_and
_Greene.html

Blacker House, Pasadena, California, USA
D. L. James House, Carmel Highlands,
  California, USA
Gamble House, Pasadena, California, USA
N. Bentz House, Santa Barbara, California, USA

The Museum of Modern Art, USA
www.moma.org

The collection includes Settee by Gustav
Stickley.

11 West 53 Street
New York
New York 10019-5497
USA

Moderne

The Museum of Modern Art, USA
www.moma.org

The collection includes Adjustable Table by
Eileen Gray.

11 West 53 Street
New York
New York 10019-5497
USA

The Virginia Museum of Fine Arts, USA
www.vmfa.state.va.us

The collection includes Canoe Sofa by
Eileen Gray.

200 N. Boulevard
Richmond
Virginia 23220-4007
USA

Modernism

Buildings designed by Le Corbusier
www.greatbuildings.com/architects/Le_
Corbusier.html

Carpenter Center, Cambridge,
  Massachusetts, USA
Centre Le Corbusier, Zurich, Switzerland
Convent of La Tourette, Eveux-sur-Arbresle,
  near Lyon, France
House at Weissenhof, Stuttgart, Germany
Maisons Jaoul, Neuilly-sur-Seine, Paris, France
Museum at Ahmedabad, Ahmedabad, India
Notre-Dame-du-Haut, Ronchamp, France
Ozenfant House and Studio, Paris, France
Palace of Assembly, Chandigarh, India
Philips Pavilion, Brussels, Belgium
Shodan House, Ahmedabad, India
Unite d'Habitation, Marseilles, France
United Nations Headquarters, New York, USA
Villa Savoye, Poissy, France
Villa Stein, Garches, France
Weekend House, Paris, France

The Museum of Modern Art, USA
www.moma.org

The collection includes works by Ludwig
Mies Van Der Rohe, including paintings and
architectural sketches for building designs.
Also included are works by Peter Behrens.

11 West 53 Street
New York
New York 10019-5497
USA

Op art

The National Gallery of Art, USA
www.nga.gov

Features paintings by Larry Poons, Victor
Vasarely, and Bridget Riley.

National Mall
Between Third and Seventh Streets at
Constitution Avenue, NW
Washington, DC
USA

The Victoria and Albert Museum, UK
www.vam.ac.uk

The collection includes paintings by Bridget Riley.

Cromwell Road
South Kensington
London SW7 2RL
UK

Organic design

The Design Museum, UK
www.designmuseum.org

The collection includes work by Charles Rennie Mackintosh.

Shad Thames
London
SE1 2YD
UK

Herman Miller
www.hermanmiller.com

Manufactures designs by Alvar Aalto, Charles and Ray Eames, and many other modern designers.

Knoll Museum
www.knoll.com

Founded in 1938, Knoll has been recognized as a design leader worldwide. The Knoll Museum features work by Eero Saarinen and Alvar Aalto.

East Greenville
Pennsylvania
USA

Vitra Design Museum
www.vitra.com

For over 50 years, Vitra has been manufacturing the furniture of Charles and Ray Eames. The Vitra Design Museum holds one of the largest collections of modern furniture design in the world.

Buildings designed by Frank Lloyd Wright
www.greatbuildings.com/architects/Frank_Lloyd_Wright.html

Boomer Residence, Phoenix, Arizona, USA
Coonley House, Riverside, Illinois, USA
D. D. Martin House, Buffalo, New York, USA
Ennis House, Los Angeles, California, USA
Fallingwater, Ohiopyle, Pennsylvania, USA

Pop art

The Guggenheim Museum, USA
www.guggenheim.org

The collection includes paintings by Robert Rauschenberg, Roy Lichtenstein, and Andy Warhol.

1071 Fifth Avenue at 89th Street
New York
New York 10128-0173
USA

The Museum of Modern Art, USA
www.moma.org

The collection includes S&H Green Stamps, Jackie II, and Untitled from Marilyn Monroe by Andy Warhol.

11 West 53 Street
New York
New York 10019-5497
USA

Tate Liverpool, UK
www.tate.org.uk/liverpool

The collection includes works by Andy Warhol, Jasper Johns, and Robert Rauschenberg.

Albert Dock
Liverpool L3 4BB
UK

Tate Modern, UK
www.tate.org.uk/modern

The collection includes work by Roy Lichtenstein.

Bankside
London SE1 9TG
UK

Postindustrialism

The products of Ron Arad, UK
www.ronarad.com

62 Chalk Farm Road
London NW1 8AN
UK

The Design Museum, UK
www.designmuseum.org

The collection includes designs by Tom Dixon.

Shad Thames
London
SE1 2YD
UK

The products of Tom Dixon, UK
www.tomdixon.net

4 Northington Street
London WC1N 2JG
UK

The design work of Tom Dixon is included in the collections of Cappellini, Habitat, and Inflate.

Postmodernism

Buildings designed by Mario Botta
www.greatbuildings.com/architects/Mario_Botta.html

Residence in Riva San Vitale, Ticino, Switzerland
Residence in Cadenazzo, Switzerland
School in Morbio Inferiore, Switzerland
SFMOMA, San Francisco, California, USA

Buildings designed by Michael Graves
www.greatbuildings.com/architects/Michael_Graves.html

Alexander House, Princeton, New Jersey, USA
Crooks House, Fort Wayne, Indiana, USA
Hanselmann House, Fort Wayne, Indiana, USA
Portland Building, Portland, Oregon, USA

The Museum of Modern Art, USA
www.moma.org

The collection includes designs by Mario Botta, Shiro Kuramata, and Michael Graves.

11 West 53 Street
New York
New York 10019-5497
USA

Buildings designed by Aldo Rossi
www.greatbuildings.com/architects/Aldo_Rossi.html

Hotel Il Palazzo, Fukuoka, Japan
Il Teatro del Mondo, Venice, Italy

Rationalism

Buildings designed by Giuseppe Terragni
www.greatbuildings.com/architects/Giuseppe_Terragni.html

Casa del Fascio, Como, Italy

Scandinavian modern

Buildings designed by Alvar Aalto
www.greatbuildings.com/architects/Alvar_Aalto.html

Finnish Pavilion, New York, USA
Flats at Bremen, Neue Vahr district, Bremen, Germany
Flats at Hansaviertel, Hansaviertel, Berlin, Germany
House of Culture, Helsinki, Finland

Artek, Finland
www.artek.fi

Manufactures the furniture designs of Alvar Aalto.

The Danish Design Center, Denmark
www.ddc.dk

Features works by Arne Jacobsen.

HC Andersens Boulevard 27
DK 1553 Copenhagen
Denmark

The Design Museum, UK
www.designmuseum.org

The collection includes many designs by Arne
Jacobsen, Verner Panton, and Alvar Alto.

Shad Thames
London
SE1 2YD
UK

**The House of Copenhagen Collection / The
Museum of Modern Art**, USA
www.moma.org

Features designs by Arne Jacobsen, Hans
Wegner, and Bruno Mathsson.

11 West 53 Street
New York
New York 10019-5497
USA

Iittala, Finland
www.iittala.com

Manufactures glassware designs by Aino and
Alvar Aalto.

IKEA, Sweden
www.ikea.com

Manufactures Scandinavian modern–style
furniture and accessories.

Secession

**Buildings designed by Josef Franz Maria
Hoffmann**
www.greatbuildings.com/architects/Josef_
Hoffmann.html

Stoclet Palace, Brussels, Belgium

The Toyota Municipal Museum of Art, Japan
www.museum.toyota.aichi.jp

The collection includes Armchair by Koloman
Moser.

5-1 Kozakahonmachi8–chome
Toyota Aichi 471-0034
Japan

Space age

The Metropolitan Museum of Art, USA
www.metmuseum.org

The collection includes designs by Richard
Sapper.

1000 Fifth Avenue at 82nd Street
New York
New York 10028-0198
USA

The Museum of Modern Art, USA
www.moma.org

The collection includes designs by Richard
Sapper and Marco Zanuso Sr.

11 West 53 Street
New York
New York 10019-5497
USA

de Stijl

The Centraal Museum, the Netherlands
www.centraalmuseum.nl

The modern art collection provides a broad
survey of Dutch visual art of the twentieth
century, featuring work by Theo Van Doesburg,
and the world's largest collection of designs by
Gerrit Thomas Rietveld.

Nicolaaskerkhof 10
Utrecht
The Netherlands

The Guggenheim Museum, USA
www.guggenheim.org

The collection includes many paintings by Piet
Mondrian.

1071 Fifth Avenue at 89th Street
New York
New York 10128-0173
USA

The Museum of Modern Art, USA
www.moma.org

The collection includes work by Piet Mondrian,
Gerrit Thomas Rietveld, and Theo Van Doesburg.

11 West 53 Street
New York
New York 10019-5497
USA

Buildings designed by Gerrit Thomas Rietveld
www.galinsky.com/buildings/schroder

The Rietveld Schroder House, Utrecht, the
Netherlands

Streamlining

The Pompidou Centre, France
www.cnac-gp.fr

The collection includes many designs by
Raymond Fernand Loewy, Norman Bel Geddes,
and Walter Dorwin Teague.

Place Georges Pompidou
75004 Paris
France

**Smithsonian Cooper-Hewitt, National Design
Museum**, USA
ndm.si.edu

The archives contain the papers, promotional
materials, clippings, and photographs
of designers and design firms including
Henry Dreyfuss.

2 East 91st Street
New York
New York 10128
USA

Surrealism

The Museum of Modern Art, USA
www.moma.org

Includes *The Persistence of Memory* by Salvador
Dali and *Les Chants de Maldoror* by Comte de
Lautréamont.

11 West 53 Street
New York
New York 10019-5497
USA

The Peggy Guggenheim Collection, Italy
www.guggenheim-venice.it

The collection includes photographs by Man
Ray and paintings by Salvador Dali.

Palazzo Venier dei Leoni
701 Dorsoduro
30123 Venice
Italy

The Pompidou Centre, France
www.cnac-gp.fr

The collection includes many works by Salvador
Dali, Paul Nash, and Man Ray.

Place Georges Pompidou
75004 Paris
France

Tate Modern, UK
www.tate.org.uk/modern

The collection includes *Lobster Telephone*, *Metamorphosis of Narcissus*, and *Mountain Lake* by Salvador Dali.

Bankside
London SE1 9TG
UK

Vorticism

Tate Britain, UK
www.tate.org.uk/britain

The collection includes many sculptures by Jacob Epstein and Henri Gaudier-Brzeska.

Millbank
London SW1P 4RG
UK

The Walker Gallery, UK
www.liverpoolmuseums.org.uk/walker

The collection includes work by Henri Gaudier-Breska.

William Brown Street
Liverpool
L3 8EL
UK

Wiener Werkstätte

Buildings designed by Josef Franz Maria Hoffmann
www.greatbuildings.com/architects/Josef_Hoffmann.html

Moser House, Vienna, Austria

The Museum of Modern Art, USA
www.moma.org

The collection includes work by Otto Prütscher, Koloman Moser, and Josef Franz Maria Hoffmann.

11 West 53 Street
New York
New York 10019-5497
USA

Further reading

General

Albrecht, Donald; Lupton, Ellen; Holt, Steven Skov. *Design Culture Now*. Laurence King Publishing, 2000

Albus, Volker, et al. *Icons of Design: The 20th Century*. Prestel Publishing Ltd, 2004

Antonelli, Paola. *Objects of Design from The Museum of Modern Art*. The Museum of Modern Art, 2003

Bocola, Sandro. *The Art of Modernism*. Prestel Publishing Ltd, 1999

Byars, Mel. *The Design Encyclopaedia*. Laurence King Publishing, 2004

Byars, Mel. *100 Designs/100 Years: Innovative Designs of the 20th Century*. RotoVision SA, 1999

Cirker, Hayward and Blanche. *The Golden Age of the Poster*. Dover Publications, 1971

Conran, Terence; Fraser, Max. *Designers on Design*. Conran Octopus, 2004

Dixon, Tom (ed.); Hudson, Jennifer. *The International Design Yearbook 2004*. Laurence King Publishing, 2004

Dormer, Peter. *Design Since 1945*. Thames & Hudson, 1993

Eggers, D. (illustrator). *Area*. Phaidon Press, 2003

Fiell, Charlotte and Peter. *Design of the 20th Century*. Taschen, 1999

Fiell, Charlotte and Peter. *Designing the 21st Century*. Taschen, 2001

Fiell, Charlotte and Peter. *Graphic Design for the 21st Century*. Taschen, 2003

Gombrich, E. H. *The Story of Art*. Phaidon Press, 1995

Gorman, Carma (ed.). *The Industrial Design Reader*. Allworth Press, 2003

Hiesinger, Kathryn; Marcus, George. *Landmarks of Twentieth Century Design*. Abbeville Press, 1993

Hillier, Bevis. *The Style of the Century*. Herbert Press, 1998

Johnson, Michael, et al. *REWIND: Forty Years of Design and Advertising*. Phaidon Press, 2002

Julier, Guy. *The Thames & Hudson Dictionary of Design Since 1900*. Thames & Hudson, 1993

Lupton, Ellen; Miller, Abbot J. *Design Writing Research*. Phaidon Press, 1999

Meggs, Philip. *A History of Graphic Design (3rd Edition)*. John Wiley & Sons, 1998

Pile, John. *The Dictionary of 20th Century Design*. Da Capo Press, 1994

Poynor, Rick (ed.). *Communicate: Independent British Graphic Design since the Sixties*. Laurence King Publishing, 2004

Raizman, David. *History of Modern Design*. Laurence King Publishing, 2004

Riley, Noel; Bayer, Patricia. *The Elements of Design*. Mitchell Beazley, 2002

Sparke, Penny. *Design Source Book*. Chartwell Books, 1986

Sparke, Penny. *A Century of Design: Design Pioneers of the 20th Century*. Mitchel Beazley, 1999

Antidesign

Cook, Peter (ed.); Webb, Michael (introduction). *Archigram*. Princeton Architectural Press, 1999

Lang, Peter; Menking, William. *Superstudio: A Life Without Objects*. Skira Editore, 2003

Art deco

Bayer, Patricia. *Art Deco Interiors: Decoration and Design Classics of the 1920s and 1930s*. Thames & Hudson, 1998

Delhaye, Jean. *Art Deco Posters and Graphics*. Rizzoli International Publications, 1978

Striner, Richard. *Art Deco*. Abbeville Press, 1994

Art nouveau

Amaya, Mario. *Art Nouveau*. Schoken Books, 1985

Bliss, Douglas. *Charles Rennie Mackintosh and Glasgow School of Art*. Glasgow School of Art, 1979

Duncan, Alistair. *Art Nouveau*. Thames & Hudson, 1994

Gerhardus, Maly. *Symbolism and Art Nouveau*. Phaidon Press, 1979

Selz, Peter; Constantine, Mildred. *Art Nouveau Art and Design at the Turn of the Century*. The Museum of Modern Art, 1959

Arts and Crafts movement

Cumming, Elizabeth; Kaplan, Wendy. *The Arts and Crafts Movement*. Thames & Hudson, 1991

Naylor, Gillian. *The Arts and Crafts Movement*. Trefoil Books, 1971

Pevsner, Nikolaus. *Pioneers of Modern Design*. Penguin Books, 1975

Bauhaus

Carmel-Arthur, Judith. *Bauhaus*. Carlton Books, 2000

Smock, William. *Bauhaus Ideal, Then and Now: An Illustrated Guide to Modernist Design and Its Legacy*. Academy Chicago Publications, 2004

Whitford, Frank. *The Bauhaus: Masters and Students By Themselves*. Conran Octopus, 1993

Wingler, Hans. *The Bauhaus*. The MIT Press, 1969

Beaux-arts

Drexler, A. *The Architecture of the Ecole Des Beaux-Arts*. Secker & Warburg, 1977

Steffensen, Ingrid. *The New York Public Library: A Beaux-Arts Landmark*. Scala Editions, 2004

Biomorphism

Aldersey-Williams, Hugh. *Zoomorphic: New Animal Architecture*. Laurence King Publishing, 2003

Feuerstein, Gunther. *Biomorphic Architecture: Menschenund Tiergestalten in Der Architektur/ Human and Animal Forms in Architecture*. Edition Axel Menges GmbH, 2002

California New Wave

Farrelly, Liz. *April Greiman: Invention and Experiment*. Thames & Hudson, 1998

Greiman, April. *Hybrid Imagery: The Fusion of Technology and Graphic Design*. Phaidon Press, 1990

Constructivism

Bann, Stephen. *The Tradition of Constructivism*. Da Capo Press, Reprint Edition 1990

Lodder, Christina. *Russian Constructivism*. Yale University Press, 1983

Rickey, George. *Constructivism: Origins and Evolution*. George Braziller Inc., Revised Edition 1995

Contemporary style

Kirkham, Pat. *Charles and Ray Eames: Designers of the Twentieth Century*. The MIT Press, Reprint Edition 1998

Mink, Janis. *Joan Miro: 1893–1983*. Taschen, 2000

Czech Cubism

Cooper, Philip. *Cubism*. Phaidon Press, 1995

Margolius, Ivan. *Cubism in Architecture and the Applied Arts*. David & Charles, 1979

Dadaism

Blackwell, Lewis; Carson, David. *The End of Print: The Graphic Design of David Carson*. Chronicle Books, 1995

Blackwell, Lewis. *Edward Fella: Letters on America*. Princeton Architectural Press, 2000

Hall, Peter. *Sagmeister: Made You Look*. Booth-Clibborn Editions, 2002

L'Ecotais, Emmanuelle. *The Dada Spirit*. Editions Assouline, 2003

Deconstructivism

Giusti, Gordana Fontana; Schumacher, Patrick. *Zaha Hadid: The Complete Works*. Thames & Hudson, 2004

Johnson, Philip. *Deconstructivist Architecture*. The Museum of Modern Art, 1988

Libeskind, Daniel. *Breaking Ground: Adventures in Life and Architecture*. John Murray, 2004

Deutsche Werkbund

Burckhardt, L. (ed.); Sanders, P. (translator). *The Werkbund: Studies in the History and Ideology of the Deutscher Werkbund, 1907–1933*. The Design Council, 1980

Esthetic movement

Baal-Teshuva, Jacob. *Tiffany*. Taschen, 2001

Loring, John. *Louis Comfort Tiffany at Tiffany & Co*. Harry N. Abrams Inc., 2002

Whiteway, Michael. *Christopher Dresser 1834-1904*. Skira, 2002

Whiteway, Michael (ed.). *Christopher Dresser: A Design Revolution*. V&A Publications, 2004

Futurism

Hulten, Karl (ed.). *Futurism and Futurisms.* Abbeville Press, 1986

Kozloff, Max. *Cubism/Futurism.* Charter House, 1973

Marinetti, Filippo Tommaso; Flint R. W. (ed.). *Marinetti: Selected Writings.* Farrar, Straus and Giroux, 1971

High-tech

Slessor, Catherine. *Eco-tech: Sustainable Architecture and High Technology.* Thames & Hudson, 2001

International Style

Rams, Dieter. *Design: Dieter Rams.* Gerhardt Verlag, 1981

Japonisme

Lambourne, Lionel. *Japonisme: Cultural Crossings between Japan and the West.* Phaidon Press, 2005

Meech, Julia, et al. *Japonisme Comes to America.* Harry N. Abrams, Inc., 1990

Wichmann, Siegfried. *Japonisme: The Japanese Influence on Western Art Since 1958.* Thames & Hudson, 1999

Wiedermann, Julius; Kozak, Gisela. *Japanese Graphics Now!.* Taschen, 2003

Various. *Japanese Design: Modern Approaches to Traditional Elements (Vol I).* Gingko Press, 2001

Jugendstil

Blaschke , Bertha; Lipschitz, Luise. *Architecture in Vienna 1850 to 1930: Historicism, Jugendstil, New Realism.* Springer-Verlag New York Inc., 2003

Brinckmann, Justus. *Jugendstil.* Havenberg, 1983

Krekel-Aalberse, Annalies. *Silver: Jugendstil and Art Deco 1880–1940.* Arnoldsche Verlaganstalt GmbH, 2001

Minimalism

Castillo, Encarna. *Minimalism Designsource.* HarperCollins Publishers, 2004

Jodidio, Philip. *Tadao Ando.* Taschen, 2004

Meyer, James. *Minimalism: Art and Polemics in the Sixties.* Yale University Press, 2004

Pawson, James. *Minimum.* Phaidon Press, 1998

Mission style

Cathers, David. *Furniture of the American Arts and Crafts Movements: Stickley and Roycroft Mission Oak.* New Amer Library Trade, 1983

Roycrofters. *Roycroft Furniture Catalog, 1906.* Dover Publications, 1994

Moderne

Duncan, Alastair. *American Art Deco.* Thames & Hudson, 1999

Weber, E. *Art Deco in America.* Hacker Art Books, 1985

Modernism

Behrens, Peter, et al. *Steel and Stone: Constructive Concepts by Peter Behrens and Mies van der Rohe.* Lars Muller Publishers, 2002

Cohen, Jean-Louis. *Le Corbusier.* Taschen, 2005

Cuito, Aurora (ed.). *Mies van der Rohe.* Te Neues Publishing Company, 2002

Frampton, Kenneth. *Le Corbusier: Architect of the Twentieth Century.* Harry N. Abrams Inc., 2002

Op art

Follin, Frances. *Embodied Visions: Bridget Riley, Op Art and the Sixties.* Thames & Hudson, 2004

Greenberg, Cara. *Op to Pop: Furniture of the 1960s.* Little, Brown and Company, 1999

Moorhouse, Paul (ed.). *Bridget Riley.* Tate Publishing, 2003

Organic design

Antonelli, Pada; Lovegrove, Ross. *Supernatural: The Work of Ross Lovegrove.* Phaidon Press, 2004

Pearson, David. *New Organic Architecture: The Breaking Wave.* University of California Press, 2001

Pop art

Honnef, Klaus. *Warhol.* Taschen, 2000

Mink, Janis. *Lichtenstein.* Taschen, 2000

James, Jamie. *Pop Art.* Phaidon Press, 1996

Livingstone, Marco. *Pop Art: A Continuing History.* Thames & Hudson, 2000

Postindustrialism

Collins, Michael (ed.). *Tom Dixon.* Phaidon Press, 1991

Sudjic, Deyan. *Ron Arad.* Laurence King Publishing, 2001

Postmodernism

Alessi, Alberto. *The Dream Factory: Alessi Since 1921.* Konemann, 1998

Bertens, Hans. *The Idea of the Postmodern.* Routledge, 1995

Poynor, Rick. *Design Without Boundaries.* Booth-Clibborn Editions, 1998

Rationalism

Schumacher, Thomas L. *Surface–Symbol: Giuseppe Terragni and the Architecture of Italian Rationalism.* Princeton Architectural Press, 1991

Scandinavian modern

Fiell, Charlotte and Peter. *Scandinavian Design.* Taschen, 2002

Ellison, Michael. *Scandinavian Modern Furnishings 1930-1973: Designed for Life.* Schiffer Publishing, 2002

Fleig, Karl; Aalto, Elissa (eds). *Alvar Aalto: Complete Works.* Birkhauser Verlag AG, 1990

Secession

Fliedl, Gottfried. *100 Years of the Vienna Secession.* Hatje Cantz, 1997

Fleck, Robert. *Vienna Secession 1898-1998: The Century of Artistic Freedom.* Prestel Publishing Ltd., 1998

Space Age

Rawsthorn, Alice, et al. *Marc Newson.* Booth-Clibborn Editions, 1999

Topham, Sean. *Where's My Space Age: The Rise and Fall of Futuristic Design.* Prestel Publishing Ltd., 2003

de Stijl

Friedman, Mildred. *De Stijl: 1917-1931 Visions of Utopia.* Abbeville Press, 1982

Overy, Paul. *De Stijl.* Thames & Hudson, 1991

Streamlining

Arceneaux, Marc. *Streamline: Art and Design of the Forties.* Troubador Press, 1975

Lichtenstein, Claude; Engler, Franz. *Streamlined: A Metaphor for Progress: The Esthetics of Minimized Drag.* Lars Muller Publishers, 1994

Loewy, Raymond. *Industrial Design.* Overlook Press, 1979

Surrealism

Duchamp, Marcel. *Duchamp Cameo.* Harry N. Abrams Inc., 1996

Hubert, Renee Riese. *Surrealism and the Book.* University of California Press, Reprint Edition 1992

Nadeau, Maurice. *The History of Surrealism.* Harvard University Press, 1989

Swiss school

Gerstner, Karl; Kutler, Marcus. *Die Neue Grafik/ The New Graphic Art.* Hastings House, 1959

Kusters, Christian; King, Emily. *Restart: New Systems in Graphic Design.* Thames & Hudson, 2001

Margadant, Bruno. *The Swiss Poster: 1900-1983.* Birkhäuser Verlag, 1993

Müller, Lars (ed.). *Josef Müller Brockmann: Pioneer of Swiss Graphic Design.* Verlag Lars Müller, 1996

Vorticism

Beckett, Jane; Edwards, Paul (ed.). *Blast: Vorticism, 1914–1918.* Ashgate, 2000

Black, Jonathan (ed.). *Blasting the Future: Vorticism and the Avant-Garde in Britain 1910–20.* Philip Wilson Publishers, 2004

Wiener Werkstätte

Fahr-Becker, Gabriele. *Wiener Werkstätte: 1903-1932.* Taschen, 2003

Neuwirth, Waltraud. *Wiener Werkstätte: Avantgarde, Art Deco, Industrial Design.* Neuwirth, 1984

Picture credits

The publishers would like to thank the following sources for their kind permission to reproduce their images in this book

Antidesign

Cactus coat rack, designed by Guido Drocco and Franco Mello of 'Studio 65', 1972 (painted polyurethane foam), 'Bocca' sofa designed by 'Studio 65', 1972 and 'Gherpe' Shrimp light designed by 'Superstudio' (plastic), Studio 65 & Superstudio (20th Century) / Private Collection, Bonhams, London, UK / www.bridgeman.co.uk

VIP chair. Marcel Wanders for Moooi (www.moooi.com)

Art deco

Duck money box. Photo: Luke Herriott

Wooden clock. Photo: Luke Herriott

Fashion plate. Worth evening dress, fashion plate from Gazette du Bon Ton, 1925 (litho), Barbier, Georges (1882–1932) / Bibliotheque des Arts Decoratifs, Paris, France, Archives Charmet / www.bridgeman.co.uk

Chrysler building. Photo: Lindy Dunlop

De La Warr Pavilion. Photo: Lindy Dunlop

Peach-glass table. Made by James Clark Ltd. of London, 1930s (glass & wood), English School, (20th century) / Royal Pavilion, Libraries & Museums, Brighton & Hove / www.bridgeman.co.uk

RCA Victor Special, John Vassos. V&A Images/Victoria and Albert Museum

Marine Court. Photo: Luke Herriott

Star Cinema, off York Road, Leeds, 11th May 1938 (b/w photo), English Photographer, (20th century) / © Leeds Library and Information Service, Leeds, UK / www.bridgeman.co.uk

Crystal Palace Ball chandelier. Courtesy of Tom Dixon

Art nouveau

Sagrada Familia. Photos: Lindy Dunlop

Interior of the Horta House. The Staircase, 1898–1901 (photo), Horta, Victor (1861–1947) / Horta House, Rue Americaine, Brussels, Belgium, Paul Maeyaert / www.bridgeman.co.uk © DACS 2005

Abbesses Metro Station. Photo: April Sankey

Parc Guell. Photo: Lindy Dunlop

Plate 54. V&A Images/Victoria and Albert Museum

Electric fan. Photo: Luke Herriott

Gal lip balm. Photo: Luke Herriott. Courtesy of Perfumeria Gal www.gal.es

Casa Batllo. Photo: Lindy Dunlop

Casa Mila. Photo: Lindy Dunlop

Pewter teapot. Photo: Luke Herriott

Arts and Crafts movement

Writing desk by A. H. Mackmurdo, c. 1886, William Morris Gallery, Walthamstow, UK / Bridgeman Art Library

Net Ceiling paper. Photo: Luke Herriott

Enameled silverwork, 1901–1903 (mixed media), Ashbee, Charles Robert (1863-1942) /Cheltenham Art Gallery & Museums, Gloucestershire, UK/Bridgeman Art Library

Decanter with silver mounts, c. 1904–1905, Ashbee, Charles Robert (1863-1942)/Victoria and Albert Museum, London, UK/Bridgeman Art Library

Sponge vase. Marcel Wanders for Moooi. www.moooi.com

Hotel Pattee guest services directory and logo. Courtesy of Sayles Graphic Design. www.saylesdesign.com

Crocheted lampshade. Design by electricwig, produced by Trico International. Photo: Tas Kyprianou

Swallows wallpaper. Photo: Keith Stephenson. Courtesy of Absolute Zero°. www.absolutezerodegrees.com

Bauhaus

Armchair designed for the Bauhaus by Marcel Breuer, oak lath and linen, 1924, Christie's Images, London, UK / www.bridgeman.co.uk

Staatliches Bauhaus, 1995, built 1925–1926 (photo), German School, (20th century) / Dessau, Germany / www.bridgeman.co.uk

Cover of issue number 7 of Offset Buch und Werbekunst 1926, Schmidt, Joost (1893–1948) / Private Collection / www.bridgeman.co.uk © DACS 2005

Bauhaus Design (color litho), German School, (20th century) / Private Collection, The Stapleton Collection / www.bridgeman.co.uk

Barcelona chair. Photo: Luke Herriott. Courtesy of Nicole Kemble

Tykho radios, Marc Berthier. Courtesy of Lexon (www.lexon-design.com)

Apple iMacs. Courtesy of Apple Computer, Inc.

Lift 01 poster. Design and Art Direction Vince Frost

CD Player, Naoto Fukasawa. Courtesy of Muji. www.muji.co.uk Tel: +44 (0)20 7323 2208

La Valise. Ronan & Erwan Bouroullec © Paul Tahon

Beaux-arts

Detail of the facade of the New York Public Library, opened in 1911 (photo), Carrere, John (1858-1911) and Hastings, Thomas (1860-1929) / Fifth Avenue, Manhattan, New York City, USA / www.bridgeman.co.uk

Biomorphism

Eames chairs: Clockwise from Top: DAR (Dining Armchair Rod); RAR (Rocker Base Armchair); DAR (Dining and Desk Chair); A Production 'X' Base DAX (Dining and Desk Chair), all designed by Eames, Charles (1907–1970) and Ray (1912–1988), 1953 (fiberglass, metal, and wood), Eames, Charles (1907–1980) and Ray (1912–1988) / Private Collection, Bonhams, London, UK / www.bridgeman.co.uk

30 St Mary Axe (top and bottom right). Photos: J. A. Dunlop

30 St Mary Axe (bottom left). Photo: Grant Smith. Courtesy of Foster and Partners

California new wave

Identity and business cards for Vertigo. Design: April Greiman. Courtesy of April Greiman, Made in Space

Cal Arts View book. Design: April Greiman. Courtesy of April Greiman, Made in Space

China Club identity. Design: April Greiman Signage: April Greiman & Jayme Odgers Courtesy of April Greiman, Made in Space

Cal Arts catalog. Design: April Greiman Photo: Jayme Odgers Courtesy of April Greiman, Made in Space

Constructivism

Ministry of the Interior, Cuba. Photo: April Sankey

3-D Objects. Dextro 2001

Contemporary style

Red and Black on a Blue Background, Miro, Joan (1893–1983) / Christie's Images, London, UK / www.bridgeman.co.uk © Successio Miro, DACS, 2005

A Cross Patch Textile, designed by Ray Eames (1912–1988), 1945 (hand printed silk-screen mounted on cloth), Eames, Ray (1912–88) / Private Collection, Bonhams, London, UK / www.bridgeman.co.uk

Ball clock, George Nelson. Photo: Andreas Sutterlin. Courtesy of Vitra (www.vitra.com) and Herman Miller (www.hermanmiller.com)

Hang it All, Charles and Ray Eames. Available from www.twentytwentyone.com

Jason chair, Carl Jacobs. Photo: Luke Herriott

Alto Writing Desk. Norway Says

Prototype chair, Egg Designs. Design: Greg and Roche Dry, Egg Design 2004

Czech Cubism

Prague building. Photo: Lindy Dunlop

The Studio Corner dish (ceramic), Picasso, Pablo (1881–1973) / Pushkin Museum, Moscow, Russia / www.bridgeman.co.uk © Succession Picasso/DACS 2005

Clarice Cliff. (LtoR) A pair of Oranges and Lemons pattern vases, a Cubist pattern Archaic series vase, a Farmhouse pattern vase,

a pair of Sunburst pattern vases, a Castellated Circle (Green Circle) vase, a geometrical design conical bowl, a Picasso Flower (orange colorway) pattern Stamford Jardiniere and a geometrical design conical bowl by Clarice Cliff (1899–1972) (ceramic) / Private Collection, Bonhams, London, UK / www.bridgeman.co.uk
Clarice Cliff is a registered trademark of Josiah Wedgwood & Sons Limited, Barlaston, Stoke-on-Trent, England
America's Answer! Production poster, Jean Carlu © (2005) The Museum of Modern Art/Scala, Florence © ADAGP, Paris and DACS, London 2005
Louvre Pyramide. Photo: April Sankey
AIGA Wisconsin poster, Jim Lasser. Courtesy of AIGA

Dadaism
Front cover of Bulletin Dada No. 6, February 1920 (color litho), Duchamp, Marcel (1887–1968) / Galleria Pictogramma, Rome, Italy / www.bridgeman.co.uk © Succession Marcel Duchamp/ADAGP, Paris and DACS, London 2005
Collage M2 439, 1922, Schwitters, Kurt (1887–1948) / Marlborough Fine Arts, London, UK / www.bridgeman.co.uk © DACS 2005
AIGA Biennial Conference poster, Stefan Sagmeister © Sagmeister Inc., New York
Treetrunk bench. Droog Design, Jurgen Bey Photo: Marsel Loermans

Deconstructivism
Radio in a Bag, Daniel Weil. V&A Images/Victoria and Albert Museum
The Jewish Museum © Jüdisches Museum Berlin. Photo: Jens Ziehe, Berlin
Exterior, facade. The Richard B. Fisher Center for the Performing Arts at Bard College. Photo © Peter Aaron/Esto
Exterior, detail. The Richard B. Fisher Center for the Performing Arts at Bard College. Photo © Peter Maus/Esto

Deutsche Werkbund
Display of Tropon goods, from Deutsche Werkbund Jahrbuch. V&A Images/Victoria and Albert Museum
Deutsche Werkbund Ausstellung poster, Peter Behrens. V&A Images/Victoria and Albert Museum © DACS 2005
Apartment block, Ludwig Mies van der Rohe. Courtesy of the Weissenhofseidlung. www.weissenhofseidlung.de Photo: Jörn Vogt
MR Side Chair, Ludwig Mies van der Rohe. Courtesy of Knoll International Ltd. www.knoll.com

Esthetic movement
House and Studio for F. Miles Esq, Chelsea. Engraved by C. P. Edwards, Godwin, Edward William (1833–1886) Private Collection, The Stapleton Collection / www.bridgeman.co.uk
Toast rack. "90029" design Christopher Dresser, 1991 (1878) Courtesy of Alessi
An esthetic interior showing works by William Morris (1834–1896) and William de Morgan (1839–1917), English School (nineteenth century)/The Fine Art Society, London, UK/Bridgeman Art Library
My Lady's Chamber. Frontispiece to The House Beautiful by Clarence Cook, published New York, 1881 (color litho), Crane, Walter (1845–1915) / Private Collection, The Stapleton Collection / www.bridgeman.co.uk
The Yellow Book. V&A Images/Victoria and Albert Museum
Royalton bar stool. Courtesy of Philippe Starck
Juicy Salif. Photo: Luke Herriott. Courtesy of Lindy Dunlop.

Futurism
Zang Tumb Tumb. Book cover for Zang Tumb Tumb, written and designed by F. T. Marinetti (1876–1944) 1914, Marinetti, F. T. (1876–1944) / Private Collection / www.bridgeman.co.uk © DACS 2005
Electric Power Plant. 1914 (pen & ink, pencil, on paper), Sant'Elia, Antonio (1888–1916) / Private Collection, Milan, Italy / Accademia Italiana, London / Bridgeman Art Library
War Party tapestry, Fortunato Depero. War Party (tapestry), Depero, Fortunato (20th century) / Galleria Nazionale d'Arte Moderna, Rome, Italy, Alinari / www.bridgeman.co.uk © DACS 2005
MAXXI, Center of Contemporary Arts, Rome. Courtesy of Zaha Hadid Architects
Shift bookend. Sara de Bondt for "Shift! Re-Appropriated"

High-tech
Lloyds of London. Photos: J. A. Dunlop
Aeron chair, Donald T. Chadwick. Photo: Robert Z. Brandt
Apple Pro Mouse. Courtesy of Apple Computer, Inc.
"Blow up" design Fratelli Campana, 2004. Courtesy of Alessi
Rolling Bridge. Thomas Heatherwick Studio Photo: Steve Speller

International Style
Cabinet with four drawers, Charles Eames, 1940 © (2005) The Museum of Modern Art/Scala, Florence
The Citicorp Centre, designed by Hugh Stubbins & Associates, 1978 and the Seagram Building, designed by Miles van der Rohe and Philip Johnson, 1954–1958 / New York City, New York, USA, Roger Last / www.bridgeman.co.uk

Roberts radio. Photo: Luke Herriott. Courtesy of Bob Phipps
Multipurpose Kitchen Machine, 1957, Braun AG (Frankfurt) © (2005) The Museum of Modern Art/Scala, Florence
Toio Floor Lamps, 1962 (Flos S.p.A., Brescia, Italy), Castiglioni, Achille (b. 1918) © (2005) The Museum of Modern Art/Scala, Florence
Berlin buildings. Photo: Luke Herriott
Custom Greetings Cards. Courtesy of Daniel Eatock. www.eatock.com

Japonisme
Dummy vase. Decorated in imitation of cloisonne, Minton & Co, c. 1870 (porcelain), Dresser, Christopher (1834–1904) / Private Collection, The Fine Art Society, London, UK / www.bridgeman.co.uk
Teapot. V&A Images/Victoria and Albert Museum
Side Chair. Herter Brothers Company, c. 1876–1879 (cherry, gilt, and upholstery), Herter, Christian (1839–1883) and Gustave (1830–1898) / © Museum of Fine Arts, Houston, Texas, USA. Funds provided by the Stella H. and Arch S. Rowan Foundation / www.bridgeman.co.uk
Compagnie Francaise des Chocolats et des Thes. Reproduction of a Poster Advertising the French Company of Chocolate and Tea (litho), Steinlen, Theophile Alexandre (1859–1923) / Private Collection, The Stapleton Collection / www.bridgeman.co.uk
Shu Uemura cleansing oils. Designed by Ai Yamaguchi

Jugendstil
Lady's Bureau. c. 1897 (wood), van de Velde, Henry (1863–1957) / Musee d'Orsay, Paris, France / www.bridgeman.co.uk
Tropon. 1898 (litho), van de Velde, Henry (1863–1957) / Calmann & King, London, UK / www.bridgeman.co.uk
Riga buildings. Photos: Lindy Dunlop
Thinking Man's Chair. 1986, Cappellini. Photo: James Mortimer

Memphis
Casablanca sideboard, Ettore Sottsass. V&A Images/Victoria and Albert Museum
Kariba fruit bowl, Memphis. V&A Images/Victoria and Albert Museum
Installation in the Coop Himmelb(l)au pavilion, 1994 (mixed media), Lichtenstein, Roy (1923–1997) & Lucchi, Michele de (b. 1951) / Gröningen, the Netherlands, Wolfgang Neeb / www.bridgeman.co.uk © The Estate of Roy Lichtenstein/DACS 2005
Kozmos Blocks, Karim Rashid. Courtesy of Karim Rashid Inc.

Minimalism
Primate Kneeling Stool, 1970 (Zanotta, S.p.A., Italy), Castiglioni, Achille (b. 1918) © (2005) The Museum of Modern Art/Scala, Florence
Kissing salt and pepper shakers, Karim Rashid. Karim Rashid Inc. 2005
UMBRA Garbino, Karim Rashid. Karim Rashid Inc. 2005
Bend Chair. Photography Pelle Wahlgren/Swedese Möbler AB
Teatro Armani, Milan. Richard Bryant/arcaid.co.uk
iPod Shuffle. Courtesy of Apple Computer, Inc.

Mission style
Desk Chair, Roycroft Shop. c. 1905–1912 (oak wood), American School, (20th century) / © Museum of Fine Arts, Houston, Texas, USA, Funds provided by the Alice Pratt Brown Museum Fund / www.bridgeman.co.uk
Trico Café furniture, Michael Marriott. Courtesy of Michael Marriott
Double Decker table. Marcel Wanders for Moooi (www.moooi.com)

Moderne
Aram Designers Adjustable Table, Eileen Gray © (2005) The Museum of Modern Art/Scala, Florence
Mirror Ball pendant. Courtesy of Tom Dixon

Modernism
The Fagus Shoe Factory. Designed by Walter Gropius (1883–1969) and Adolph Meyer, 1910–1911 / Alfeld-an-der-Leine, Germany / www.bridgeman.co.uk
Table lamp, William Wagenfeld. V&A Images/Victoria and Albert Museum © DACS 2005
Laccio tables, Marcel Breuer. Courtesy of Knoll International Ltd.
MR Side chair, Ludwig Mies van der Rohe. Courtesy of Knoll International Ltd. www.knoll.com
The German Pavilion at the International Exposition in Barcelona. Designed by Ludwig Mies van der Rohe (1886–1969) 1929 Barcelona, Spain / www.bridgeman.co.uk
Pontresina Engadin poster, Herbert Matter © (2005) The Museum of Modern Art/Scala, Florence
Missed Day Bed, Michael Marriott. Courtesy of Michael Marriott
Second phone, Sam Hecht for Muji. Courtesy of Muji. www.muji.co.uk Tel: +44 (0)20 7323 2208

Op art
Impact fabric, Evelyn Brooks. V&A Images/Victoria and Albert Museum
Bridget Riley. Untitled (Winged Curve), 1966 (screenprint on paper), Riley, Bridget (b. 1931) / Private Collection / www.bridgeman.co.uk

Mexico City logo. Design: Lance Wyman
Tile. Designed by Edward Barber & Jay Osgerby

Organic design
LCW Chair, Charles and Ray Eames. Photo: Hans Hansen. Courtesy of Vitra (www.vitra.com) and Herman Miller (www.hermanmiller.com)
La Chaise, Charles and Ray Eames. Photo: Hans Hansen. Courtesy of Vitra (www.vitra.com) and Herman Miller (www.hermanmiller.com)
Atomic coffee maker. Photo: Luke Herriott. Courtesy of Lindy Dunlop
Tulip armchair, Eero Saarinen. Courtesy of Knoll International Ltd. www.knoll.com
Sydney Opera House. Courtesy of the Sydney Opera House
Henry Moore. Maquette for Reclining Connected Forms (bronze on wood base), Moore, Henry Spencer (1898–1986) / Private Collection, Agnew's, London, UK / www.bridgeman.co.uk
The work illustrated on page 151 has been reproduced by permission of the Henry Moore Foundation
Flow fruit bowl. Courtesy of Gijs Bakker
Kareames chairs, Karim Rashid. Courtesy of Karim Rashid Inc.
Ty Nant bottle, Ross Lovegrove. Design: Ross Lovegrove Photo: John Ross
Tea and coffee set. Courtesy of Alessi

Pop art
Panton stacking chair, Verner Panton. Photo: Gary French. Courtesy of Leonie Taylor
Crak poster, Roy Lichtenstein. V&A Images/Victoria and Albert Museum © The Estate of Roy Lichtenstein/DACS 2005
Totem coffee pot, Portmeirion Pottery. Photo: Luke Herriott
Sgt Pepper's Lonely Hearts Club Band, The Beatles. Photo: Luke Herriott © Peter Blake 2005. All Rights Reserved, DACS
Campbell's Soup, 1968 (screenprint), Warhol, Andy (1930–1987) / Wolverhampton Art Gallery, West Midlands, UK / www.bridgeman.co.uk © The Andy Warhol Foundation for the Visual Arts, Inc./ARS, NY and DACS, London 2005
Patterns 07. Courtesy of Büro Für Form San Francisco 2012. Courtesy of Morla Design. www.morladesign.com

Postindustrialism
Speaking coffee maker. Droog Design: Elbert Draisma
Clouds. Ronan & Erwan Bouroullec © Paul Tahon
The Locker, Egg Designs. Design: Greg and Roche Dry, Egg Design, 2004

Postmodernism
Svincolo standard lamp by Ettore Sottsass, 1979 and a Tindouf Tambour fronted cabinet by Paolo Navone, 1979, both for the Bauhaus Collection (Studio Alchimia), Navone, Paolo (20th Century) / Private Collection, Bonhams, London, UK / www.bridgeman.co.uk
Bird kettle. Courtesy of Alessi
View of the Museumsinsel Gröningen, built 1989, Mendini, Alessandro (b. 1931) / Gröningen, the Netherlands, Wolfgang Neeb / www.bridgeman.co.uk
Tea urn with feet. Courtesy of Virginia Graham
Kila lamp. IKEA Ltd., Stockist no. 0845 3551 141, www.ikea.co.uk

Rationalism
Gualino Office Building, Mario Pagano © 2005 Scala, Florence
Berlin buildings. Photo: Luke Herriott
Air-Chair. 1999, Magis. Photo: Walter Gumiero

Scandinavian modern
Armchair 41, Alvar Aalto. Courtesy of Artek. www.artek.fi
Glasses, Aino Aalto. Courtesy of Iittala. www.iittala.com
Aalto vase, Alvar Aalto. Courtesy of Iittala. www.iittala.com
Ant chair, Arne Jacobsen. Courtesy of Danish Design Center
Egg and swan chair, Arne Jacobsen. Courtesy of Danish Design Center
Candlesticks, Arne Jacobsen. Courtesy of Danish Design Center
AJ Lamp, Arne Jacobsen. Courtesy of Danish Design Center. Photo: Piotr Topperzer
Unikko textile. Courtesy of Marimekko Corporation
Low Pad. 1999, Cappellini. Photo: Walter Gumiero
Papermaster magazine table. Courtesy of Norway Says
Benjamin stool and Buskbo coffee table. IKEA Ltd., Stockist no. 0845 3551 141, www.ikea.co.uk

Secession
The Stadtbahn, Otto Wagner. The Stadtbahn Pavilion of the Vienna Underground Railway, design showing the exterior and a view of the railway platform, c.1894–1897 (colored pencil), Wagner, Otto (1841–1918) / Historisches Museum der Stadt, Vienna, Austria / www.bridgeman.co.uk
J. M. Olbrich interior, from Deutsche Kunst und Dekoration. V&A Images/Victoria and Albert Museum
Alfred Roller poster. V&A Images/Victoria and Albert Museum
Decades typeface. Courtesy of Corey Holms www.coreyholms.com

Index